NLP Business Masterclass

Skills for realizing human potential

David Molden

Prentice Hall
FINANCIAL TIMES

An imprint of Pearson Education

London • New York • San Francisco • Toronto • Sydney • Tokyo • Singapore
Hong Kong • Cape Town • Madrid • Amsterdam • Munich • Paris • Milan

PEARSON EDUCATION LIMITED

Head Office:
Edinburgh Gate
Harlow CM20 2JE
Tel: +44 (0)1279 623623
Fax: +44 (0)1279 431059

London Office:
128 Long Acre
London WC2E 9AN
Tel: +44 (0)20 7447 2000
Fax: +44 (0)20 7447 2170
Website: www.business-minds.com

First published in Great Britain in 2001

© Pearson Education Limited 2001

The right of David Molden to be identified as author
of this work has been asserted by him in accordance
with the Copyright, Designs and Patents Act 1988.

ISBN 0 273 65016 5

British Library Cataloguing in Publication Data
A CIP catalogue record for this book can be obtained from the British Library

10 9 8 7 6 5

Typeset by Northern Phototypesetting Co Ltd, Bolton
Printed and bound in Great Britain by Bell & Bain Ltd, Glasgow

The Publishers' policy is to use paper manufactured from sustainable forests.

About the author

David Molden

Born and educated in the UK, David began his career in the IT industry as a computer engineer, stepping into his first managerial role in 1972. As National Service Manager with Computacenter he became increasingly interested in personal development until, in 1992, he was appointed head of training and development, and began to integrate NLP principles into management and leadership training.

Always looking for innovative and effective ways of developing people, David has become something of an expert in challenging orthodoxy, and seeking ways of increasing the leverage for change. He is author of *Managing with the Power of NLP* (FT Pitman Publishing, 1996), co-author of *Realigning for Change* (FT Prentice Hall, 1999), a professional member of the Association for Neuro Linguistic Programming, and a director with Quadrant 1 consultancy, where he works as a facilitator, coach and trainer for organizations that want to harness the full potential of their people.

Acknowledgments

First and foremost, recognition must go to the pioneers of NLP – John Grinder and Richard Bandler – for their initiative and energy in bringing the tools of NLP to our attention, and to all the early developers, especially Robert Dilts for his prolific work with modeling and logical levels.

Thanks also to:

◆ all the friends who have helped me to expand my horizons, including Dr Wyatt Woodsmall, Magic Marvin Oka, Dr Willie Monteiro, Brad Waldron, Michael Chase and Sifu Richard Williams;

◆ clients at Computacenter, Bristol Myers Squibb, Philip Morris, Alstom, National Power, The Army, Cereal Partners, Brown & Root, and the Institute of Management for providing me with a wide variety of challenging assignments;

◆ Alan Black, Brad Waldron, David Robinson, Denise Parker, Graham Yemm, Jane Revell, Jon Symes, Marcus Muir, and Mark Underwood, who have contributed material to Sections 3 and 4 – your creative input has enhanced the book for readers seeking practical and effective solutions to their business problems;

◆ my friends and work colleagues for coaching me from day to day;

◆ all the readers of my book *Managing with the Power of NLP* for your encouraging feedback;

◆ the team at Pearson Education for your support, energy and effort;

◆ above all, Ju, Ross and Charlie, for giving me the space to complete the project, and our dog, Bonnie, for accepting my neglect – we now have the spring and summer to catch up with each other.

Contents

Introduction

One of my favorite books is *The Empty Space* by Peter Brook (Penguin Books, 1968), the world-famous theatre director. In it, Brook explains Brecht's belief that, in making an audience take stock of the elements in a situation, the theatre is serving the purpose of leading its audience to a more just understanding of the society in which it lives, learning in what ways that society is capable of change. As an example, Brook describes a scene where a girl, who has been raped, walks on to a stage in tears. If her acting touches us sufficiently, we automatically accept the implied conclusion that she is an unfortunate victim. However, suppose a clown were to follow her, mimicking her tears, and suppose, with his talent, he succeeds in making us laugh. His mockery destroys our first response.

Imagine the organization as a stage, the employees as both the actors and the audience. In taking stock of the many situations that occur each day, emotions are stirred in response to the way people act out their roles. These responses are often inappropriate, exaggerated or, perhaps, misguided, manifesting in conflict, inertia, apathy, and withdrawal. Change becomes a struggle, learning suffers, and progress is impeded. If the way forward for organizations – as Brecht suggests for societies – is to take stock of the elements in a situation and learn in what ways the organization can change, then this book can be considered a handbook for the change agent.

Neuro-linguistic Programming (NLP) is a set of principles, models, and tools for learning, communication, and change. It describes the workings of the mind and how verbal and non-verbal language is used to communicate our thoughts. This, though, is not a book on psychology; for it contains a battery of techniques to help you realize your full potential as a human being in the world of business.

You may be reading about NLP for the first time, in which case you will find this book a simple and direct interpretation, making both the theory and the vast array of techniques easily digestible. If you have some NLP knowledge, or you have attended a training seminar, the comprehensive coverage of the principles, patterns and techniques will provide you with a creative reference manual you will want to use for many years to come. Whatever your level of knowledge and skill, if you want to have more of an influence in the business world, you have in your hands a practical companion packed with tried and tested ways to achieve superior performance.

This book is the result of a collaborative effort, combining the experience of ten highly trained and successful NLP business consultants. Together they have over 50 years' experience of using NLP to help make companies and their employees more successful. In Section 1, you will learn the key principles on which NLP is based and, like any discipline, the techniques will only work when underpinned by sound principles. The eight chapters of Section 2 explain the core patterns of thinking and behavior to give you a solid foundation on which to begin developing your skills. Section 3 consists of 13 chapters of tools, techniques and skills fully tried and tested by the contributors – a substantial compendium of effective ideas for creating change. Section 4 is dedicated to modeling excellence, five chapters revealing how you can be the best at whatever you choose, with examples from customer service, consulting skills, effective memory, getting rid of bad habits, and the model team.

At the time of writing this book, my colleagues and I were designing a new course in NLP for use in business. The course and the book were given the title "Masterclass" in recognition of the demanding expectations of our clients. I wanted to write a book that could be used with the training, so it had to have sufficient theory supporting the reference material, and a large practical section crammed with ideas for putting NLP to use in a variety of business situations, plus a section on modeling to enable you to generate whatever excellence you desire. I think a book with this amount of content and coverage deserves to be called "Masterclass", but you will judge this for yourself. I invite you to write to me with news of your achievements using these powerful ideas. Your feedback will be highly valued.

Section 1

Principles of NLP:
the foundations of success

Introduction

The human race lives by its principles. Some principles form constitutions or religions. Others have been turned into civil laws. While the majority of people uphold our civil laws, some choose to violate them and risk the consequences. At a lower level than this, we develop principles of our own to help us make decisions and get things done on a day-by-day basis. While most people support our societal principles and apply them universally in their lives, this is not always the case with principles we create for our personal use. Take, for example, a manager closely monitoring the work of employees in her department. Perhaps she is working from the principle "you have to keep an eye on people otherwise they will let you down". As a role model for aspiring future managers, her behavior could encourage others to do the same. However, it is unlikely to attract universal support as a general management principle and the results will be quite uncertain.

Like any other discipline, NLP is underpinned by a number of governing principles with universal application. You can test universal principles with cause and effect. The followers of Hare Krishna understood the power of universal principles when, in the 1960s and 1970s, it was difficult to walk through any railway station without being given a flower or religious script. On accepting the gift, you would be approached a few seconds later with a request for a donation. Very few people could resist the powerful principle of reciprocation and the followers made millions from this simple technique. As people became wise to this, they would avoid making a donation by resisting the gift, preventing the principle from taking effect.

Some people seem unaware of the principles they use to get by in the world, and their success is more the product of chance and coincidence than a well thought out strategy based on sound principles. The universal principles of NLP will give you the best possible chance of living and working at the cause rather than at the effect end of other people's actions. They apply in all contexts and for all people, but they will work for you only if you choose to believe in them and if you use them consistently to guide your thinking and your actions.

It is worth considering the outcome of having no principles or of applying sensible principles incorrectly. There are certain laws, or principles, of the universe that will deliver results every time, when applied correctly. Archimedes demonstrated the principle of leverage. He is quoted as saying, "give me a place to stand and I will move the earth". He was referring, of course, to a lever that, if large enough and positioned on a pivot according to the principles of leverage, could easily move the earth from its current position in the universe. If you get the pivot in the wrong place it becomes ineffective, and without knowledge of the principle you stand very little chance of moving anything using these tools.

The universal principles of NLP will give you the best possible chance of living and working at the cause rather than at the effect end of other people's actions.

Organizations can swamp their employees in minutiae, such that they become blind to the principles that would actually help them make better progress. The progression of individual tasks through a busy day does not necessarily result in the progression of strategic and global objectives. When heartless carrying out of tasks takes priority over the satisfaction and emotional charge of a job well done, hearts and minds become disengaged from the work, resulting in poor quality, wherever you look.

NLP has many principles to guide the practitioner. In this book I have drawn on ten core principles to underpin your learning of the material and help you integrate new ideas and techniques into the business environment. They cover three main areas of human endeavor:

◆ breaking free from limiting habitual behavior;

◆ understanding and respecting other people for their unrealized potential;

◆ taking responsibility for our thinking and actions.

Ten principles of NLP

1 Generate new, don't repair old.

2 Feedback nourishes, failure saps energy.

3 Influence and control are gained through flexibility.

4 Resistance indicates a lack of rapport.

5 Intention and behavior are different.

6 People have all they need to change.

7 If it's possible for one person, it's possible for others.

8 The meaning of my communication is in the response.

9 Perception is reality.

10 I am in charge of my mind and responsible for my results.

Section 1 explains what each of these principles means, with real-life examples to demonstrate the consequences of acting from both within and without the guidance of the principle. The overriding belief, which will result in maximum gain from the techniques you will learn in this book, is:

Violate these ten principles and suffer the consequences or choose to apply them universally in all your interactions and you will achieve success limited only by your imagination.

1

Leave the swamp alone and you will escape the hungry alligators

I hear this metaphor often. I hear it from people who find themselves bogged down by urgent detail, causing them to fire fight for survival. They will tell you that when you are up to your neck in alligators it's difficult to remember that your goal is to drain the swamp. Metaphors are powerful influences on behavior, so wouldn't it be better to develop useful ones? The likely consequence of working from the alligator metaphor is that you become a fire fighter. If you drain the swamp, you should expect the alligators to go for you – after all, it is their swamp and you are a handsome meal. So, who decided to drain the swamp and why? I wonder what principles this metaphor might be based on? Single-mindedness? Unquestioning commitment to duty? No concern for human life? These principles seem to be very unsound and they are certainly not universal.

> **When you are up to your neck in alligators it's difficult to remember that your goal is to drain the swamp.**

This chapter explains three key principles to prevent you from becoming trapped in the alligator metaphor. They will increase your personal creativity and provide you with a solid platform from which to rid yourself of useless habits. They will also help you to launch some new ways of thinking and acting.

Principle 1 Generate new, don't repair old

A great deal of time can be spent repairing systems that don't work very well, are outdated or have been neglected. It is understandable to repair something for nostalgic or aesthetic purposes – for example, a classic car or a valuable antique. If we repair something for the purpose of making it more effective, then we might question that purpose, especially when the repair is likely to bring only small improvements. The Japanese perfected the art of continual improvement, but, in the process, they sacrificed creativity and innovation. The world is now changing so fast that small continual improvements are no longer enough to secure future success. If something ceases to be effective, don't repair, generate new. Smart people are generating new ways of doing business every day. Compare these two examples.

❖ example

A factory manager once asked a consultant to help fix his troubled production line. The problem was described as a requirement for people with a high tolerance for boredom to operate short-cycle production runs. The facility had been designed by a team of consultants for optimum productivity, but the operators were making mistakes because they were getting bored and becoming distracted. The factory manager wanted to improve on this by recruiting people who would not get bored operating the line. I am pleased to report that the consultant in question refused the assignment and offered to help design a more humane process with even higher productivity goals.

In contrast to this, in a different company, designers had created a new, fully automated facility to increase productivity by 300 per cent, and significantly improve product quality. The new design incorporated a training program to help employees with traditional trade skills learn how to operate the new equipment. The training helped them to work as a team, brainstorm problems, think creatively, solve problems as a team, make decisions as a team, and take ownership of the entire production process. These are life skills, providing employees with personal development that will be valuable to them in the future, whatever they decide to do.

In the second example, the productivity gains were realized, and the new working methods brought ancillary benefits as the workforce became generally more creative and competent at teamworking. In the first example, the exact opposite happened as managers spent their time immersed in the details of error reports, blame apportionment, defensive behavior, and developing boredom assessment tests.

In my entire consulting experience, I haven't met one business leader who is happy with their company's ability to communicate. For some companies, the desire to communicate more effectively has resulted in information overload, as they have just done more of the same. More irrelevant e-mails, more unproductive meetings, more reports that no one has time to read, more conferences to emphasize key messages that few people know how to put into action. One company I have been working with has achieved more than most in its quest to improve communications, and it has done so by generating new methods. They already have e-mail, meetings, reports, conferences and an intranet. What's new is their appointment of a dual-role communications link person (CLP) for every team. The job of a CLP is to filter the plethora of communications so that individuals spend time only with information of use to them. Amazing progress has been made, and the thinking behind it generated something completely new, rather than tried to fix what was already there but not working very well.

The principle of "generating new" applies to personal contexts as much as it does to teams and organizations, which has to be the case as it is individuals who make groups what they are. On our management courses, our delegates have told us of many instances where they have "run out of ideas" for improving performance. What they often mean is that they have exhausted the possibilities that occur to them from within their cultural ways of thinking. When we help them to break through the limitations created by cultural norms, all kinds of exciting possibilities begin to take shape. Generating "new" means thinking and doing things differently. The degree of difference you are prepared to make will be determined by your courage, belief, creativity, and inspiration.

> *Our delegates have told us they have "run out of ideas". What they often mean is that they have exhausted the possibilities that occur to them from within their cultural ways of thinking.*

Think of the new concepts introduced in the past few years that are changing the world we live in. Digital TV, DVD, the Internet, e-commerce, MP3 music format, multimedia, mobile phones, computerized stock trading, GPS navigation systems, are all the result of generating new, not repairing the old. It's not that continual improvement should be discarded – in fact, it ought to be an everyday process – but it should be used for the things that are working, not broken. Of course, we want to improve our performance, but an improvement strategy alone is unlikely to create the shifts in thinking needed to compete in the future. Think about the time you spend at work each day. What proportions of it are used repairing the old, improving what works, and generating new? Are you happy with this split?

■ Principle 2 Feedback nourishes, failure saps energy

The way we conceptualize long-term goals is becoming obsolete. In the early decades of this century, it was reasonable to set long-term goals of ten years or more. Today, "long-term" is getting shorter. Who will be bold enough to predict the business environment five years from now when we have experienced so much change in the past decade?

This has an impact on the way we think about success and failure. If we set a five-year goal and fail to meet it, have we been incompetent? Had we lost focus? Perhaps the environment moved on and, as a consequence, our goal became unrealistic. Long-term success relies much more on the flexibility to change and revise goals in response to the environment. If we want to continue to set realistic goals for ourselves and for our business, then success and failure must be viewed through a different lens, otherwise we may become fixed in the timespans of the past.

If we want to continue to set realistic goals then success and failure must be viewed through a different lens.

First, the notion of failure is – has always been – inappropriate. This is as much to do with our mindset as it is the changing world. If you fail, then you need only take a small step to think of yourself, or a colleague, as a person who has failed or, in more succinct terms, you/he/she is a failure. To think in this way lowers self-esteem and saps your energy. You don't need to be told that you have failed too many times for the label "failure" to become self-fulfilling.

In our ever-changing world, it's easy to fail when the goalposts have moved. To continue with this image, picture a football game in which the goalposts frequently disappear and reappear in another location. A team's strategy and tactics would have to continually evolve to account for the moving target. This is what it can be like doing business in today's environment.

Why not banish the term "failure" from the context of human endeavor and restrict its use to non-biological systems? My fountain pen fails when it runs out of ink and my TV failed when the tube stopped working. For people, we will replace "failure" with the concept of "feedback", and introduce a simple loop mechanism called a TOTE.

The TOTE

A TOTE[1] is a completed event. The letters stand for test–operate–test–exit. It helps to remind us that success in life is actually a very simple process of four stages (see Figure 1.1). The four stages are:

◆ know what you want to achieve and determine the measure you will use to know when you have succeeded (Test);

◆ have flexibility in thinking and behavior so you can change if you're not getting what you want (Operate);

◆ continue this loop until you achieve it (Test–Operate);

◆ move on to another goal when you've finished (Exit).

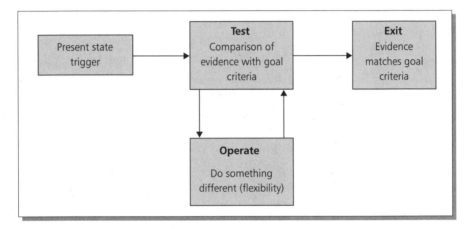

Fig 1.1 ◆ The TOTE feedback loop

While this may seem like a simple enough concept, it is surprising how frequently habitual behavior prevents people from being more successful. Think about the way you manage your finances. What about presentations you have given? Consider the ways in which you communicate with people at work. How many of your interactions would benefit from more flexible behavior? What about the way you make decisions? If any of these events trigger the same thinking and behavior that you used last time, it is highly probable your results will also be the same. Whatever you want to improve, the TOTE reminds us of the four simple stages to go through, and we shall be returning to this at various stages in the book.

The TOTE is a universal feedback model and the quality of the results you get from using it will depend on your attitude and skill in giving feedback to others, receiving it from others and from yourself, then integrating feedback into your behavior. Whether or not we have succeeded in achieving a goal, it is certain that we will have amassed a mountain of feedback in the process of trying to achieve it. When we are out of tune with feedback, we are not receptive to it. Mountains are there to be climbed, so, as it can help you to be more successful, work towards being tuned in to it with your ears, eyes, feelings, and your heart.

Giving feedback

Can you think of someone at work whose performance you find annoying at times? What is it about their performance that annoys you? Is it a lack of focus? Poor attention to detail? Inappropriate communication style? Lack of consideration for others? Would you like to help this individual improve their performance? Have you given them some feedback?

When giving feedback, the intention behind it is extremely important. If you answered "yes" to the first question above, and you get annoyed at someone's performance, your being annoyed is unlikely to result in a positive outcome for the other person. Feedback given when you are emotionally charged with annoyance is more likely to feed your own ego than to help the individual concerned. At worst, your attempt to give feedback will be interpreted as a put-down. If you are sincere in your interest to help someone improve their performance, feedback will be more readily accepted when it is interpreted as being well-intentioned and sincere. Emotions like annoyance, frustration, and impatience will be picked up intuitively and have the opposite effect to what you wanted.

Feedback is often considered to be of just two types – positive or negative. This thinking is not very helpful. I can only surmise that the intention of negative feedback is to feed the ego of the giver. Positive feedback is not always useful either. To be told that your performance was "excellent" may be considered as feedback, but how useful is it? It is a generalization and completely devoid of any information you could use to improve the next performance. So, feedback should contain a message. The message might be made up of some encouragement and some specific information about how to improve the performance. This would be delivered in a sincere and well-intentioned style.

> *A large amount of the feedback in organizations today is interpreted as criticism. It is only given when something goes wrong.*

Feedback from our management students shows that a large amount of the feedback in organizations today is interpreted as criticism. It is only given when something goes wrong. Giving praise and encouragement for a job well done is sometimes perceived as "being soft". Yet, when we have asked our students if they would like more specific feedback, the overwhelming response has been "YES!" This is a classic example of cultural limitation at work. No one wants to be labeled a softy, but everyone would like more praise, encouragement and specific feedback. For a Catch-22 such as this, extraordinary courage is required to break the cultural norms.

Receiving feedback

Essentially, there are two ways in which feedback can be received, regardless of how it is given. One way is regressive in its effect and is one of the biggest blocks to learning and personal development. The other way is progressive and a real catalyst to learning.

Suppose a colleague tells us that our style of communication at a meeting alienated a key person in the organization. A regressive response might be to get defensive and conjure up excuses to validate our communication style – for example, "She isn't interested in this project anyway" or "She is always resistant to new ideas." Another regressive response is to take the attitude "I know that – do you think I haven't noticed?" There is no learning to be had with any such responses. If we really want to learn how to get better results with our communication style, we first need to change our response to feedback so that we can begin to make progress.

You could take away half the reporting from an organization without affecting the business.

Let's take the same example above and respond in a progressive way. The attitude to adopt is one of gratitude, acceptance, and curiosity. We can be thankful that someone is able to provide us with feedback and accept the feedback without prejudice or bias. Above all, we can be curious to seek out more details, to help us decide what to do differently the next time we have an opportunity to influence this particular person. We begin to question and, as a result, glean more useful information from which to learn.

Organizations know the importance of feedback, but sometimes the principle is lost in the huge amounts of data produced to measure business performance. In the worst case, I have observed managers putting pressure on employees to produce an increasing variety of reports in the hope that performance will be recorded positively. This is not smart. It would be better to invest more energy in putting things right than in churning out meaningless reports. I have a theory that you could take away half the reporting from an organization without affecting the business. This would free up an enormous amount of energy that could be channeled into more creative pursuits. The knack in benefitting from this unproven theory is in knowing which half to get rid of. It's important to measure your progress and just as important to know what to measure and why you are measuring. Feedback from your system is only useful if the information contained in it shows you where to make changes.

Integrating feedback

Being receptive to feedback is a prerequisite for continual learning, but it is only a beginning. Unless you make a change to your behavior, you have only put the feedback into your head, it has not been integrated into your range of behaviors.

The majority of our behavior is habitual. The stock phrases we use in conversation, the places we go, the rituals we play out, and the attitudes we adopt in response to other people and situations are mostly habitual. We use them without even thinking about them. They are automatic. When we learn something new, we are actually taking on new habits and, in many cases, we must unlearn the old habit before the new one can take root. The classic example of this is aircraft pilot training, where the pilots are learning to operate a new layout of flight controls in a plane they have been flying for many years. Even after quite extensive practice with the new control layout, in emergency conditions, some of the pilots revert to old habits and move their hands to the old locations to hit the emergency warning switches.

The key to integrating new behaviors – whether physical, attitudinal or verbal – is preparation, planning, and repetition. You will discover many methods and techniques to aid integration throughout the practical sections of this book. Practice each one at least three times.

Principle 3 Influence and control are gained through flexibility

In the earlier part of the last century, control was exerted by means of authoritarian methods. The boss set the rules and there were dire consequences for anyone stupid enough to break one. Times have changed, and authoritative power has given much ground to more subtle influencing skills for controlling business. Consider the following example.

❖ example

A young manager was told that, if he wanted to be considered for promotion, he would have to do something about his aggressive communication style. I was asked to coach him and soon discovered the cause of his aggressiveness. He had a strong need for people to do things his way and any deviation from this caused him great frustration, which came across to others as aggressive.

The manager was being very rigid in his insistence on people adopting his way of doing things. He had no flexibility whatsoever to listen and take on other people's ideas because he believed his job, as manager, was to show people the best way of doing things. In this way, he could know what people were doing and so exert more control. His one and only strategy for improving performance was focused on other people and what they needed to do to improve. Although his intention was to have more control, the result of his behavior left him with less control and, as a wider consequence, his prospects for promotion had diminished.

I am pleased to say that this manager did become more flexible as a result of the coaching and was put forward for promotion some time later.

The concept of control is probably the biggest worry for most managers as they are encouraged to empower their staff and allow people to learn from mistakes. Learning to control business in the new era of leadership will require courage and breakthroughs in terms of the way people "normally" get things done. There is very little "normality" in the future. Think about the principles of inflexibility and courage in this example.

❖ example

A large transport company was struggling to meet customers' demands while operating unprofitably and experiencing a growing number of accidents. Senior managers considered the problem to be a lack of new ideas and I was invited in to receive a brief.

I was told that managers had plenty of opportunity to meet and come up with fresh solutions, but that they kept talking about the old ways of doing things. I asked if they had learned basic creativity tools, but that wasn't the problem, they said. They wanted to teach all their managers how to give their meetings more structure and stop wasting time talking about the way things used to be. I might have been just slightly convinced of this as a solution had the briefing meeting been conducted in a structured way. The room was very small, uncomfortably hot with no natural light, and we had numerous interruptions from people dealing with crisis situations – not the best environment for encouraging creative thought. However, it was an excellent example of how to run unstructured, problem-oriented meetings, and of rigid thinking.

Behavioral inflexibility can be observed in any number of situations at work:

◆ meetings with rigid agendas produced with little consideration for the interests and outcomes of attendees;

◆ training courses that instruct and offer no opportunity to draw on the experience of delegates;

◆ business goals that become outdated and yet remain alive;

◆ a business need borne out of the personal motivation of an individual rather than from collective input;

◆ the interfering manager creating mistrust and low motivation.

The list of situations could be endless. The key difference between flexibility and rigidity is in the focus for change. A rigid or inflexible person will tend to look at how other people or the system can be changed. A flexible person will think about how they themselves can change in order to bring about change in other people or the system. The rigid person will think, "What they need to do is … ." The flexible person will think, "How can I behave differently in order to influence them?" This book will show how vastly different these two ways of thinking are and how, by developing behavioral flexibility, you will increase your powers of influence and control in your organization, career, and personal life.

Note

1   G. Miller, E. Galanter, and K. Pribram (1960) *Plans and the Structure of Behaviour*, Holt, Rinehart & Winston.

2

What we think about people matters

As the world of work changes, the success of a company increasingly relies on the relationships between people doing work for that company. The traditional boss is becoming extinct as more people are working in project teams, with their direction and motivation often provided from different sources. Creative thinking, team problem solving, self-management, and self-direction are becoming standard in the way people work together.

The focus for non-technical training and development is being turned towards the quality of the relationships between any two people. This might be considered as the basic unit of productivity.

With relationships as the foundations of company performance, the focus for non-technical training and development is being turned towards the quality of the relationships between any two people. This might be considered as the basic unit of productivity. It matters today, more than at any other time, to get relationships at work on to a stable and productive footing and, in this environment, what we think about people matters.

What you believe about another person will color your judgment of them, and this will influence the relationship you have with that person. Consider this example.

❖ example

Some years ago a young manager was recruited into a salt mining company. His brief was to help the production workers embrace change. Whatever he asked them to do, no matter how small a change, he would get plenty of reasons for keeping things as they were. People dug their heels in and refused to cooperate. He soon began to think of them as stubborn and, in some cases, even stupid. Things got worse and the manager began to get frustrated and stressed.

I asked him to stop telling people to do things for two weeks and, instead, just listen to them and agree with whatever they said, even if they were knocking the company.

The next time we met, he told a different story, of how they had been mismanaged in the past, treated badly and undervalued. He said that he now thought of them as seeking acceptance for past labors and appreciation for the work they were doing now, never mind the changes to come.

This change of understanding led the manager to behave differently. He spent more time listening and learning, giving praise and encouragement, and empathizing with their problems. Very soon, changes began to happen as the manager focused more on his relationships with the workers than on the work itself.

Relationships that motivate and create high performance have trust, sincerity, and understanding at their core. The four principles in this chapter will help you to achieve this in any situation.

Principle 4 Resistance indicates a lack of rapport

Rapport is essential to working relationships, especially if you want to be influential. We will resist being influenced by someone with whom we have no rapport – that is human nature. We like to have some degree of common understanding and an acceptance of a person before being comfortable with their attempts to influence us. We are more likely to respond positively to a colleague's ideas and suggestions when we have a rapport with them.

Often we find that attempts to influence begin in the wrong place. Ideas meet resistance from other ideas, resulting in a battle for the best idea. Some people may find this mental jousting productive and character building, but it certainly isn't the most creative or rational approach to getting things done in organizations. It also kills rapport for most people and then buy-in becomes a major issue.

Resistance is a challenge to someone else's idea. It could be a small idea – perhaps to move office furniture around or make some small change to a factory layout – or it could be a big idea – a relocation, perhaps, a merger or major diversification. No matter what size the idea, however, resistance is a well-recognized response indicating a reluctance to accept the result of other people's thinking.

It is best to avoid resistance in the first place by starting in the right place with your ideas. The following scenario provides an example of both starting in the wrong place and then removing resistance by starting somewhere else. In this particular case, consider how the resistance was turned into creative teamworking and higher levels of self-esteem and initiative as the team began to put their energy into helping the much-needed changes take effect.

❖ example

A small team of computer analysts worked in a City bank. Their job was to provide a service for users of desktop computers. Customer service was at an all-time low, and falling, and the management finger of blame was pointing at the analysts.

A mature manager was informed of the severity of the situation and told to sort it out. His idea was to observe the team in action, give them some feedback and send them on a customer service training course. For the first day, he sat in his office looking out on the team and making notes. Things got worse over the next four weeks and another manager was given the same brief. This second manager's idea was to bring in some outside help to restructure the way the team was working, so, each day, new faces were observed in meetings with the manager. The situation continued to deteriorate.

Both these managers neglected the importance of rapport. They began with an idea, which the team decided to sabotage. They were not going to cooperate with anyone, why should they? No one seemed to be the least bit interested in their problems.

Then came the third manager, this time with a lot more knowledge about the power of relationships. She began by meeting every team member and taking an interest in their work. She held informal meetings and let them air their mounting grievances. She listened, understood, empathized, and agreed with much of what they said. Yes, they had been subjected to incompetent management and, yes, no one had ever asked them for their ideas, of which they had plenty.

Very soon, the team's energy diverted from resisting and sabotaging change as they decided to channel it into improving customer service. This was a much more satisfying and worthwhile outcome for their effort. No training was attended. The situation was turned around solely on the strength of the team's relationship with its manager. She really understood the influential power that comes from building trust, sincerity and understanding.

Resistance is created by the approach taken to bring about change in an individual, a team or an organization. If you say, "We are going to make some exciting changes", don't be surprised if you get resistance. Alternatively, if you say, "Tell me what it's like here", then listen, understand, and agree in a sincere way, you can begin to work with people's energy towards progress. Follow with, "What would you like to happen?", then, "That sounds sensible, I would like to work with you on this and exchange my ideas with you." In this way, you are working on the relationship as well as the ideas and you are less likely to meet resistance. Any resistance you do get will be much easier to work with.

> *If you say, "We are going to make some exciting changes", don't be surprised if you get resistance.*
> *If you say, "Tell me what it's like here", you can begin to work with people's energy towards progress.*

Principle 5 Intention and behavior are different

Having established that productive relationships require understanding, we can turn our attention to all the ways in which misunderstandings occur. What if we could begin to grow an awareness of the cause of problematic relationships? What if we could develop an expert insight into the ways in which relationships go wrong? This is a good place to begin if we want to learn how to influence. We can start by looking at the differences between the things people say and do, and the intentions behind their actions. In many cases, problems stem from our misinterpretations of behavior and intention. Think about the implications of well-intentioned behavior in this example.

❖ example

A project manager was rising in the unpopularity stakes because of his interfering behavior. Unlike other project managers, he would ask project teams for more than the usual level of reporting. On receiving the reports, he would call people and ask questions about small details of procedure and method, regardless of how well the project was going. His actions were interpreted as "interfering" and "meddling". People began to feel mistrusted.

However you describe, or label, this behavior, the intention behind it was to manage projects successfully. The project manager didn't intend to interfere or meddle, but, because of his low self-confidence and poor skills in motivating and influencing people, he would feel a need to closely monitor his projects for fear they might go awry. He knew that his relationships with people in the project teams were weak, and this led him to mistrust what people put in their reports. His behavior was an attempt to compensate for his lack of influencing skills, but it was not getting him what he wanted.

When we are confronted with puzzling, unreasonable or exaggerated behavior, we instinctively want to label it with words like aggressive, dismissive, threatening, disinterested, interfering, uncommitted, scathing, critical, and so on. However, there is a positive intention behind all behavior. This is the case even for the most destructive behavior. Often the intention then will be emotionally driven – for example, feeding the ego or covering up feelings of insecurity, isolation or incompetence. If we misinterpret behavior by giving it a label according to our response to it, we will damage our relationship with the individual or group, and limit our ability to influence.

Being aware of the differences between intention and behavior allows us to recognize three very important aspects of our own communication. First, that in seeking to achieve our most deep-rooted intentions, success will be determined by the range of behaviors available to us. In other words, the degree of flexibility we have in getting what we want. In the previous example, the project manager had no flexibility whatsoever, which is why he continued to use the same behavior to try to achieve his goals even when it was not working. Most of his projects were highly problematical.

> *Being aware of the differences between intention and behavior allows us to recognize important aspects of our own communication.*

Second, pay attention to the labels you are giving people. Understand that people are generally well intentioned and work with them to help them succeed. False labeling will affect your behavior towards others and this will damage your relationships with them. If your behavior is not getting you what you want, change it; do something different.

Third, whenever you are confronted with unreasonable behavior, work with it, understand it, find agreement, and get some rapport going. Once you have rapport, then you can begin to influence. Suspend judgment, at least until you have done your utmost to gain rapport and influence. Be aware that once you have formed a judgment about a person, you have limited your chances of influencing them.

■ Principle 6 People have all they need to change

Think about your own desires for a moment. Is there something you would like to achieve but do very little to get? Millions of people want to be rich, but the only effort they put into achieving this is to buy a lottery ticket.

How high do you set your sights? Is there a limit to what you believe you can achieve in your lifetime? What do you feel you are capable of?

> *At the age of 14, Michael Dell, now CEO of Dell Computers, was asked what he wanted to do with his life. He replied, "I'm going to compete with IBM."*

Notice Michael Dell's words "going to", as if it were just a matter of time. Self-confidence, strength of will, and commitment such as this are rarely observed in everyday life, but if Michael Dell can muster these essential qualities of success, so can you.

Before going any further, it is important to talk about success. NLP is generally recognized as being a set of principles and tools for achieving success. This can mean different things to different people. Someone I know is very successful at achieving charitable goals. She is poor in material terms, but very rich when it comes to living a satisfying and meaningful life. Some people use NLP to be more effective at working with the underprivileged and influence government committees and other powerful organizations. So, the meaning of "success" varies depending on the mind and heart of the individual.

A person needs only three things in order to be successful. The first is the know-how. Let's suppose you want to become the chief executive officer or some other high-ranking position of an organization. There are plenty of training courses, books, videos, and other CEOs you can get the know-how from. The second thing you need is the opportunity to become a CEO. There are plenty of companies around wanting CEOs, so it is quite possible for you to become one. You may encounter cultural obstacles, such as sexual or racial discrimination or the "who you know" syndrome adopted in some boardrooms, but, if you really want to become a CEO, these things will not stop you. This brings us to the third need: you must want to be a CEO. In fact, wanting is not quite enough; it's more a matter of how much.

The inner resources driving successful people are not primarily the know-how or opportunity, but more the desire, self-belief, confidence, and courage to take risks.

The inner resources driving successful people are not primarily the know-how or opportunity, but more the desire, self-belief, confidence, and courage to take risks. Without these resources you may never realize the success you dream about. We all have these inner resources, we all have the ability to draw on as much confidence and courage as we want, but some people have difficulty tapping into it. NLP is all about developing personal creativity, and this book will help you to find your inner resources and become a more creative person. One of the things you can do with your new creative ability is achieve your biggest dreams. It will show you how to help other people gain access to their inner resources and begin to achieve more of their true potential also. Consider this example.

❖ example

Many years ago, I interviewed a young woman for an administrative role. During the interview she told me, in a very poker-faced way, that her previous boss had sacked her for being miserable. I also discovered that her boyfriend was cheating on her and her family gave her very little support. She said that she wanted a job where she could keep her head down and focus on her work.

I employed her and, very soon, noticed that her self-esteem was very low – perhaps a result of a tactless and hurtful boss and an uncaring boyfriend.

Over the coming months, the team gave her plenty of praise and we gradually added to her responsibilities. Over the next year, this young woman increasingly showed us a lively and engaging personality, while becoming very popular with our customers. She found the work enjoyable and ended up with responsibility for over £2m of training budget, a handsome new boyfriend, a team she could trust, and excellent career prospects. She had always been capable. What my team did was to help her discover her inner resources of confidence and self-esteem.

Principle 7 If it's possible for one person, it's possible for others

The models and techniques of NLP originated from modeling successful people. Therapists were the first subjects of modeling, followed by entrepreneurs, business leaders, salespeople, negotiators, athletes, and public speakers. Most of what you will discover in NLP today came from the early modeling assignments in the 1970s–1980s.

This principle has far-reaching implications for organizations, particularly those for which skills are crucial to future success. Later in the book we will be looking at the reasons for people doing well in some jobs and not so well in others. When a person finds themself in a job they don't enjoy, they are unlikely to perform consistently well. The choice available is either to find a different job or learn to enjoy and do well at the current one. We will be looking at this principle for a number of roles, such as customer service, sales, and leadership, but here we will take just a brief look at it.

At the heart of being competent, there is more than just knowledge and experience. Can you think of two people who have received the same training for a job, but one of them is performing better than the other? It's very common. Of course, attitude is also important to competence, but this still doesn't give us enough information to model superior performance.

A good friend of mine had a fast-track management career, taking him from junior manager to functional senior manager in under four years. His success came from an ability to get high performance from his team and deliver value to his customers. He grew his first team from 8 to 32, with significant revenue and profit growth, in just 18 months. Today, he is a very popular and effective member of the senior management team in a large division of his company.

If you were to model this excellence, you would need to find out the *values* driving it. You would want to know the *beliefs* that make success possible, and you would want to learn the *strategies* that are used to form the thinking behind the behavior. We also want to listen to the *language* being used, notice *physical* characteristics, and search for key *distinctions* being made. When we have modeled these aspects of performance, we can replicate it for ourselves, and others.

In the section on modeling, you will learn how to model any type of performance. When organizations model performance from elsewhere, it is called *best practice*. This is popular with manufacturing companies. Rank Xerox, ICL, Motorola, and Rover have successfully used best practice to improve their businesses. With NLP, we can apply the principle of best practice to individuals. It's one thing to improve a production facility, but when you can help individuals to achieve excellence, in any field of endeavor, you can get high performance wherever it is needed.

> *Whenever you hear the phrase "I can't ...", you are being confronted with a limiting belief. Whenever I have come across this, there has always been someone in the same organization who can.*

A common way in which people limit themselves is by forming beliefs about what is possible and what isn't, for them. Whenever you hear the phrase "I can't ...", you are being confronted with a limiting belief. Whenever I have come across this, there has always been someone in the same organization who can. Counter-examples are good for breaking down limiting beliefs, and they often make excellent role models. We will go into much greater detail later in the book as you learn the models and techniques required to do this successfully. For now, it is sufficient for you to believe in the principle that if it's possible for one person, it's possible for others.

3

Excuses and scapegoats wanted for blame role

I t's a poor workman who blames his tools, the old saying goes. The complexity of organizations today makes it easier than ever to pin the blame on someone or something other than yourself. You can choose to put the blame with other departments, the IT system, a new process, an old procedure or an uncooperative management team and leave yourself free of the responsibility for things not working out as planned. Scapegoats are also very easy to find. Pick on the administrator, the personnel officer, the computer analyst or whoever will find it difficult to defend himself.

The three principles delineated in this chapter are about taking responsibility for your actions and the way others respond to you. More specifically, they will help you to keep a rational mind, uncontaminated by conjecture, false perception, and limiting beliefs about yourself and others. They will encourage you to develop an appetite for learning from experience, and accept that your very presence has an influence on others, whether intended or not. Sometimes, when we influence people unintentionally, the result can be problematical. A healthy curiosity will help you to become increasingly competent at influencing yourself and other people in ways that will result in more success for you and your organization. This curiosity is more focused on changing your own thinking and behavior than seeking to change others, because by changing ourselves we can have more influence with different people. Think about the implications of unintentional influence in the following example.

❖ example

A marketing team was having problems with a creative design agency. Every time the agency was given a brief they would come up with substandard solutions. Only after being given a final ultimatum would the agency produce acceptable design ideas. This pattern occurred on every project, consuming vast amounts of time. Why couldn't they get it right first time? On each new product the marketing team would follow the same procedure at briefing meetings and they would get the same poor result. A pattern for creating substandard work had been established and the marketing team saw the agency as the problem. Odd, though, that the agency was doing terrific work for other clients. Why the difference?

When the marketing team began to take responsibility and understand that it was as much a part of the pattern as the agency, it started to get different results. The first thing it did was re-establish rapport and introduce a different meeting format in a more creative environment. This allowed the agency to be open about some of the limitations imposed on them, and a more trusting and productive relationship developed.

If you hold a position of authority, there is a dangerous default position when it comes to influencing: you can just tell other people what you want them to do. Also, your power allows you to assume that you don't need to change. That's why you have the power, isn't it, so that you can force others to change?

Don't be fooled by this. The day of the authoritative manager is long gone; we are in a new era now of learning and cooperation, where survival and success require well-developed communication and influencing skills. Using power to influence is a clumsy, lazy, and ineffective method, resulting in only short-term gains at best. Few people want to work with a power-abusing manager.

Principle 8 The meaning of my communication is in the response

When we communicate a message to someone else, we first translate our thoughts and feelings into language. The next step is to choose a medium and trust that the intended target will receive the message. The message, when received by the target, will be interpreted and a response generated. It's a complicated system and it often breaks down. When it does, the true meaning of the message will be found in the response. Consider the scenario below.

❖ example

I was working recently with the new executive team of a large engineering business. The parent company had decided that, to ensure future success, a major reorganization was required. Many of the production units were being run down and sourced from external suppliers, and what used to be a substantial production site, the size of a small village, was being sold off, plot by plot, to build retail parks.

The executive team had created a new mission statement, with a list of core values and a set of measures for each department. These new messages were communicated in a variety of ways to all the staff, but resistance was high. The majority of employees resisted change, making it extremely difficult for any progress to be made. Listening to the executive team, I heard them voice frustration – such as "That's not what we wanted!", "We have put momentous effort into communicating, so what's the problem?", "How could they think that way?", "Why can't they understand?", "How else can we get the message across?"

The new mission, values, and measures had little currency for the majority of employees, who seemed more interested in keeping the past alive. Here was a new management team rushing in to change the way employees worked together. In a company that had experienced very little change, the strategy was so bold and different that few people could understand what it really meant and how it would affect them.

Rather than continuing to communicate the same messages, the team realized its responsibility to communicate in a more meaningful way and began to use everyday language in place of the lofty high-level wording contained in the mission and values. This allowed the team to really connect with people and be better understood by the majority. To get to this position, the team accepted responsibility for the response they had been getting to their communication.

Confusion and misinterpretation also occur on a smaller scale. When I think about the art of delegation, many of my management students have had bad experiences. Managers often delegate tasks they have been doing for some time. Their familiarity with the task can lead them to form assumptions about the information required for someone else to perform the task well.

When performance falls short of expectations, it is often the performer who is in question, not the process of delegation. Your experience of this will depend on the quality of your relationships. If a relationship is open and supportive, the employee may feel safe in asking for clarification, but if not, they are unlikely to run the risk of looking foolish by saying that they don't understand.

A simple rule to follow here is: whenever you get a response you consider to be inappropriate in some way, rather than reiterate the same message, work with the response and be curious to understand it. In the next two sections you will learn a number of techniques for working in this way, so that more of your messages hit home and get the response you want.

Principle 9 Perception is reality

Reality exists only in the mind of the individual and, as no two minds are alike, we need concern ourselves only with perception. Consider how the following example elucidates this statement.

❖ example

A friend of mine works with a large IT company. Her job is to manage the customer's perception of service and she spends a lot of time communicating specific and precise information to customers. She knows all too well that, particularly in a service business where you don't get to see the product, customers will form their own perceptions of the quality of your service. Often these perceptions are formed from experiences of a previous supplier or what other people have said. Sometimes – and this is the eerie part – perceptions are formed from no evidence or experience at all, it's all pure conjecture of the mind. So, to help customers form an accurate perception of service, a continuous stream of evidence and information is supplied, at all levels, with feedback mechanisms to measure the quality of each service interaction. It's a painstaking process, but one that makes the job of providing service so much easier. Any service person will tell you that being tarred with the brush of false perception makes it difficult to satisfy the customer.

What causes people to form false perceptions? Well, we must have some view of how things work in order to get our job done, but often we *generalize*, *delete*, and *distort* the real world, then make our decisions based on the resulting perception of it. It's like using a road map to navigate by. Maps become out of date very quickly and they give you only minimal information. Road maps omit weather conditions, road works, other vehicles, accidents, pedestrians, road signs, and a host of other details. We represent the real world like a road map and very often forget how much more there is to the world outside our own understanding, or representation, of it.

Our opinions and beliefs are nothing more than generalizations of the world, formed from a limited amount of evidence. How much evidence we seek out before forming a belief will depend on each situation and our understanding of how we form our perceptions. Some people need very little evidence indeed and may even adopt the belief of a friend for the sole purpose of maintaining the friendship. This is how groups, teams, and entire divisions within companies form collective false perceptions. A team can give the impression that they are performing well, even when they are not, by creating the perception that other teams are performing badly by comparison.

Road maps omit weather conditions, road works, other vehicles, accidents, pedestrians, road signs, and a host of other details. We represent the real world like a road map.

In the process of communicating, we also distort reality by filling in missing details from our own experiences. When we are listening to someone's account of something that happened, we hear only an abridged version. The detailed version would be unbearably pedantic and lengthy. For example, imagine a factory team leader explaining a problem to her manager.

> *"Mike pressed the button to start the machine, but it had been loaded with the wrong batch of materials. I caught it just in time before the entire batch was used, but it has made us short for the next job, and we will be over our target for waste this week. I've had a word with Mike and with Jane. I'm always telling Jane to keep a close eye on machine loading, but I guess it hasn't sunk in yet."*

In this scenario, it would be very possible for the manager to accept the team leader's account and put responsibility for the problem with Jane or Mike. The manager will build a picture of the scenario, and the sequence of events. This visual representation may include details from personal experience of similar situations involving these people. This is how we interpret meaning, and a certain percentage of this is pure conjecture. Do you think that Mike and Jane would give the same account of what happened? I doubt it very much. Each is likely to distort the facts just as much with the language they use to convey what happened. The brevity of our language makes it easy for us to be foolish with the things we say.

Be aware of the perceptions you form about the world around you. Think back to some recent decisions you have made at work. In the process of making each decision, what proportions of evidence and conjecture were used? Be honest with yourself.

■ Principle 10 I am in charge of my mind and responsible for my results

This may seem like a commonsense principle, and it is, but how many times do you hear people say things of the likes of:

"They make me mad."

"I'm not in the right state of mind for this right now."

"I deplore the way he assumes control, it's infuriating."

"I get so angry when she does that."

"I doubt if they would listen to me."

What do these statements actually mean?

Let's suppose someone called Frank is behind these statements. They all imply that someone else is controlling Frank's state of mind. Frank gives over control to someone else and he gets angry, mad or becomes infuriated as a result. In the last statement, Frank has used his crystal ball to predict the future. How can he know if they will listen or not until he tries talking to them? Perhaps the last time Frank tried to talk to them they didn't listen to him and so, rather than take responsibility for finding a better way to communicate with this group, Frank decides they wouldn't listen anyway. I call that creative failure. What a waste of thinking power.

What about the second statement? Have you ever caught yourself saying this? Again, it implies that your mind chooses its own states and you have no control over this. Here's an example to highlight the importance of managing your state of mind.

❖ example

Karen – a young training consultant on my team – was given the responsibility for the design and delivery of training for the company's Quality program, which was managed by Mike, an authoritative man with an eye for detail. Mike had an urgent tone to his voice, and kept records of every conversation and e-mail. When he called you on the phone, he would hit you with a barrage of questions, all about some detail or other. It was rare that you would have an immediate answer and having to wait would frustrate him. I could always tell when Mike was on the phone to Karen because her state would change. Her shoulders would fall and her voice would become frail. Her skin colour would go quite red and her breathing would speed up. Her entire body would tense up and, at the end of the call, she would slam the phone down.

Karen asked to be given different responsibilities because she said she could no longer handle Mike, although she did enjoy working with the Quality team. I asked if she would reconsider if I could help her handle Mike, and she agreed. We used a few NLP techniques to break down her response to Mike's voice tones and, in a few short weeks, Karen was in control of her state and found Mike an interesting challenge instead of a stressful threat.

Responses like the one in the above example are learned. We respond once or twice in a particular way and it soon becomes a habit that is difficult to break. Like Pavlov's dogs, whose salivation was triggered by the sound of the dinner bell, Karen's state was anchored to Mike's voice. However, unlike Pavlov's dogs, we humans can change our anchored responses. We just have to learn how to do it. One of the simplest ways to experience this is by taking a few minutes to do the following exercise.

◉ exercise

Think back to a time in your life when things were not going too well for you at work. Bring back the images into your mind and recall what people were saying. Run a movie in your mind's eye of the events leading up to this situation. How do you feel as you think about it? If the memory is strong enough, you are probably feeling very much the same way you felt at the time.

Now, before reading further, take a walk around the room and inhale a few deep breaths. Done that? The walking and breathing are important – read on only when you have done it.

Now, bring a more enjoyable experience back into your mind. Again, run the movie and put in the sounds. How does this feel? Which feeling do you prefer? Which feeling puts you in a more resourceful state of mind?

You have just changed your state of mind at will; see how easy it is. The walking and breathing helped you to get out of the first unpleasant state. As the mind and body are one system, we can change our state of mind by changing our physiology.

You will learn later in the book how all your behavior is dependent on your state. If you allow others to press your hot buttons and create negative states, you are limiting your powers of influence. State control is a major component of NLP, and you will learn a number of techniques for increasing your flexibility by developing superb state management skills.

In the next section, you will learn more about how we communicate, and begin to develop an awareness of certain patterns of communication that most people miss. The principles in this chapter underpin all the NLP models and techniques you will learn from this point on. Without a full understanding and a solid belief in these ten key principles, the techniques will not work for you. So, make sure you have fully absorbed this section before reading on.

Section 2

Patterns of NLP:

an awareness of difference

Introduction

The world is a complicated structure of patterns. Many of these patterns recur while others evolve, and new ones are being created as you read these words. Some patterns are of a universal nature, such as the seasonal cycle, tides, religious celebrations, and so forth. Other patterns are less the effect of universal laws and ritual, more the result of habitual thinking and behavior. Our daily domestic routines are patterns of human behavior, as are many of our social activities.

Organizational culture is held together by patterns of behavior, some useful, others less so. It is commonplace to have meetings at regular intervals, perhaps weekly or monthly. The number of people I have met who get value from their regular meetings is about equal to those I have met who don't. This phenomenon prompts me to ask the question "Why perpetuate a pattern that wastes time and alienates people?" The answer is not quite so simple as the question. To understand it fully we need an awareness of the powerful forces at work in the human psyche; forces that most people are oblivious to, yet are heavily influenced by. Consider the forces at work in this example.

❖ example

I was leading a discussion on organizational change at a management seminar when one of the delegates told us of a very aggressive vice-president who had ruled by fear for ten years. Employees were only ever called into his office for a dressing down, displaying all the textbook traits attributed to poor leaders.

One day, the VP left the company and his successor was selected for his more people-oriented leadership style. After a few weeks in the job, he realized that fear had taken strong root and his team lacked initiative, creativity, and humor. The team members were also very closed and would rarely share information with other people. Cynicism was at a high level while commitment was low.

He recognized that the team's behavior was a result of ten years of leadership by fear, and respected that they might find it difficult to break the negative habitual patterns that were preventing them from improving their performance.

He wanted to do something to help the team change, so, to make an immediate impact, he put a notice on the company bulletin board. It read, "At 5pm on Friday 10 February, behind the parking lot, I will be burning the desk used by my predecessor. Please come and share this ceremony with me." He burned the desk in front of about 150 employees.

This example shows the creativity of a thoughtful leader. Someone who understood the powerful effect of office furniture perhaps? Well, this is not such a crazy statement. Habitual behavior is a pattern that is switched on by a stimulus of some kind. Very often the stimulus can be a feeling created by the things you see around you. I have several friends who have a buying pattern consisting of only three stages: they see something in a shop window, feel how good it will be to have it, then buy it. This pattern is more commonly called the "see it, buy it" strategy, but there is always an emotional feeling in the middle. In the example above, consider the type of emotions attached to the VP's power-desk. How many times had employees been in the office and felt bad while sitting in front of that desk? The pattern in this case would be "see the desk, feel bad, withdraw effort, and keep a low profile".

When you begin to explore patterns at this level, you can uncover the real drivers of behavior. We may think we are in control of our actions, but are we really? We are creatures of habit. Some habits get us desired results, others use our energy in less productive ways. In this section, you will discover the answer to the question "What makes us tick?" The more you understand about patterns, stimuli, how habits are formed and broken, and how we communicate with others and with ourselves, the easier it will be for you to develop behavioral flexibility and have a bigger influence in your organization.

> *We may think we are in control of our actions, but are we really? We are creatures of habit.*

There is a precision to our habits. Indeed, the preciseness of repeated behaviors is quite amazing – whether it's a driving habit, such as the way you operate the steering wheel, a facial expression, how you do the shopping or how you write a report. If you could put each of these behaviors under a microscope you would see their precision. What if you were to apply this to other skills, such as planning, implementation, decision making or time management? You would see a very similar precision in these thought patterns.

By breaking old patterns and creating better ones, we progress as human beings. This is how we learn, develop and become more successful. It is the realm of difference – finding more effective ways of achieving the things we want for ourselves, and we begin by putting our habits under the microscope to reveal the stimuli driving them.

4

Road maps for living our lives

How do you live your life? What has caused you to take the route you have embarked on? Think about your profession for a moment. What causes one person to become an accountant and another to become an engineer? How is success natural for one person, yet elusive to another? Upbringing? Schooling? Social environment? Genetic factors? Well, these factors have probably all had an influence in creating your personal road map for living your life, a map that you share with no one else – not even your family or closest colleagues and friends.

No two maps are alike and this uniqueness provides us with a lens through which we can view the world and form personalized opinions about it. To take a simple example, the lens of a pessimist is cloudy, obscuring the world with problems, while an optimist keeps the lens clear by polishing it with solutions. One of the challenges we face in our work is dealing with the different maps of the people we work with.

In a customer complaint situation, a sales executive might focus on the client relationship, a designer the product specifications. Their unique road maps make this so and provide the richness of a variety of perspectives. Unfortunately, in some cases, this diversity of perspective results in negative behavior. Individuals dismiss, fail to notice or have little respect for each other's alternative views.

In this chapter, you will learn how perceptions of the world, or maps of reality – which are so important to the communication process – are formed. The individual elements included in this chapter will build into a communication model that you will use to understand and increase your awareness of how we communicate and how we mis-communicate.

Some elements will be covered here in depth; others will be dealt with more fully in later chapters.

▦ Surely, you don't mean that, do you?

Respect is the foundation of effective communication. Would you listen and cooperate with someone you didn't respect? How much disrespect is generated in your organization? Sometimes disrespect can be coarse, but it can also appear in more subtle forms. What would cause one person to disrespect the views of another? One of the clues we use to recognize disrespect is language. Choose any one of the following to complete a sentence beginning "That's … ":

◆ not rational

◆ not logical

◆ not possible

◆ not practical

◆ not proper

◆ not sensible

◆ not feasible

◆ not right.

The adjectives are irrelevant to some extent. When used in a particular situation, there may be some truth in any of these statements, but it is the adverb "not" that causes problems in a relationship. The word "not" negates and dismisses, so is it any wonder that it causes friction between people? This simple word is often responsible for creating feuds because it is really saying, "The map you are using to navigate your thinking is wrong." In this context, the word "not" is more often interpreted as a direct attack on the person, on their ideas, and it can be "wrong" only if compared with the other person's unique map. So, who is to judge? Consider the following example.

❖ example

A close friend of mine has a wild imagination. He often comes up with ridiculous scenarios, obscure references, and bizarre observations of the world. He is a deep thinker and so brings some fresh perspectives to the way we usually see things. I enjoy his company and look forward to hearing his latest insights. This is not the view of other people, however. Some find him difficult to communicate with, consider him eccentric, a little loose in the head, perhaps, and they avoid him at parties and other social gatherings.

How could they think that about such a wonderful person? Of course, they are comparing him with their unique road maps for living their lives and forming judgments that stem from these. In fact, if they took some time to listen to what he is saying they might actually broaden their thinking around certain life issues, but their own road maps make them unreceptive, so what he says has very little meaning for them. The more we judge other people, the more we become fixated with our own road map, using it as a standard for others. There is little need to describe the obvious flaw in this thinking. A fixation with our own map is the best way to limit our learning and flexibility. No one is a perfect example of a human being.

Whose reality is the true reality?

Does anyone see the world as it truly is? You might read Albert Einstein's theory of relativity to get an answer to this one. Einstein gave us the scientific revelation that your view of what is happening in the world depends on where you are looking at it from. Try this simple exercise to experience this for yourself.

⊙ exercise

Stand on a chair and, with your finger going in a clockwise direction, draw an imaginary circle in the air at waist height, horizontally to the floor. Keep the movement going and ask someone to sit on the floor in front of you and look up at the circle you are drawing. Ask them in which direction the circle is going. They will tell you it is going anti-clockwise.

Who is right in this example? Both of you are right. You are just looking at the same thing from different perspectives.

Getting beneath the surface

Let's take a deeper look beneath the surface and explore the way we each create our unique map of reality. We have already identified that each person has a unique range of influences on their life. Children tune in to the significant parent figures around them; peer groups, cultural norms and daily experience all contribute to making the person. The nature–nurture debate remains unresolved today, there being insufficient evidence to assess the contribution of genetics to personality. So, let's work with the facts.

Biological filters

A fully functional person senses the outside world through their eyes, ears, nose, mouth, and by touching. Our senses are used to tune in to what is around us and pass information to the brain for processing. The senses are exposed to huge amounts of data, including all the information coming to our eyes, such as objects and their size, location, depth, color, movement, shadow, and so on. The things we hear in the foreground and background, the tone, volume, pitch, resonance, direction, and so forth. Smells and tastes and our feelings of touch and internal kinaesthetic sensations are all signals coming in via our senses. If we paid attention to all this information at once, we would overload and break down, so we filter most of it out. In fact, research[1] has established that we are only able to consciously pay attention to seven plus or minus two pieces of information at any one time.

We are only able to consciously pay attention to seven plus or minus two pieces of information at any one time.

While the senses are responsible for filtering information and deleting it from conscious awareness, the selection process – deciding what we pay attention to and what we don't – is the responsibility of our psychological filters.

Psychological filters

There is more to the brain and its functioning than most people realize. The processing power required to solve arithmetical problems, the imagination to create a work of art, make decisions, use logic, sequence things, and other functions is what we usually think of as being brain power. Yet, there are other processes at work, not always associated with the brain – those more often referred to as functions of mind. It is these mental functions that tell our sensory inputs what to look for and what to ignore. They create the road map and cause most of our communication breakdowns, and other people-related problems encountered in organizations.

Memory

When Charles Dickens wrote "It was the best of times; it was the worst of times", the famous first line from *A Tale of Two Cities*, I am sure he was expressing his understanding of how we remember experience. When an experience is charged with emotion, whether positive or negative, it becomes a more powerful memory, easily accessible to our conscious mind. Often the bad times will be packed away as we avoid talking about them until the memories fade, while the good times make great stories, so we regularly relive them with our friends. Pessimists seem to enjoy conveying only their bad experiences of the world; what dark minds they must have.

However, we should not think of memory just as a feature of the mind. The body is able to remember patterns of movement, which is why it is possible for a skilled driver to drive a vehicle without thinking consciously about the controls or for a juggler to launch the balls in the air and the rest be automatic. Some of the memory used to perform sequential physical tasks may be as much a part of the body as it is the mind, while it is certainly the mind that kicks off a pattern.

So, there are also patterns in the ways in which we use our physical and mental memories. One person may think pessimistically, another optimistically. Some people find it easier to recall memories than others, and the life we lead will have an influence on the types of emotions we attach to each stored memory. For those people with more stored negative emotions than positive, there is some good news. You can use your imagination to change that, if you want. Do the following exercise and discover this for yourself.

⦿ exercise

Bring into your mind the memory of an experience where things didn't go too well for you. Imagine a movie of it in your head and run it for a few seconds. Describe the events like a story and notice the qualities of the film – color, contrast, depth, size, location (in your mind's eye), volume, tone, and so on.

As the experience peaks, notice how you feel. Now, break this state of mind by changing your breathing or turning your body around 180 degrees.

Next, make up an alternative storyline, as you would have liked it to turn out. Then, recreate the movie, using this new storyline, and intensify all the qualities of the film. Crank them up really high. How does this feel? Which feeling would you rather have?

Is this exercise changing history? Yes it is. It's changing the history department in your mind. From now on, all your "history books" can have attached whatever emotion you choose. It won't change other people; it will just help you to be more resourceful in your life. If you had any difficulty creating images in your mind, stay with me – you'll get some help with this later. Not everyone finds it easy to work with mental images, but we all think in pictures, that's how the mind works – it's just that some people have very dark and distant pictures.

The quickest way to bring back a memory is with the olfactory sense – smell. When a memory contains a distinct smell, that smell will bring the experience flooding back into your conscious mind. While the smell is most often the trigger to a memory, it is the mental images that carry the emotion. This is why, in NLP, we work with visual communication a great deal of the time.

Getting back to the filtering process, I said that the mind tells the senses what to take in and what to filter out. The visual memory plays a part in this and is the cause of many false assumptions and distortions. Here's a simple exercise.

◉ exercise

I am going to tell you a story. As I tell it, I want you to remember as much of it as you can by picturing it in your mind.

Some time ago, a friend asked me out. She said she had been cooped up in the house for a week and needed to get out and enjoy herself. We went bowling, and I let her win. Later, we saw a film and then had dinner at her favorite place. I didn't drink, as I was driving, and I dropped her at her home later in the evening.

What do you remember?

Did you picture any of the following?

She asked me out over the phone.
She was 55 years old.
We went bowling at an outside, grass bowling green.

We had dinner at McDonald's.
My friend wasn't drinking either.
We rented a video and watched it at my house.
My car was a Volvo estate.
Her home is on the tenth floor of a block of flats.

Did you picture anything else? Perhaps you saw a different bowling scenario or a different restaurant. Did you imagine a younger friend perhaps? Did we go to the cinema? Were we face-to-face at the beginning? What car did I drive? What type of house did my friend live in? What styles of clothes were we wearing?

When we communicate our experiences, we miss out a lot of the details. If we didn't, we would send people to sleep! When we are listening, we remember in pictures, so very often we fill in the missing details because clear and well-defined pictures make remembering easier. Guess where these extra details come from? They come from your own experience. In the example above, you may have seen a familiar cinema, car, house or bowling alley. These may be places you have been to or seen on television.

We remember in pictures, so very often we fill in the missing details because clear and well-defined pictures make remembering easier. Guess where these extra details come from?

This ability to fill in the gaps is one contributing factor to poor listening skills. How many times each day does this kind of misinterpretation occur in business? How often are you the cause of distorted information? Take care with the movies in your mind when you are listening.

Values

We are now going to delve into the deep-rooted drivers behind human energy expended in the name of work. Our much-cherished values are a very potent force, generating the most creative energy – and the most destructive. Consider the following scenario.

❖ example

A very proficient and highly experienced person – I will call him Trevor – was recruited as technical training manager for a young, fast-growing computer company. Trevor impressed his interviewers and was given the position.

In the first two weeks, he demonstrated excellent abilities in building concepts and working them through to implementation schedules. This was a very bright individual. Unfortunately, his values got in the way and he left after only four weeks.

The first signs of trouble were female employees complaining about his abrupt and directive style of communication. It got so bad that a number of women said they would leave unless Trevor changed. He certainly wasn't a team player, yet his peer group could see no evil. They were confused. It came to a head one evening when a long-serving and highly respected manager resigned. She could take no more. When the head of training confronted Trevor, a number of powerful values were revealed.

Trevor had done enough menial jobs and now he was a manager he expected others to respect him. He observed a pecking order and, while being subservient to his bosses, he showed contempt for those he considered beneath him. This category included all females, who, he thought, should make his coffee and look after other basic needs in the office. This is how he had been brought up, and he was raising his children the same way. While these values may have worked for him in previous organizations, in this young, free-spirited company they were his undoing. He refused to change and chose to leave the company.

We come up against values every day in our work and social lives. You may have experienced problems caused by individuals holding opposing values on the following subjects.

◆ **Time**

Punctuality has more meaning for some than others. Is it OK to be late sometimes? Is punctuality that important?

◆ **Quality**

Not everyone buys into this, do they? What values does a person pursue when resisting the push for better quality?

◆ **Dress code**

Formal or smart casual? The rituals of working attire can be stifling or liberating, depending, of course, on your own values concerning this issue.

◆ **Protocol**

Is it OK to communicate up? Across? Can I ask anything of my boss? What will he or she think? Should we approach the boss? What are the unwritten taboos? Some bosses make it very clear what is OK and what is not OK to talk about, and those with whom you shouldn't communicate. This is a value judgment at work.

◆ **How to do the job better**

What's needed to improve? Training? Assessment? Teamworking? Better control systems? Working harder? Who knows best here? Bringing together such diverse values for improving the way work gets done requires individuals to get down from their personal hobby horses and respect each other's personal values for making improvements. In many cases, the CEO's values rule.

◆ **Working style**

What time do people arrive at your workplace in the morning? What time do they leave – in the afternoon, the evening? Who sets the pace for work in your part of the organization? Is this pace OK with everyone? Working to a regime that goes against your personal values will create an inner conflict. This will create stress and lead to physical and mental illness.

We may think that we know what our values are, and for the more obvious big subjects, most people probably do. I'm thinking here of the major influences on the ways in which we organize our lives. Issues such as GM foods, Third World debt, transport policies, lifestyles, law and order, professional ethics, family values, and other high-level ideals. Underneath these values are more day-to-day values, such as personal finance, social preferences, table manners, and other domestic rituals, and the work-related values we mentioned above.

Our values hold the key to our motivation; each decision made can be traced up the hierarchy to a high-level value.

These values are organized in a hierarchy, those at the top exerting power over a wider range of decision making than those at the bottom, which will address a narrower band of experience. Very often, the lower-level values conflict with the higher-level ones.

Our values hold the key to our motivation; they decide the needs we feel we should be feeding and each decision made can be traced up the hierarchy to a high-level value.

Observe the logic in the hierarchy shown in Figure 4.1 and consider how the potential for conflict occurs the lower down you get.

In this case, having adopted a high value for conserving energy, conflict is occurring as behavior attempts to support the value (taking the train to work). It may take this person some time to resolve the conflicts between environmental concerns, performing well at work and keeping a balanced family life. At the level of action, we can construct any logic to keep our high-level values intact. This is where value conflicts occur and the areas between world, family, and work values can become very blurred indeed.

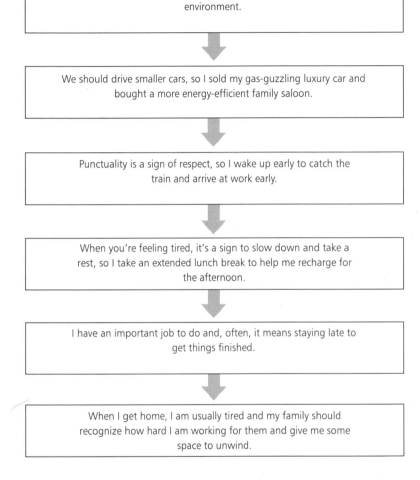

It's important to conserve energy and stop polluting the environment.

We should drive smaller cars, so I sold my gas-guzzling luxury car and bought a more energy-efficient family saloon.

Punctuality is a sign of respect, so I wake up early to catch the train and arrive at work early.

When you're feeling tired, it's a sign to slow down and take a rest, so I take an extended lunch break to help me recharge for the afternoon.

I have an important job to do and, often, it means staying late to get things finished.

When I get home, I am usually tired and my family should recognize how hard I am working for them and give me some space to unwind.

Fig 4.1 ◆ Example of a hierarchy of values

Now, none of this has absolutely anything to do with the quality of decision making. Indeed, we all make decisions from time to time that either backfire or fail to have the desired effect. It's the intention behind the decision that is fixed to the value driving it, not the action resulting from the decision. Work through the following example and consider the links between intentions, values, decisions, and results.

❖ example

The head of an internal service department is feeling a little inadequate in his job role. He really wants to do well and is very pleased with his progress to date. However, the personal stakes are now higher and his peer group is a very smart bunch of professionals. He is finding them very difficult to handle.

He has strong values relating to his status and position in the company and wants to be recognized as a person who gets things done and provides leadership for others. This value drives an intention to influence his peer group with his ideas for how they should be using his service.

Unfortunately, his words have very little meaning for them, so there is no buy-in and his ideas fall on stony ground. This makes him frustrated and even more determined to push his ideas, but he has not yet developed the flexibility required to be effective at this level in the organization. (Figure 4.2 outlines what is happening here.)

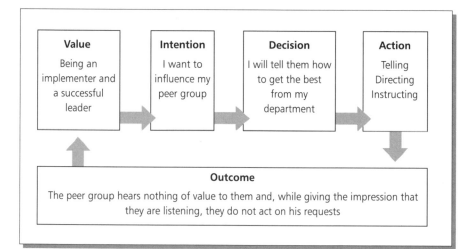

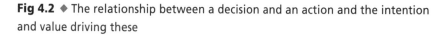

Fig 4.2 ◆ The relationship between a decision and an action and the intention and value driving these

In this particular example, the department head would do well to consider his values concerning learning and providing service. While the value of leadership is at a higher position on his hierarchy than learning and service provision, he may never develop the flexibility needed to achieve his intended outcome.

High-level values are often called *ends values*, the lower-order values *means values*. These lower-order means values are created to meet a particular ends value. When our value hierarchies are aligned to our actions, we can muster the energy we need to be effective quite easily. Problems come when something in our life changes and shifts begin to occur in the higher-order

When our value hierarchies are aligned to our actions, we can muster the energy we need to be effective quite easily.

ends values. This can send a shudder down the hierarchy, and we may begin to question the meaning behind some of our actions. Here's a simple exercise to get you thinking about your own values, the intentions they are driving, and the link to your actions. If you have strong supporting links between each answer, you are well aligned. If not, you might want to ask a few more questions about your reasons for doing what you do.

⊙ exercise

Values

Describe one activity you engage in at work. This might be a report you produce, a meeting you attend or something you do with a team.

Now, think about your decision-making process for engaging in this activity. What thoughts influenced your decision to engage in this activity?

What is your intended outcome for being engaged in this activity? What do you want this activity to get for you? What do you want to achieve by doing this activity?

Why is the previous statement important to you? Why do you want this for yourself? What high-order need is this activity satisfying for you?

At organizational level, values are extremely important. It is so easy to alienate employees by inappropriate or inept articulation of company values. In an ideal world, there will be an alignment of values held by individuals, the teams they work in, and the organization they belong to. All too often, however, the high-level business language of the boardroom is used to express values that managers then recite to their teams almost like a creed. Words such as *a "world-class service operation"* may enthuse top executives, but what does this mean to the service engineer at the customer interface? Values like these that aspire to some ideal must be interpreted for different people in the organization. For the service engineer, this might be as much to do with their tools and systems as the professionalism of their interaction with a customer.

> *Words such as a "world-class service operation" may enthuse top executives, but what does this mean to the service engineer at the customer interface?*

Beliefs

Do you believe in magic? How about alien visitors from another planet? What about abortion? Smacking naughty children? How about your personal potential as a human being? What do you believe in? There is no right or wrong answer to any of these questions, except when measured against personal standards, and the answers you get depend on who you ask.

Here we have another very powerful filter of our experiences. Beliefs are generalizations; they are formed from small amounts of inconclusive evidence. Our beliefs are generalizations of our subjective experiences, but we can also take on the beliefs of a majority where we have little evidence of our own to go on. There is insufficient evidence to prove, in every case, whether smacking a child will cause harm or instil a sense of discipline. Despite this, most people have a belief about smacking children, formed from their personal experiences.

Beliefs help us to get through life. We must believe in some things in order to make decisions each day. If I didn't believe that my team needed me as their leader, I might question the reason for going to work. If I hold no beliefs about fun, relaxation, health, learning, and personal growth, I am likely to stagnate as a human being. What I believe about these things will have a strong influence on my personality, my demeanor and my future. Beliefs are closely linked to our values.

While a value is something we hold as important in our lives, our beliefs cluster around providing support to keep the value intact. The more beliefs we can generate for a value, the stronger the value becomes. Beliefs are most commonly broken when we experience counter-evidence, but, even then, we may fabricate tenuous excuses to try to keep our belief from falling apart. Here's an example for you to consider.

❖ example

I ran a workshop for a group of middle managers in a British engineering company who were resisting changes recently brought in by their new French owners. This was a large company with a long tradition of manufacturing heavy equipment for the engineering industry.

One manager said, "These new marketing methods, designed to increase flexibility and choice for customers on a global basis, will never work." "It's destined to fail," he added. Here was a belief at work. Where it had come from, who knows? Even though there was nothing he could do about the change, he continued to devalue it and talk about its eventual failure. Senior managers began to perceive him as a stubborn pessimist and a liability to the success of the implementation project, but he didn't seem to care.

The group offered him a number of examples where this type of marketing method was working for other similar companies. His organization was merely following a much proven global trend. Still he refused to accept it and his reasons were getting weaker. Eventually, the only argument he could muster was, "The French will mess it up, and the lads here will never go along with such a ridiculous idea."

I later discovered that the value at the centre of his beliefs about the new marketing methods was to do with his professional status. He had a great deal of experience in the industry and no one had asked for his input regarding the changes. He felt hurt by this lack of recognition and the method used to communicate the changes. He was on holiday when the news was announced and was informed, on his return, by a colleague.

This is not yet the complete canvas on beliefs. Once we have formed a belief, we tend to seek evidence to make it true. This evidence gathering is often distorted and ongoing. A bit from here, a bit from there, it all gets packed around our values. If you think that a member of your team is being lazy, you are likely to find the evidence to prove it, even if you twist it a little. So, you saw her chatting to friends by the coffee machine three times today and you might compute this to mean "lazy". You could be right, but you could also be very wrong. What if she had just found her husband cheating and she needs to talk it through with someone? Is this lazy or is it more a need for emotional support in a time of crisis? Beware of the self-fulfilling nature of beliefs.

Beliefs can be extremely damaging to individuals and organizations. They can prevent cooperation, stifle creativity, limit possibilities, damage relationships, and constrain valuable human resources. They can also be liberating, empowering, and a vehicle for success. You can choose what to believe. You don't have to accept the evidence you have filtered to form a belief, you can choose to believe in anything you want. Success, effectiveness,

> *Don't sit around waiting to be recognized, stretch your beliefs and take charge of your journey.*

and achievement are more to do with belief than anything else. There are many super-intelligent people around whose lives are a mess. Equally, there are many unqualified people who have made fantastic successes of their lives. The majority of successful people are self-made. Their energy comes from within, generated by an unswerving belief in themselves and their ideas. Don't sit around waiting to be recognized, stretch your beliefs and take charge of your journey.

Over the next week, listen for other people's beliefs. They are easy to recognize. They often appear in language with such phrases as these:

◆ "I/we *can't* solve this ...", "You *can't* do it that way ..."

◆ "That *won't* work ...", "They *won't* help us ..."

◆ "It *isn't* going to succeed ...", "It *isn't* how we usually do it ..."

◆ "It's *not* worth the effort ...", "It's *not* possible ..."

How often do these negative phrases appear in your conversations? In what way are they limiting your potential? How would your organization be different if more people adopted beliefs that were empowering and liberating? Isn't it better to hear people say phrases like these?

◆ "I/we *can* do this ...", "We *will* do our best to make that work ..."

◆ "I am/we *are* creative ..." "We *can* learn much from this project ..."

◆ "I/we *will* be innovative ...", "We *are* a strong team ..."

◆ "We *will* work hard to achieve the most demanding goals."

These words are small, yet so powerful. They act like acupuncture points, either opening or closing the pathway for constructive energy to flow along. Some organizations have created such a culture of negative energy that, for many people, achievement is limited to getting through the day. That is a sad state of affairs.

You either can or you can't – the choice is yours. Later in this book, you will learn some simple techniques for changing beliefs that are limiting. Make a note in the margin if you can think of beliefs you want to change and refer back to this when you get to the exercise.

Decisions

We go through life making decisions. We make them about what we like and dislike, our future, and about who we are. Often our decisions are made unconsciously, from very little research, and they do not always serve us well. Having decided on a particular course in life, with certain criteria attached, we will focus our energy within those parameters and miss a whole lot of other experiences. Some decisions help us, others hinder, so it is important to evaluate past decisions and check their validity when set against the future you want for yourself. Think about the implications of past decisions in the following example.

❖ example

A coaching client once revealed to me a decision he had made as a young computing trainee. He had decided to steer his career towards management because he saw this as a route to financial and employment security. This decision led him to invest time in management courses and generally to maneuver himself into any situation that would give him exposure to management practices. That was six years ago. He is now stuck in a job managing a team that is performing badly and he is not enjoying it one bit. His computing skills are now out of date, and he has arrived at an impasse in his career.

This is just one example of a past decision leading to poor results. You can imagine the inner conflict this person must have felt as he tried to get his team to perform. You might also consider how the team perceived him as a manager who disliked his job and was underperforming. Decisions about who you are can have a major impact on your value and belief systems and on the filtering process generally.

Language

We have already touched on some elements of language and there will be many more throughout this book. Language is another filter of our experience. It acts to direct our attention towards some things and away from others. What we say, both to other people and to ourselves in our self-talk, helps to form our perceptions of the world.

The language we use also reinforces our values and beliefs. The simple words and phrases we use every day have such a big impact on our lives. We will be going into language in more depth in later chapters, but, for the time being, consider the following.

⊙ exercise

Imagine that you can digitally record all of your internal dialog for an entire day. You are going to capture your self-talk – the things you say to yourself as you contemplate situations throughout the day. Just before you go to bed, you play it back to yourself and a friend. Are you pleased with what you are hearing? Does it energize you or leave you feeling low? Do you want to change any of it?

Metaprograms

As a young manager, some years ago, I had a boss who was always interfering in small details. I used to think he didn't trust me, but later realized that he acted like this with everyone. I now know that his behavior was very natural, for him. He just really revelled in details. This was his preference, and also his downfall. As a general manager, his love for detail got in the way of further promotion. He was demoted twice because he showed no signs of the strategic thinking required of his role.

This was a *metaprogram* at work. Metaprograms run continuously in background mode and influence how we think. They give us information to help understand motivation and to select jobs we will succeed in. They are another set of psychological filters of our experience, and an awareness of them can help us communicate more effectively and have more influence with other people.

Metaprograms will be covered extensively later in this book, but the brief introduction to them here will allow you to build a complete conceptual picture of the filtering process.

Time

How we perceive time affects our ability to be effective. This has a major influence on how successful you are with long-term projects.

You may have heard the saying, "If it weren't for the last minute, nothing would get done." Some people seem to live their lives out of a personal organizer, while others are more free and easy with their time. Companies invest in time management courses to help their employees get more out of the time they spend at work. For some people this works, for others it makes very little difference. I shudder to think how many personal organizers are sitting on shelves, gathering dust, because the owners haven't found them useful.

The people who seem to gain from conventional time management courses are those who already manage their time well. For those who really need it, often the discipline required to work from an organizer is too painful for them, so they very quickly revert to old habits. You will learn how you code time for yourself and how you use this as another filter of your experience. Time is limited. It is one thing we have not learnt to manufacture, so using it productively and keeping that use at the highest quality is about all we can do with it.

> Time is limited. It is one thing we have not learnt to manufacture, so using it productively and keeping that use at the highest quality is about all we can do with it.

What next?

This chapter has introduced you to the main filters of experience, both biological and psychological. Understanding how these filters work will give you real insights into human behavior.

In the chapters that follow, you will learn techniques for reprogramming filters so that you can achieve more for yourself, and others. NLP is a technology of achievement and success, both at work and in your personal life.

Next, we will put together the elements from this chapter to build a functional model of human communication so that you can see what to change to achieve more of what you want.

Note

1   G. Miller (1957) "The Magical Number Seven, Plus or Minus Two", *Psychology Review*, 83.

5

A state of mind

In the previous chapter, I asked you to reflect on your route in life and consider how this has helped to make you the person you are today. Now we turn to results, and their most powerful determinant – your state of mind. You can have mountains of knowledge, skills and qualifications, but if your mind is charged with doubt and uncertainty, if you are feeling at a low ebb, or if you are unsure about your ability, you are unlikely to perform well in anything. Being in a resourceful state of mind helps you to access your knowledge and experience more readily. An unresourceful state of mind will make it much more difficult to tap into your natural ability and will, ultimately, limit your potential.

When an athlete prepares for a competition or a boxer for a fight, each will have spent as much time working on their mental state as they have their physical fitness. They are creating "winning" states of mind to help them succeed in their challenge. As I write this chapter, Mike Tyson has just defeated Julius Francis in Manchester, England. In the days leading up to the fight, reporters commented on Tyson's confidence and Francis' self-doubt, which came across loud and clear in their interviews. State of mind is as much about how you think of yourself, your identity, and your mission as it is technical skill. For sportsmen, state of mind is never left to the last minutes before an event. Rather, it is developed as an integral part of their overall training regime.

When an athlete prepares for a competition they are creating "winning" states of mind to help them succeed in their challenge.

A world-class chess player might create a "tactical genius" state of mind, a surgeon a "focused precision" state of mind, an artist a "creative" state of mind, a leader a "visionary" state of mind. What states of mind would help you improve your performance? Here are a few for you to think about:

◆ confident

◆ focused

◆ analytical

◆ receptive

◆ creative

◆ persuasive

◆ calm

◆ energetic.

Can you think of situations where you would like more resources like these? In the next section, there are exercises for creating any state of mind and accessing inner resources for anything you want to do well.

Here, we will put experience and filters into the functional model to show how we communicate, learn and change, and how results are created. The more we know about our own internal patterns of thinking, and how we generate our state of mind, the more flexibility we can have to influence our results and get more of what we want.

Results

Let's look at some experiences first of all to help clarify what I mean by results. Consider this scenario.

❖ example

As a young accounting executive in a mining company, Graham was being groomed for a senior role in the top team. He was an excellent accountant, with a team of eight people helping him to produce financial statements for the Board. His career to date had been highly successful. He had delivered great results to his employers, who showed their appreciation in promotion and remuneration.

However, this new senior position was proving much more of a challenge to him. Previously, his results had been achieved mainly by the application of his technical accounting knowledge and experience. Getting results in this new role would require something different.

He found that he was being asked for ideas and that his peers were making unsound financial decisions without consulting him. He felt overshadowed by the weight of authority and high-level posturing in the group. He found fitting in and contributing very difficult and he certainly wasn't getting results.

It is commonplace for a company to promote a person for doing well in one particular role, only to find that the skills, experience, and confidence required to perform well in the new role are lacking. Getting results in a new context requires the flexibility to learn, communicate differently, and perhaps change in other ways also, which may require a step change in our thinking and behavior. This is a higher level of learning than that applied to learning a technical skill. It requires the ability to adapt and evolve to cope with new situations and relationships, using our natural creativity to muster the resources we have within.

Figure 5.1 shows the reflective linkages between results and communication, learning and change. The real limitation is not technical ability, but the degree of creative thinking we are able to apply to our learning and personal development. There are many ways of putting limits on ability and they all come down to the degree of access we have to our inner creative resources, including self-motivation, belief, determination, responsibility, energy, perception, focus, and flexibility. These are the resources that, when enabled, empower us to create more of the results and more of the future we want.

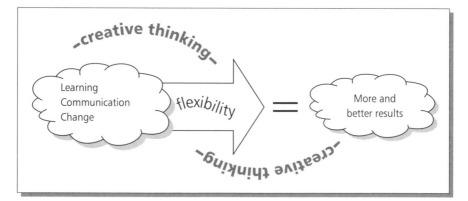

Fig 5.1 ◆ Getting better results

Behavior

Once we have opened our mouths and words have blurted out, we cannot reverse the process. We know the importance of thinking before speaking and acting. Forgetting to think first can land us in trouble. It is our behavior that directly connects to results, even though our thinking may be responsible for generating the behavior. I may think up a strategy for persuading my peers to buy in to a project, but my behavior will be judged by the perceptions of the people on the receiving end of my communication. It is not enough just to think we have the best way of influencing others; we must also pay attention to how we may be perceived by them. If our strategies are not getting us the results we want, we can carry on doing the same or we can do something different. The former is the choice of ignorance and incompetence; the latter requires flexibility and making a conscious decision to do something different.

If our strategies are not getting us the results we want, we can carry on doing the same or we can do something different.

Behavior often conforms to rules and norms within an organization. Even with a conscious effort to think differently, strong behavioral patterns can prevent change from taking place. A team of ten people may resist change simply because it is easier to stay the same. Successful team leaders are also change agents, with the ability to influence large groups. This is where the effort you are putting in to learn NLP will pay off in large amounts, as you become increasingly influential with work teams and in all other areas of your business and personal life. The larger an organization becomes, the more fixed patterns of behavior you will find and the more you will require influencing skills to make a difference. Take a few moments to do the following exercise.

exercise

Think about your own patterns of behavior. Take a typical week in your working calendar and recall the meetings and the written communications you engaged in.

How much of this was a repetition of something you have done before? How much of it was different to what you had done before?

Scrutinize what you did, what you said, and how you said it. How much of it got the results you wanted? How much of it didn't?

If you could go back in time and live that week again, which parts of your behavior would you change, and why? What about your listening skills, your perception?

If some of your behavior is not getting you what you want, the first step towards changing it is to recognize what you want to change, then create some alternatives. This may sound simplistic, yet I bet you know lots of people who keep repeating ineffective behavior, even though the results are clearly not contributing to higher-level goals. This is where it is useful to have some kind of feedback mechanism.

Feedback

The principle of feedback was introduced in Section 1. It is such a vital part of our learning process, and to NLP, that it appears in a variety of forms throughout this book. Here, I briefly describe feedback from a systems view.

If you think about human communication as a system, the input arrives at the brain for processing via the senses and the output of the system is behavior. Electromechanical systems also have feedback mechanisms. They feed back some of the output to compare with what was required (the system regulatory control). Adjusting the input, then, compensates for any difference between what you want from the system and what it produces (see Figure 5.2).

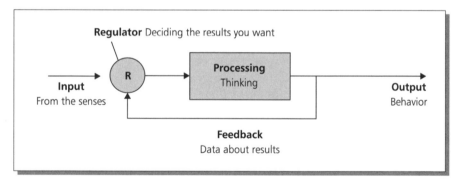

Fig 5.2 ◆ Feedback in a system

People are no different in this respect. Without feedback about our behavior, we may lose control. Our inbuilt feedback mechanism is called "learning". We all have some aptitude for learning, but, unlike electro-mechanical systems, we can choose to learn or not to learn. The ability to choose can be our most valuable attribute or the most under-used. Because learning is a choice, much of the feedback available to us can become redundant if we choose to ignore it. Quality of life is dependent on the quality of learning, and feedback is the fuel for life's journey.

We shall be returning to organizational patterns later in the book. Here, we are building this functional model of communication shown in Figure 5.3, incorporating the filters described in Chapter 4 and showing the influences on mental states.

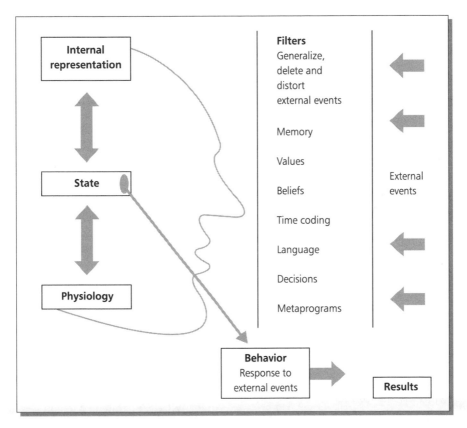

Fig 5.3 ◆ Functional model of communication

Physiology

Up to now, we have been concentrating on the senses, mind, and behavior. While we mostly recognize behavior in the form of words and actions, there is much more to observe for the trained eye. I am referring, of course, to body language, or physiology, and the insight it can give us into patterns of thought and behavior. Consider the following example.

❖ example

I was in a meeting with a CEO and his team. As we talked, we watched through the window as the factory employees were arriving at the site for the beginning of their shift. We noticed that a number of them were looking down at the floor, some shoulders were drooping, others were walking as if with leaden feet, no one was smiling, their faces looked heavy.

"They're miserable before they get to work," said the CEO. "All they talk about is the old days – they're just not interested in the future. They don't seem to realize that we are changing and they will have to face up to it eventually."

While this may have been true for some of the workers, it is pure conjecture to attach a meaning to body language without sufficient evidence. However, very evident, from my perspective, was the body language and voice tones used by the CEO as he told me about his workers. He was very forward and gesturing quite strongly with a cutting palm in the workers' direction. His voice became higher pitched as he began to stroke his brow.

What did this mean? This particular pattern of physiology was noticeable whenever he met a difficult problem, perhaps a frustration. I could have guessed that he was feeling angry or frustrated at their reluctance to embrace change, but that might be a conjecture too far. It was certainly not a resourceful state and this may be all we need to know.

Physiology is a very large part of any communication and it is easily misinterpreted. The words may be giving one message and the physiology another. If a colleague says to you, "I'm with you the whole way", do you believe them? What if their voice is wavering slightly, and their head is tilted a little to the side, and they are looking down? Are you less convinced? Body signals reflect the state you are in, and if the state doesn't match the words, suspicion is intuitively raised. The most extreme form of this incongruence between words and physiology is the businessman who says "yes" while moving his head from side to side.

Physiology is a very large part of any communication and it is easily misinterpreted. The words may be giving one message and the physiology another.

When you begin to recognize more non-verbal signals, you can check for incongruence in others. These mixed messages require follow-up action, as problems are sure to arise if left unattended. Let's suppose you are meeting with a supplier and you request some extra services. The supplier answers your request with "Yes, of course we can provide that for you, no problem", accompanied by incongruent body language and tone of voice. If you leave this unchallenged, you may be let down. It would be better to explore the reality of the supplier providing the extra services and anticipate any problems before they affect you.

Physiology reveals hidden messages, many of which we would rather keep to ourselves. Some people may be better at disguising them than others, but they are there in varying degrees nonetheless. Most of the time, we are totally unaware of the messages we are giving out – so deep within our psyche are their roots. The more aware you become of these signals, the more effective your communication will be. Here's a list of the things to watch and listen for in yourself and other people:

◆ posture

◆ head position and movement

◆ hand and arm gestures

◆ rhythmic tapping of hands and feet

◆ muscle tension

◆ shoulder movement

◆ frowning

◆ jaw movements

◆ crow's-feet around the eyes

◆ skin tone

◆ lip size and color

◆ lines around the mouth

◆ breathing:
  – high in the chest
  – abdomen
  – low in the abdomen
  – frequency of breaths

◆ eye movements

◆ voice characteristics:
  – tone
  – timbre
  – speed
  – volume
  – pitch
  – projection.

Sensory acuity

Your skill in recognizing patterns in body language and voice characteristics will help you to understand others' states of mind and so be more influential. These signals contain important information as to the state a person is in. It's only common sense – if you can help to put someone in a pleasurable state, they are more likely to respond well to your attempts to influence them than if they are in a negative state.

Developing your sensory acuity – that is, the skill of fine-tuning your senses so that you observe and hear much more of what is actually going on for people – is at the heart of NLP.

This requires some effort. Developing your sensory acuity – that is, the skill of fine-tuning your senses so that you observe and hear much more of what is actually going on for people – is at the heart of NLP. A heightened awareness of these unconscious communication signals makes the techniques you will learn later all the more effective. The use of any technique is a response to an external event, so the more you develop your sensory acuity, the more information you will have to work with.

In the example above, noticing the CEO's physiology as he talked about his workers gave vital cues to his attitude and communication style with them. He was very well-intentioned and wanted to enlist their support for his change program. Unfortunately, initial attempts at communicating the desired future fell on deaf ears and suspicious minds. From that point on, it became a struggle and, rather than taking responsibility for changing his communication style with the workers, the CEO saw the problem solely as the workers' reluctance to cooperate with his requirements. The majority of them were clearly not in a state of mind to be influenced, and the CEO ignored this or didn't consider it important.

Calibration

Whoever you want to influence, if you help the person to create a positive state of mind, the job will be half done before they start. Calibrating a person's "good state" will enable you to notice it at other times, then you will be able to tell whether your attempt to influence is working or not. This applies to selling, negotiating, coaching, teaching and training, presenting to groups, managing and leading people, teambuilding, facilitating change initiatives, getting commitment at meetings, literally anywhere you may want to have more of an influence. Here's a scenario to work through. As you read it, consider how patterns of thinking and behavior influence results.

⊙ exercise

Imagine that you are in a meeting with Lydia, one of your peers, and your aim is to get her to buy into a project. You have initiated the meeting and you are responsible for the project. You want to get Lydia to commit some of her people to your project. As usual, life is hectic and there are already too many projects putting demands on too few people and other valuable resources, but she seems keen to help.

You have presented Lydia with your project objectives and criteria, and you have answered her questions. She has expressed a concern that her people are spread across too many projects, but has agreed to participate. You continue by asking her about recent projects that went wrong and, as she is telling you about these bad experiences, you are calibrating her state by noticing certain physiological cues. She is stroking her jaw, widening her nostrils, breathing higher in the chest, sitting bolt upright, her voice tone has become harsher, and she is playing with the ring on the middle finger of her right hand. You give this state a name so you can remember it more easily – you call it "Jaws" to remind you how dangerous it can be.

Having calibrated the Jaws state for Lydia, you can be quite sure that whenever you notice this state, she will not be feeling her best. We cannot say for sure that it will always be linked to project problems, but it is safe enough to connect it with something negative going on inside her mind. This pattern should warn you if, for example, it appears at the same time as she is giving you her commitment to collaborate with you.

Calibration is a key skill in NLP. A close colleague of mine has a state I call Searcher, which I have learned to recognize and use to my advantage. Her skin color gets redder and she will either stop talking altogether or slow her speech down, and any words she does use are voiced in a deeper tone than usual. I have learned that Searcher means she has discovered something in a conversation that doesn't seem to fit and she begins to search for possible connections. Often this will result in either the discovery that there are no connections or the development of a new vein of thought entirely. Whatever the result, it has proved to be an extremely valuable supplement to my own thinking, so I give her all the space she wants until the state changes.

There will be exercises later in this book to help you develop sensory acuity and calibration skills, but you could begin now by making a conscious effort to see and hear more from people every day. Refer to the list earlier in this section on physiology for guidance on the important signals to watch and listen for.

State

We can all create our states of mind whenever we want, but some people believe they have no control over this. It is commonplace to hear people saying, "I'm in the wrong frame of mind for this." One of the most powerful aspects of NLP is the array of techniques used to generate any state of mind. The phrase "state of mind" is not quite correct. Although it is the one generally used to describe how you are feeling in your mind, it is more accurate to use "state". This can be extended to "state of being", recognizing that the mind and body are one system with many interconnections between them.

The communication model (Figure 5.3) shows how we observe and respond to the world. This is the functional model of NLP, depicting the process of turning our representation *of* the world into results *in* the world. We have covered most of the elements of this model, so you can now put them together to show what influences our experiences of the world.

The map is not the territory

Although we take in external events via our senses, we do not all see the world in the same light. It's like using a road map to find your way to a destination and the map will give you certain general information, but not show other traffic, pedestrians, road works, weather conditions, and other changeable events. These details ensure that each traveler experiences a different journey, even though the map is the same. In a similar manner, we all live in the same world and think that we experience events in the same way, but the reality is far from that. Two people may be looking at the same event and thinking entirely different thoughts. In fact, the chances of two people having the same thoughts is extremely slight, if not impossible. Consider the following scenario.

❖ example

Two friends are walking down a busy city street as someone in a sleeping bag sitting in a shop doorway beckons to them, asking for money. One friend gives a hard look and comments, "These people should take responsibility for their lives. Begging will just keep them on the streets." The second friend casts a more sympathetic eye and remarks, "What has our society become? Surely we should be putting more effort into helping these people get off the streets?"

In this example, it is the same event being witnessed by two people and the result is completely different thoughts and responses. This is an example of filters at work, and you can imagine how each person's filtering produces very specific states.

Once you realize how easy it really is to change your filters, you can create any state you want. From the communication model, you will see that all behavior is state dependent – that is, what we do and say will be determined by the state we are in. If we are in a "down" state, we are unlikely to behave at our optimum and this will show in our results.

Internal representation

When we have filtered external events, we end up with a unique internal representation of them. This will consist of images, sounds, and feelings that we create as our own internal map of the external territory. Our internal representation influences our state, which affects our physiology, and the three components interact to form behavior.

I have explained how to change a state by making physiological changes, such as breathing and posture, and the same can be achieved with the internal representation. You were guided through this in an earlier exercise where you adjusted the qualities of images in your mind. One way to think about this is to imagine you have a control panel for changing the qualities of your internal representations, called *submodalities*. Figure 5.4 shows the more common changes you can make, some being simple digital off/on functions, such as the switch for black and white or color, while others are more analog in design, with a range of amplification, such as volume and contrast.

Have a go at the controls using a representation of a pleasurable past event. Choose one that brought positive feelings and results you were particularly pleased with.

⊚ exercise

First of all, bring a pleasurable experience back into your mind and notice all the qualities of the representation. If this is an experience you would like to replicate in the future, intensifying the representation will make it more powerful and easier to recall when you want to. The intensity of your state makes a big difference: the more intense, the more resourceful you will be; low-intensity states lead to mediocrity.

Visual submodalities

If your image is black and white, switch it to color. If it is framed, make it panoramic, and switch to 3D if you have a flat, two-dimensional picture. Try changing the size of the image, making it small then enlarging it as much as you can. Tilt the image in different directions and notice the physical location in your mind's eye. If it is located up and to the front of you, bring it down a little and move it to your left. Try different locations. Next, turn up all the visual controls of contrast, brightness, color, hue, and focus, one at a time. Do you have any movement? If so, slow it down, then speed it up and stop the action at its most intensely satisfying moment.

Auditory submodalities

Do you have sounds? Are they mono or stereo? Alter the volume, bass, and treble. Change the location the sound is coming from. What other auditory qualities can you change?

Kinaesthetic submodalities

Now play around with the feelings. Do you have texture, pressure or temperature in this representation? If so, change the controls and feel for any difference in intensity. If you have other feelings associated with the representation, adjust those, too. Now, can you see yourself in this image or are you just looking at the image? Looking at yourself is called a dissociated state. If you have this, then flip the switch to associated and, as you do, bring the representation slowly towards you so that it surrounds you and you become part of it. You are likely to experience a direct and highly intense feeling as you make this association. If you don't get this, it is possibly because the experience you chose is not memorable enough for you. When you associate in this way, you are bringing back the feelings you had at the time of the experience and intensifying them using submodalities.

Did you notice any of the controls having more of an impact on your state than others? There will be one or two that, when changed, will give you an emotional rush. These are called the *critical submodalities* and will be of great service to you as you develop your ability to work with your internal representations. They are also responsible for triggering your down states, so identifying them will be valuable for dealing with all your states.

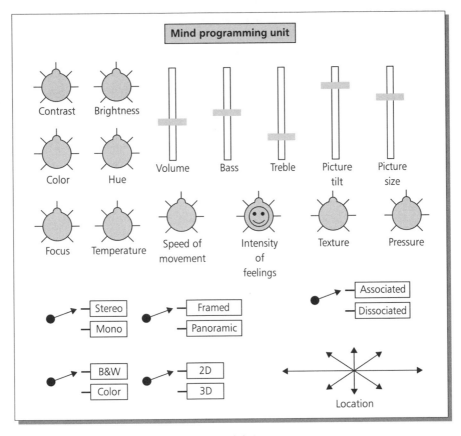

Fig 5.4 ◆ Internal representation submodalities

The submodalities I have included in the control panel in Figure 5.4 do not form the complete set. They are the more common qualities that are likely to help you manage your states more easily. You may find that you are able to identify other visual, auditory or kinaesthetic qualities in your internal representations. This is fine; use whatever works best for you.

I have chosen a short piece of Chinese philosophy to round off this chapter. A little self-indulgent perhaps, but it is one of my favorite texts. It reminds me of the importance of state management to clarify the mind and unravel the tangle of feelings created by a busy and complicated lifestyle.

True intent, true sense, and spiritual essence are the three jewels in our bodies: true earth, true lead, and true mercury. These three jewels have a primordial, whole, unified energy, which is complete without any defect. This cannot be called intent, sense, or essence – it is all one reality. But when it mixes with temporally acquired conditioning, and yang culminates, giving rise to yin, the single energy divides into three. Thus there come to be the terms intent, sense, and essence. Once the real divides, the false comes forth; the seeds of routine take command, sense faculties and data stir together, and habit energy grows day by day: true intent becomes adulterated with artificial intentions, true sense becomes adulterated with arbitrary feelings, and spiritual essence becomes adulterated with temperament. Aberration and sanity mix, the artificial confuses the real, essence and life are shaken; day-by-day, year-by-year, the real disappears and all becomes false.

Writings of an 11th-century Chinese philosopher,
Chang Po-Tuan

6

Patterns of rapport

Think of people in your life with whom you have great rapport. Your friends or some of your work colleagues perhaps. Now think of people with whom you have very little rapport, people whose attempts to communicate with you leave you confused, annoyed, frustrated or simply indifferent. Now compare the two. What are the differences in the relationships between you and these two types of person? Also, think about the people you meet from day to day. Do you get on with everyone or are some people more work than others? Rapport between people is, as you might have figured out by now, a filtering process and it works at an unconscious level. You may recall that the conscious mind is able to deal with about seven plus or minus two bits of information at a time and the rest of our thinking is managed by the unconscious part of the mind. Think of it as an iceberg where the tip showing above the surface of the water is the conscious mind at work, while the unconscious mind relates to the majority of the iceberg beneath the surface.

Rapport is mainly an unconscious process. We are often unaware of the reasons for preferring one person's company to another's, except for the obvious things, such as common interests, attractive looks, interesting conversation, and the good feelings we get from people we like. Relationships are rarely analyzed further than this, especially when we enjoy a person's company. At work, the quality of relationships between people will directly impact performance. Not liking someone, for whatever reason, is apt to result in you and the other person taking action to avoid each other. This will damage performance. With so much focus going on the emotional side of relationships in the workplace, rapport is increasingly seen as a competitive aspect to a company's ability. Emotional intelligence, NLP, and various forms of interpersonal skills training are just as likely to be found on the human resources director's strategic objectives list as is technical training, because they enhance the links between people and this connects directly with performance.

The upsurge in interest in NLP from the business community in general is as a result of its finally realizing the connections between relationships and performance. Getting the best out of people begins with a better understanding of relationships, and rapport is a key element in the process. Without rapport, your powers of influence over

At work, the quality of relationships between people will directly impact performance.

another person will be extremely low. Would you allow yourself to be influenced by someone you didn't like? A friend of mine has just bought a new car from a dealer he didn't care much for. I don't know too much about the details, but he told me they didn't hit it off from the beginning. My friend bought the car from him only because no other dealer had the color and specification he wanted at that time. Because of this he has found another dealer to supply servicing and extras. He told me that he would be avoiding the first dealer wherever possible in the future because he just didn't seem to understand his needs. Certainly there was very little rapport between them.

So, rapport is a prerequisite for any form of influencing. If you exert influence with the use of power, authority or reward without building rapport, you are not influencing but coercing and manipulating. It is important to make a distinction here. Coercion will backfire as soon as you lose your ability to coerce whereas rapport works regardless of the positional power of the influencer. Using rapport as your method of influence, you will find that people cooperate as a result of exercising choice and free will. There is no sense of needing to cooperate, but, rather, a wanting to cooperate. This is a very important difference. Rapport is long-lasting, elegant, respectful, and acknowledging in nature. Rapport connects emotional centers together and creates enjoyable bonds between people. Rapport is the intelligent approach to influencing, regardless of positional power, whereas power and authority are defaults for people in positions of power who have poor interpersonal skills and little flexibility.

■ What is rapport?

Rapport is the good feeling you get when you are in the company of someone you like. It is bonding at an unconscious level. You can see it in the lovers' gaze across the dinner table. It is the camaraderie among a rugby team in the bar after a match. It is the warmth between colleagues relaxing after a hard day's work. It is the everyday chat between friendly neighbors meeting in the supermarket.

When observing the behavior of people who have a deep rapport, you notice a certain synchronization. When rapport is strong, body language develops into a unified dance. You may have noticed, in meetings where rapport has been high, certain body language patterns – for example, leaning in and leaning out, opening notepads at the same time or perhaps folding arms in unison.

So, we can recognize when rapport is strong from the body language, and we can use this knowledge to build rapport with people we may not have a natural rapport with. If we reverse the process and start by matching the other person's physiology in some way, we can begin to build rapport. We are taking a natural process, learning how it works, and using it with a purpose in mind – to create a bond, so that we can be influential.

Blocks to rapport

At a fundamental level, rapport is about respect. It is an expression of our interest in the other person, showing empathy and respect for the person's experience. Listening and putting our own agenda on hold is a prerequisite for building rapport. When you are in a conversation with someone, it is often the case that, while the other person is talking, you are rehearsing or researching what you are going to say as soon as there is a gap in the conversation. It is not easy to listen and understand at the same time as you are preparing what you are going to say next. It is a complicated process and will certainly overload the conscious mind for many people. Listening with your full attention on the other person is the minimum requirement for understanding. Listening while viewing things from the other person's perspective is a more effective way of under-standing their model of the world than looking at them solely from your own perspective. When you can achieve this, you will be close to mastering rapport skills. Consider the following example.

> *Listening and putting our own agenda on hold is a prerequisite for building rapport.*

❖ example

A new client was telling me about a dilemma with her team. There were customer complaints left unresolved, and a lack of ownership of problems among some of the team members. As she continued to explain the situation, I listened as if it were my team, and I put myself in her position as best I could from the way she described events.

I asked a question or two about her feelings and what she would like to change, and I mirrored back some of her statements to get clarity. After a few minutes, she began to talk about the absurdity of the situation in a less stressful way and we laughed at the team's bizarre behavior. When we parted, she thanked me for such an enjoyable conversation, yet I had contributed nothing from my own experience.

The pressures of organizational life create tension and conflict. Sometimes conflict cuts deep and stress begins to take hold of the emotions. When this happens, people can become so obsessed with their own situations that they stop listening to each other and rapport breaks down. As rapport declines, so the barriers between people are strengthened and existence becomes a tactical survival game of attack and defense.

Listening and being curious are critical to the learning process and they are fundamental components to building rapport.

Understandably, we like to be listened to. Have you ever been talking to someone and suddenly noticed the person being distracted in some way? Perhaps his or her eyes moved to look in another direction. How do you feel when this happens? What do you think about the other person? What does this do to rapport? When it has happened to me in the past, I have taken it to mean that the other person was uninterested in what I was saying, so I have ended the conversation at that point and reverted to listening.

The skill of listening is, I believe, one of the most underpractised of all interpersonal skills. There is so much focus on language and words that listening is often relegated to a low priority, as something that was learnt on a course once. Everyone wants to get their message across and communicate what is important to them. In my experience, few people in organizations are listening compared with the number of people pushing their message out.

Listening and being curious are critical to the learning process and they are fundamental components to building rapport.

In this chapter, you will learn to notice patterns of rapport in other people, in groups, and within yourself. The degree of influence you have with anyone, including yourself, is directly relative to the degree of rapport you have established. So, let's turn now to the different aspects of physiology you can use to create rapport with people you want to influence.

Matching patterns of physiology

As we talk, we use our body to convey part of the message. Body movements may be comfort adjustments or supportive gestures to emphasize or punctuate the dialog. The voice also carries part of the message by means of the characteristics of the type of sound produced. Experiments[1] have been done to determine how much of our communication is achieved by the words and how much by physiology. The results claim a mere 7 percent is drawn from the actual words used, 38 percent from the tone of the voice, and a whacking 55 percent from body language (see Figure 6.1).

The sizes of the latter two portions explain why so much communication is misinterpreted. While we are listening and working out the meaning of what we are hearing, at the same time we are unconsciously doing the same thing with body language and the tone of the voice. This may result in confusion, distortion, deletion or worse.

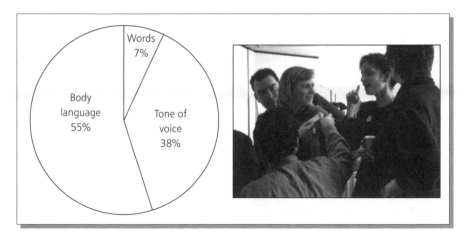

Fig 6.1 ◆ How we get the complete message

So, if 93 percent of our communication is provided by body language and the tone of the voice, we can use this to convey a message of rapport; and we know that our chances of influencing someone will be greatest when they like us, and the more we are like the other person, the more they will like us. I'm not suggesting that we emulate all the people we wish to influence. Rather, I'm saying that we connect with them at an unconscious level, in the 93 percent, conveying the message that we are like them. So, while we are listening from the speaker's perspective, we can also be creating a bond by matching certain elements of physiology. Some of the most common patterns are:

◆ body posture and position;

◆ leg positions and configuration – legs crossed, tucked under, outstretched, resting on knee, resting on desk, and so on;

◆ arm positions and configuration – folded, on top of head, hands clasped, fiddling with pen, arms tight to body, outstretched, hands tucked under seat, hands in pockets;

◆ head position – tilted up, down, to the side;

◆ rhythmic tapping of fingers, hands, feet, head;

◆ rocking motion;

◆ gestures with hands, arms, head – you do not perform a gesture simultaneously, as this would just look ridiculous, so you use similar gestures only when you are speaking;

◆ breathing – speed, depth and location (chest or abdomen);

◆ voice characteristics – pitch, tone, volume, speed, timbre.

Mirroring

You can also mirror body language by presenting a mirror image. This means that, unlike matching left with left and right with right, you mirror left with right and vice versa (assuming you are facing each other). If you make matching and mirroring moves immediate and identical, it can be easily noticed, so introduce a delay of a few seconds before changing and make your positions similar, not identical. You can also cross-match by scratching a right knee in delayed response to a right-handed head scratch. Think of it as joining in the dance, so that your combined communication can flow unrestricted.

The myths of body language

Be careful to avoid the trap of misinterpreting body language. It is not so useful to make generalizations about what particular patterns mean. For example, folded arms do not necessarily mean that a person is closed, any more than it means they are feeling cold or comfortable in that position. Hands on the head may mean that someone is feeling superior, but it could also mean that they are enjoying the stretch.

Drawing conclusions like these from body language patterns does not help to build rapport, but matching them will. Putting your body in a similar position to the other person's will help you to create the same state they are in, thus making a bond at an unconscious level between you. A young manager I was coaching told me that, during one-to-one meetings, his boss would sometimes remove his shoes and put his feet up on his desk, and that this caused him to feel uncomfortable and intimidated. I suggested that he follow suit, perhaps with an opening comment such as, "That's a good idea. You don't mind if I join you, do you?"

Putting your body in a similar position to the other person's will help you to create the same state they are in, thus making a bond at an unconscious level.

When states are similar, empathy increases and rapport is strengthened. When you are proficient at creating states when you want to, you will be able to match someone's state – regardless of how resourceful it is – and help them to change their state to a more appropriate one for the job in hand. You will learn this technique later. When we are matching, we are pacing the person's model of the world before attempting to influence by leading their thinking.

Influence

I have used the word "influence" a great deal because this is essentially the purpose of our communication. We want to have an influence on people. By "influence" I am referring to the process of engaging the thoughts of other people in such a way that they follow a direction in support of our own thinking, which concludes in a certain action being taken to our satisfaction. In this way, we are being influential in our ideas.

One of the drawbacks of launching our ideas on to other people is that they often meet their ideas coming at us and then a battle for the best idea ensues. When two people meet, they will each bring their own agenda of needs and desires.

Remember what I said about listening? If you want to influence, then you will give the other person airtime to offload their agenda and you will listen. While listening, you will be matching some of their physiology and you will have all your receptors tuned in to pick up the words and the unconscious parts of the communication.

Remember sensory acuity? We are pacing the other person's experience so that they will like us. If you ever want to reduce your personal influence, just do the opposite and mismatch. I guarantee you a high success rate.

"I really want to understand Gerald, but his MBA thesis on organizational design and post-modernism in the workplace turns me right off."

Pacing and leading

You can check if you have sufficient rapport with a person by starting to lead. If you adopt a different physiology, the other person will follow you if you have strong rapport. If not, keep pacing. At first, as you practice pacing and leading in this way, your matching may seem wooden or artificial, but persist and it will become much more natural to you after a while. When you are leading with the unconscious part of the message, you can begin to lead with the conscious part as well – your ideas. Be careful to link your ideas with theirs so that you make a natural and smooth bridge from one set of ideas to another, then continue to pace, even when you are leading.

In addition to pacing and leading using physiology, it may be appropriate to pace and lead in other ways.

Key words and metaphors

We can also match some of the words when we are talking. Even though only 7 percent of the overall message is transmitted by means of the words, they can have a very powerful influence. Pick up the key phrases used in a conversation and repeat them when you are talking. If you hear the phrase "clinch the deal", use these exact same words in your response rather than your own term – say, "close the sale". By using the same language, you are reducing the possibility of misunderstandings occurring.

By using the same language, you are reducing the possibility of misunderstandings occurring.

Similarly, if you hear the phrase, "Let's run this up the flagpole and see what happens", it will pay to work with the flagpole metaphor and respond with something like, "We'll get the flag flying at full mast in no time at all." Metaphors are an extremely powerful way of communicating. They are rich in meaning and proliferate within every organization. They include everyday terms such as "fire-fighting" and "bite the bullet" to more elaborate forms used to describe a change initiative, or a situation, such as "project Noah" and "riding the tiger". Metaphors form meaning at a deep emotional level, boosting both understanding and rapport, and, by working with a person's own metaphor, you are showing great respect for the way they perceive the world.

Values

Make a point of eliciting a person's values connected with the area under discussion. You may not share the same values, but you ought to respect the rights of others to value whatever they consider to be important. For example, a customer may tell you that negotiating a low price is important because they want to have enough money left at the end of the year to treat their team to a social event. You may not think this is important, but your customer does, so all you need to do is recognize this by saying something like, "Well, I want to make this deal with you so that when the contract is signed you are also securing the social treat you want for your team."

Mismatching a value is the quickest and most certain way to damage rapport. In consultancy, you see lots of different types of companies striving to achieve similar objectives by vastly different means. In one company I know, open communication is considered a competitive threat. This results in its spending a great deal of time blocking outside channels and making the methods highly procedural. In another company, open communication is considered strategic to its competitive advantage, so it invests heavily in the latest technology for its employees. If I am going to help either of these companies to improve their communication ability, I must begin by respecting their current values, whatever they may be, and understand why they are thinking in that way. Only then will it be safe to offer alternatives for consideration.

Styles of thinking

One of my clients thinks in models. He has about 25–30 models on his computer depicting different parts of his human resources strategy. Whenever he has explained an aspect of his company's business, he has referred to one or more of these models. I have found it rewarding to relate my ideas to one or other of the models. This allows him to grasp the idea quickly and begin to develop it for himself.

When you meet other people where you find them, you are in less danger of jarring a thought process than if you simply launch your ideas at them.

Another of my clients is on a personal mission to create major change in a short period of time. This results in very short and precise messages, so I have modified my own style to match this, and things happen very quickly indeed.

When you meet other people where you find them, and join in their style of thinking, you are in less danger of jarring a thought process than if you simply launch your ideas at them. By pacing in this way, the combined thinking moves in a much smoother and more natural way towards a conclusion.

Personal interests

You may be a devout fan of football, an ardent skier, a voluntary care worker or a regular at the local bowling alley. Personal interests are very close to our hearts and we treasure them for the sparkle they bring to our lives.

Think about your interests for a moment. Do you enjoy telling others about them? We can easily get carried away recounting the events of the match at the weekend or the skiing trip. With our friends, this is very much a part of the social interaction, bringing a pleasant respite from the seriousness of work and bonding people together.

When you are just beginning to build rapport with people you don't know so well, your stories may consume time and get in the way of understanding. In the early stages of rapport, you want to be listening, asking questions, and pacing the other person's experience. It is difficult to do this when you are giving a commentary on your last holiday.

At an appropriate time, asking someone about their personal interests can help to build rapport. If the person is comfortable talking about personal interests, you can laugh with them and share the variety of emotions connected with their experience.

Culture, ritual, and dress

When I run workshops for managers, I prefer to dress casually, believing that suits and ties are unnecessary, and sometimes a barrier, to the process of learning. Every now and again, I come across a new client who has never experienced this. In some instances, even when we have cleared the way with senior management for workshop participants to wear casual attire, some people have remained in their formal wear for the duration. In one or two extreme cases, people have simply not owned casual wear because they are always at work.

Sometimes rapport requires you to dress in a similar way to the other person. As soon as you have built rapport, you can lead the dress code with something of your personal taste, if that is appropriate. This may work with one person or a small group, but may not have an effect on an entire organization, where the mode of dress is embedded in the culture.

Ritual is something you may have to pace to build rapport, but be careful how far you take this. In one company, a culture of "work hard, play hard" had evolved into crazy drinking binges whenever employees gathered together. The occurrences became more frequent and the ritual more defined. I had to work out a survival strategy that allowed me to join in the rituals without consuming excess amounts of alcohol.

Creating rapport with a group

So far, we have been mainly dealing with influencing in one-to-one interactions. When you are in a larger group, it is still possible to create rapport and influence by pacing and leading. The same techniques can be used, but you may have to find out more about the group before and during the meeting. The techniques for more formal presentations require a little extra linguistic sophistication and we shall deal with this in another chapter.

Influencing a group requires the skills of facilitation. If you have ever observed good facilitators at work, you will have noticed how they manage the process of interaction among group members and how they draw solutions out of individuals in the group without necessarily being a technical expert. Here's a simple checklist of pacing techniques for a group.

◆ Avoid making assumptions about what each person wants to get from the meeting because they will backfire at a later stage. So, unless they offer it, ask each person for their outcomes for a meeting up front.

◆ Refer to these outcomes throughout the meeting. Use them to keep on track, clarify, and stay focused on important areas. Suggest putting their outcomes on a flipchart so everyone can refer to them throughout the meeting.

◆ Match or mirror the physiology of the person you want to have most influence with. If they are quiet and still, ask for their views on things so you have something to pace.

◆ Connect with every person. Arrive early so you can meet the attendees informally as they turn up and get some rapport going before the meeting starts.

◆ Make eye contact and acknowledge everyone in some way during the meeting. When you are speaking, make sure you engage the attention of everyone there using eye contact, gestures, key words and metaphors, values, style of thinking, and tone of voice. You don't have to do it all at once – this might cause you to blow a circuit or two – just pace enough patterns to make a connection.

◆ Pace the group's meeting style – formal, informal, structured, loose, humorous or whatever.

◆ Remember to lead at some point, having established rapport.

Rapport with yourself

I could easily have put this item at the very beginning of the book, so fundamentally important is it to your results. All the techniques in the world will do you no good if you feel uneasy about yourself in some way. How do you think about yourself and about your abilities? Do you have any inner conflict to deal with? Are you fully behind your values? Do you like yourself? If you answered "No" to any of these questions, your unease will be picked up by other people and this will limit the degree of rapport you are able to build and the amount of influence you will have.

Leadership within enables leadership without. An internal misalignment will make you indecisive. Leaving a state like this unattended to will lead to stress.

Pacing and leading is an act of leadership. You are having an influence on the direction other people will take and on their motivation to work with you. To be an effective leader of others, the first requirement is that you are able to lead yourself. Leadership within enables leadership without. An internal misalignment will make you indecisive and others will pick this up. Leaving a state like this unattended to will lead to stress and you may come across to others as having inconsistent or conflicting standards. If you like yourself as a person, you can concentrate more of your energy on other people and less on keeping up appearances for the sake of other people.

Rapport as a life skill

Building rapport should not be confined to the world of business. Becoming skilled at this will enhance all your relationships and improve the quality of your life in general. Make a point of achieving some rapport with everyone you meet. Not only is this great practice, you will probably enjoy your interactions much more. Begin with the bus driver, shop assistant, receptionist, waitress, children, neighbor ...

Note

1   Ray Birdwhistell (1970) "Kinesics and Communication", University of Pennsylvania.

7

Communication channels

In the days before the digital revolution, communication by telephone was achieved using analog lines connected together with big clunking relays. It was quite common to get a crossed line and you could end up listening to another conversation or suddenly discovering you were talking to someone you didn't know.

New digital technology has done away with this amusing quirk, but we still manage to cross our channels of communication – without the help of technology. New digital communication devices often get the blame for a great deal of our human miscommunication. I wonder how much of this blame is really a deflection of personal responsibility when communication has gone wrong, as it so often does.

With so much of the message coming from unconscious signals, is it any wonder that we get it wrong? How many times have you had a conversation with someone where reaching an understanding over a relatively simple issue was hard work? We can be with someone in the same room, using the same language, and arrive at very different conclusions.

One of the main contributors to this situation is the differences between our personal thinking strategies. The strategies of two interacting people can be mismatched, causing both people to experience a difficult communication flow. When you have a mismatch in thinking strategy with someone it is hard work getting clarity on anything.

A *thinking strategy* is the way we communicate our thoughts internally. It is the processing we do in our minds before responding with behavior. Often, mismatches in thinking strategies are the cause of difficult or puzzling interactions. It is widely recognized that children learn best from teachers they like and learn less from those they dislike. This natural selection process between teachers and children is partly the result of different thinking strategies.

When my eldest son was at his first school, the teacher asked the class where wood comes from. She was hoping to get the answer "From trees", but my son's hand shot in the air and he shouted out "It comes from God." The teacher interpreted this as a joke and didn't take him seriously.

Had the teacher been more sensitive to the differences in thinking strategies, she might have been more understanding about how he made that connection. When I asked my son about this he said, "Wood comes from the forests that grow in the earth that God made." This is not an incorrect answer. He came up with this because, as he contemplated the question, he visualized a tree in a forest and saw a God figure in the sky. He processed the question visually and saw all those things in his mind's eye. Then he felt good about having such a great answer and thrust his arm in to the air. So, his thinking strategy consisted of a visual process and a feeling. He thought he was giving a smart answer, but the teacher labeled him "joker". Until teachers receive better training, this will continue to happen to our children.

You may be thinking of situations at work where similar mismatches have occurred. They are often recognizable because of the absence of any real evidence for the mismatch – it's just such a hard slog to reach an understanding. What you will recognize is a consistency of this occurring with certain people. There will be some people you get on really well with and some you don't. Most often, these encounters where there seems to be no concrete reason for the difficulty are put down to personality, and this is extremely damaging to the relationship. We like to have a reason, so, if it isn't apparent, we can just say that the other person is "difficult", or "odd". The other person is also thinking the same about you, so, who is the "odd" one? Who is the better example of a human being? These are not useful questions. We can be much more intelligent than this and, luckily, NLP has some answers.

Rather than putting the responsibility on others to change, we can develop our sensory acuity and respond according to what we are picking up.

If we can recognize how someone is thinking, then we can communicate in ways that help the person to process more easily. Rather than putting the responsibility on others to change, which rarely produces results, we can develop our sensory acuity and respond according to what we are picking up. This ability will add to your repertoire of rapport and influencing techniques, as you learn to communicate with a wider range of thinking strategies. Before continuing, have a go at this exercise to test your intuition.

You can return to this page later and check your answers against the eye accessing cues (Figure 7.1).

⊚ exercise

Intuitive mind reading

You will be aware of how your thoughts consist of images, audio (music, words or other sounds), and your internal dialog (when you converse with yourself). You will also be aware of how thoughts can generate positive and negative feelings. Gaze into each of the pairs of eyes below and, using only your intuition, match the eyes to the following forms of thought:

◆ seeing pictures;

◆ hearing sounds;

◆ conversing with internal dialog;

◆ connecting with feelings.

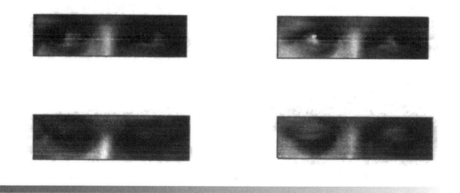

▧ Eye movements

The eyes are connected to the brain by the optic nerves. The signals from each eye go to both the left and right sides of the brain and a group of muscles is used to control eye movements. You will have noticed that people move their eyes as they think. While the eyes are responsible for one of the senses connecting us with the world outside our body, they are also connected to the brain and will perform a sequence of movements to accompany our inner processing. NLP research[1] has shown that there are distinct patterns of eye movement connected to the process of thinking. These patterns provide us with cues to a person's thinking strategy.

Awareness of eye movements is usually heightened when you are interviewing a new person for a job. If you are an experienced interviewer – particularly if you have been trained to ask behavioral questions – you will have noticed the searching eye patterns following a focused, probing question. Effective questions ask for the interviewee's own experience, so you will often get lots of eye movements as the interviewee searches for the best response. The job interview is but one context where an awareness of eye patterns can lead to improved results.

NLP research has shown that there are distinct patterns of eye movement connected to the process of thinking. These patterns provide us with cues to a person's thinking strategy.

Essentially, there are six positions relating to certain types of accessing, and the sequence of movements between these positions will give you a person's thinking strategy. The movements correspond to physical parts of the brain that are being accessed to perform certain cognitive functions. Figure 7.1 shows these positions and the related accessing cues for a typically configured right-handed person. Left-handed people tend to have a reverse configuration – that is, the left and right swap over – but not all of them do. Also, it has been noted that most cultures around the world have this configuration, except the Basques of northern Spain. Their configuration is different and, as far as I know, there has been no research to map their accessing cues, but whenever I have mentioned this to someone who comes from somewhere near to that region, they have agreed.

The patterns of eye movements generally seen are as follows.

◆ **Remembered images**
   Up and to the left is the position for visual recall (Vr), when the mind is searching for an image in the memory banks.

◆ **Constructed images**
   Up and to the right is the position for visual construct (Vc), when the mind is building an image or putting together a number of remembered images to form a new one.

◆ **Remembered sounds**
   Lateral and to the left is the position for auditory recall (Ar), when the mind is searching for remembered sounds, such as songs, and memorized words and phrases repeated by yourself and others.

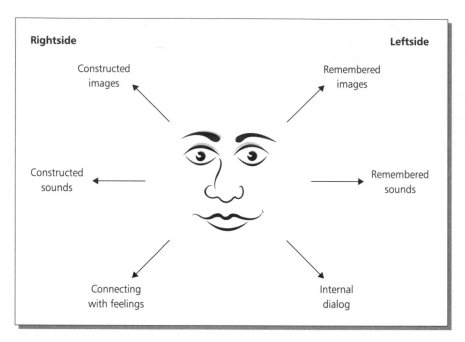

Fig 7.1 ◆ Eye accessing cues for a typical right-handed person

◆ **Constructed sounds**
  Lateral and to the right is the position for auditory construct (Ac), when the mind is thinking of words to say, or putting other auditory content together, such as music.

◆ **Connecting with feelings**
  Down and to the right is the position for accessing kinaesthetic sensations of touch and internal feelings (K).

◆ **Internal dialog**
  Down and to the left is the position for accessing auditory internal dialog (Aid). This is your inner voice, which you use to talk things over with yourself.

There is a seventh position – straight ahead, which is used to work with information once it has been accessed. For example, you might recall a memory from something you saw in a magazine (Vr), compare it with an image of something you want to achieve (Vc), then position the new image directly in front of you to manipulate it. This thinking strategy represented in notation form would be Vr, Vc.

◼ Internal representation

The eye movement patterns provide cues to the way a person is accessing information and to how they are representing the world. Remember the functional model of communication in Chapter 5, and how the filters generalize, delete, and distort external events to form an internal representation of them? Eye movement is one way of telling which of the communication channels are being used to form that representation. Is it a visual, auditory or kinaesthetic representation of the world? We actually use all three, but we may have an unconscious preference for the most developed channel and use that one most often. This is called the *representation system* and will be the one used most to process information in conscious awareness.

The visual channel

A person with a well-developed visual channel will see lots of pictures in their mind's eye. They will be able to make more distinctions in the visual channel than people with highly developed kinaesthetic and auditory channels. Their visual images will be strong and well defined. Their eye patterns will include frequent upward movements and they may stare into space as they work on the images.

Other characteristics of visually oriented people include breathing high in the chest area, and fast, high-pitched speech. These are the physiological symptoms of keeping speech synchronized with the pictures. We know that a picture says more than a thousand words and that the mind can create images very quickly. There often isn't time between sentences to draw air any further than the chest. If you are highly visual, you are probably seeing yourself in this way.

Another way to recognize when a person is using the visual channel is by the sensory words or predicates they use when talking. You will hear such a person say, "That *looks* good" "I can *see* your point" "Help me *paint a picture*" "We're starting with a *blank canvas*" and so on. The predicates indicate the channel being used in conscious awareness.

The kinaesthetic channel

A person with a well-developed kinaesthetic channel will be able to make more distinctions here than people with a preference for the visual and auditory channels. Their range of feelings will be very recognizable and meaningful to them – much more so than for people with visual and auditory channel preferences. The eyes will frequently go down and to the right as they connect with their feelings during conversations. This action causes the speech to be broken, with frequent pauses, often mid-sentence. The voice is deep and speech slow. Breathing is slower and deeper.

When the kinaesthetic channel is being used, you will hear phrases like, "How do you *feel* about this?" "Let's *run* with it" "How does this *grab* you?" "He's a little *rough* around the edges."

The auditory channel

The distinctions made in the auditory channel can include volume, tone, location, timbre, cadence, frequency, depth, echo, and many others. These words may not be used to identify auditory qualities, but a wide range of distinctions will be made nonetheless. The eyes will dart laterally, with few upward and downward movements. Breathing will be even, the air filling the chest to the diaphragm. The voice will be resonant and variable. People with a well-developed auditory channel have voices we find easy and very often enjoyable to listen to.

When the auditory channel is being used, you will hear predicates such as, "*Listen* to Mike's plan" "That *rings a bell*" "I *hear* what you say" "Let me *tune in* to your idea."

Primary system

As we age, we tend to develop a strength in one channel and use this more often than the others, which become weaker as a result. We begin to make more distinctions in the preferred channel and fewer in the other two. The preferred channel then becomes our primary representation system – the one used most often to form our internal representation of the world.

Each primary system is best suited to doing certain types of jobs, and less suited to others. Consider this example.

❖ example

A team of computer service managers had to move over 2,000 people and all their desktop computer equipment from five different buildings around London, England, into a new purpose-built block at Marylebone, near Regent's Park, central London.

The team's manager asked me to help them plan the move, telling me that previous moves had been problematical. I spent a day with them and asked them to do three things. After this, they took care of the planning and the project was completed without a single hitch. These were the three things I asked them to do.

1 "Imagine you have already completed the move and it has been successful. Look back and see all the things you had to do to make it a success." Immediately, those more visually oriented members of the team stood up and began to visualize, commenting on their images.

2 Next, I asked the others to "Listen for what is missing and comment on each identified task." This gave the auditory oriented team members something to do.

3 Next, I suggested, "Someone might like to get up and build a mind-map for the project." The remaining kinaesthetically oriented team members stood up and gathered around the flipchart.

If you ask someone with an underdeveloped visual channel to imagine the future, they may tell you that they can't visualize, or that it is difficult for them to do so. At best, they will create pictures in their mind's eye, but they may be very fuzzy pictures with little emotional energy. Also, they may want to revert to their own primary system quickly. It can be hard work using a weak channel.

The channels of communication can create conflict and stress, as, in most organizations, there is very little understanding of them. It is generally accepted among NLP trainers that roughly 45 percent of people use the kinaesthetic channel as their primary representation system, 35 percent use the visual channel, and 20 percent the auditory channel. When a strong visual person meets a strong kinaesthetic, the interaction has a high probability of creating misunderstanding or, at worst, conflict. It is possible to avoid this by matching the primary representation system of the other person. Before we look at this and other practical ways of using this information, there is more to know about thinking strategies.

The channels of communication can create conflict and stress, as, in most organizations, there is very little understanding of them.

Lead system

The lead representation system is the channel used to initiate a search for information in direct response to an external event, such as a question. It may be the same as, or different from, the primary system, switching over as soon as the initial search has been completed.

Reference system

The reference representation system is the channel used to check whether or not the information you have brought into conscious awareness is true. As with the lead system, the reference system may be the same as, or different from, the primary system, handing over to the primary system when the check has been finished.

Tables 7.1 a–d show some examples to demonstrate how these different systems are put together to make a thinking strategy. These examples are not offered as ideals, but can be considered typical strategies, created for the purpose of explanation.

Table 7.1a ◆ A popular buying decision strategy

Eye accessing cue	System	Channel	Thoughts and feelings
Up right	Lead	Visual	I imagine having a material object – a car, jacket, jewellery, holiday, etc.
Down right	Primary	Kinaesthetic	Feels really good in my stomach
Up left	Reference	Visual	Did my wife approve the last time I made a purchase like this?
Down right	Primary	Kinaesthetic	Feels bad in my stomach

In this case, the primary system is kinaesthetic, preceded by the visual lead system. The individual will have a range of feelings for different events, and the reference system has reminded him of the last time his wife disapproved, and has brought back the same feeling he had at that time. Think about the states he will have gone through to arrive at this decision. First of all, a positive state driven by the visual channel, amplified by the kinaesthetic before being put into a dive by the visual reference system, only to be negatively amplified by the primary. This is how the internal representation affects our state. We are all subject to these mini emotional rollercoasters every day, with cycle times as short as five seconds or less. Table 7.1b gives another example.

Table 7.1b ♦ A leadership strategy

Eye accessing cue	System	Channel	Thoughts and feelings
Down left	Lead	Auditory internal dialog	Tell yourself "it can be better than this"
Up right	Primary	Visual	Visualize the future
Down right	Reference	Kinaesthetic	It feels good
Up right	Primary	Visual	"First of all I will ..."

Here we have someone using her lead system of internal dialog to tell herself that things could be better. This kicks in the visual reference system and she imagines how things could be different. She is probably creating a picture or movie of how she would like the future to be. Then, the kinaesthetic reference system takes over and confirms the images are correct with a good feeling, then it's back to the primary system to begin planning in visual mode. Now to another example, shown in Table 7.1c.

Table 7.1c ♦ A procrastination strategy

Eye accessing cue	System	Channel	Thoughts and feelings
Lateral left	Lead	Auditory	Hearing the boss telling you to have the project done by the end of the month
Down right	Primary	Kinaesthetic	Feel bad about this project
Up right	Reference	Visual	"I can see so many other things to do"
Down right	Primary	Kinaesthetic	"These other things make me feel better"

This time the auditory channel is doing its best to help get the project done, but, for some reason, the kinaesthetic primary system has created a bad feeling. This may be because, at a very deep level, your unconscious knows that you will not enjoy this work. There is a quick check with the visual reference system to discover that there are plenty of other things you could be doing with your time. Next, it's back to the primary system to get those feelings of enjoyment connected with those other jobs, and we have a very effective strategy for procrastination.

Table 7.1d ◆ A motivation strategy

Eye accessing cue	System	Channel	Thoughts and feelings
Down left	Lead	Auditory internal dialog	Tell yourself, "I don't want to do this work"
Down left	Primary	Auditory internal dialog	Ask yourself, "What are the consequences of not doing this work, and of doing it well?"
Up right	Reference	Visual	Imagine the future having not done the work, then imagine the future having done it well
Down left	Primary	Auditory internal dialog	Tell yourself, "I will be in a good position for a job change when I have done this task well"
Down right	—	Kinaesthetic	Feels OK

In this example, there is very little kinaesthetic channel in the strategy. The auditory channel is doing almost all of the processing and decision making, with some visual referencing. Feelings will not be entirely absent, but they will be low in intensity.

One final example will clearly demonstrate how some strategies are more effective than others. There is a reason for some people being naturally proficient at spelling. Here is an effective spelling strategy:

◆ hear the word (auditory – lead);

◆ imagine how it looks written down (visual – primary);

◆ compare it with how you have seen it before (visual – reference);

◆ compare it with how you have heard it before (auditory – reference);

◆ get a good feeling if it's right, bad feeling if wrong (kinaesthetic).

The visual components make this an effective strategy. There are so many different, often conflicting, phonetics in language that learning to spell using the auditory channel alone is just about impossible. Compare the sound and letter composition of the following words:

buyer liar tyre fire

bear prayer dare where stair

Using the auditory channel as the main learning strategy is hard work. These two examples above demonstrate clearly the advantage of a visual strategy.

Most of us use a very small number of strategies, which can change according to our life experiences. A traumatic event can create a whole new range of emotional feelings, and exaggerated visual and auditory experiences can bring more color and sound into our representations of the world.

With NLP, what most people regard as intuition and mood, you are able to define more precisely by what is going on in your head when you have these sensations. This will give you more control over your mind and, therefore, more scope for improving your results. It will also help you to understand more about other people and, as a result, you will be more confident and influential.

> With NLP, what most people regard as intuition and mood, you are able to define more precisely.

By now, you have perhaps been reflecting on some of your own thinking strategies. Do you have a strategy for leadership? How about high-energy motivation? Do you want an improved strategy for problem solving or decision making? How about a creative thinking strategy?

You can have any strategy you want – all you have to do is build it using the most appropriate communication channels. Robert Dilts[2] has modeled the strategies of many people, including Albert Einstein, Walt Disney, and Aristotle. He has recorded their strategies so that other people can learn to use them. In Section 3, you will find an exercise to help you create your own designer thinking strategies, and in Section 4 you will learn how to model strategies from other people and use them for yourself. But first there is more to learn about neurology and the functional model of communication.

◼ Smell and taste

So far, I have concentrated on the three communication channels – visual, auditory, and kinaesthetic (VAK) – yet there are two more information pathways to the mind: olfactory (smell), and gustatory (taste). Someone working in the perfume industry is likely to have a well-developed sense of smell, making many more aromatic distinctions than people whose work does not require them to use their sense of smell. The same can be said of a gourmet chef and their gustatory sense. A particular sensory channel is developed by increasing the variety and range of distinctions you can make using it. As you do this, you will develop a language to label each new distinction. Think of all the words an experienced wine taster will have in their vocabulary to describe smells and tastes.

These two senses may be used in strategies where it is important to make these types of distinctions and form part of an internal representation regardless of that.

Developing your weaker channels

The more you can interchange between your channels, the more flexibility you will have to develop strategies that work well for you. Here are some simple exercises to help you develop more flexible mental patterns. If you are left-handed, try it twice – once with the left-handed eye positions, then reversed. Notice which way seems most natural and in which configuration it is easier to intensify the representation.

⊚ exercise

Visual channel – recall

Put your eyes in the Vr position and bring a pleasant memory into your conscious mind.

Now move the picture so that it is slightly above the horizontal and straight out in front of you. Focus on this picture and make as many visual distinctions about it as you can.

Refer back to the control panel in Chapter 5 to remind you of some of the qualities you can change. Can you make more than twice this number of visual distinctions in your image?

Visual channel – construct

Put your eyes in the Vc position and let your imagination go wild. Create an image of a future time using any context you want. Keep your eyes in the Vc position as you make as many visual distinctions as you can and until you have a completed image.

Now intensify the image qualities. Can you intensify this image more than this?

Auditory channel – recall

Put your eyes in the Ar position and bring a remembered sound into your conscious mind. It could be a piece of music you enjoy or the sound of someone you like talking.

Make as many auditory distinctions as you can and intensify them. Can you make any more than this?

Auditory channel – construct

Put your eyes in the Ac position and make up a sound. It should be like nothing you have heard before. What would your partner sound like if he or she were singing a foreign song in the voice of a chipmunk? Be sure to concentrate on the sound, not the images.

Build up the sound with as many different qualities as you can, then intensify them. Can you add any more auditory qualities to this sound?

Auditory internal dialog channel

Put your eyes in the Aid position and begin to talk to yourself using thought only. Choose a decision you have yet to make and debate the implications of making it now.

As you do this, alter the qualities of the voice you are using. How wide a range can you develop? Can you create a serious voice? How about a fun voice? Can you make it sound like Bugs Bunny? Give it the voice of James Bond 007 – a man with a mission.

What else can you change? Move the location to different parts of your head. Move the voice to somewhere outside your head – send it out into the universe and listen to it speaking from another planet.

Kinaesthetic channel

Put your eyes in the K position and begin to connect with your feelings.

Now I'm going to ask you to do two things and I want you to use only the kinaesthetic channel, so if you hear your Aid cutting in, turn it off. If you see images, turn them off also. You are working now with feelings alone, so, first of all, begin to feel negative and, just for a few seconds only, intensify the sensation so that you feel bad. Next, stand up, turn around, take a deep breath, sit back down in another place, and read on.

This time, reverse the process and begin to feel good, really good – so good that you are oozing with positive emotions. Now keep this going and keep intensifying.

Can you extend this great feeling to more parts of your body? Can you project it outside your body also? How long can you stay in this state of having such positive energy swirling around inside?

The more you do this exercise, the easier it will be for you to create winning strategies and states. Concentrate on the channels you are weakest in, and the visual channel.

Visualization is the most effective way of working with states, so it will pay to work on this every day and integrate it into your thinking strategies. Just one tip when practicing – choose experiences that make you feel good.

Notes

1   Robert B. Dilts (1977) "EEG and Representational Systems"; L. Owens (1977) "Eye Movements and Representational Systems"; "Test of the Eye Movement Hypothesis of Neuro-linguistic Programming", *Perceptual and Motor Skills*, vol. 41, Thomason, Arbuckle and Cody.

2   Robert B. Dilts (1994) *Strategies of Genius*, vol. 1, vol. 2, Meta Publications, Inc.

8

The language of influence and change

If one person in the last century comes to my mind over any other as having brought about change in the face of immense adversity and resistance, it is Nelson Mandela. His lifelong fight for freedom and the abolition of apartheid for the people of South Africa demanded great energy, belief, determination, skill, and, above all, an ability to connect with the people. To achieve his purpose, he knew it was as important to change the attitudes and perceptions of the government, including his jailers of 27 years, as it was to win the hearts and minds of all the people of South Africa.

One of Mandela's great strengths during this struggle was his ability to influence by means of language. As a trained lawyer, he established the first black law practice in Johannesburg, fighting battles in the courtroom, probing and searching the smallest of details to gain a legal advantage in his quest for justice and freedom. As his crusade for a new South Africa progressed, he learned to influence people outside the courtroom also, and found himself increasingly in demand as a speaker within the ANC, using language in a different way, to win support for the fight, both from home and abroad.

> It is impossible to talk to someone and not have an influence, but the results are not always in the speaker's favor.

The words we use have an influence. It is impossible to talk to someone and not have an influence, but the results are not always in the speaker's favor. The words Nelson Mandela chose to create such incredible change were very carefully crafted for maximum impact; the craftwork for the courtroom being very different from the craftwork used to engage the people.

This chapter is all about the use of language to create change for you and for others. You will learn how to craft your words and phrases to develop deeper rapport, engage and motivate, increase understanding and clarity, challenge, and create change. Whether it's a boardroom meeting, a company presentation, an informal team get-together or a one-to-one conversation, what you do with words has an immediate influence. Words may constitute a mere 7 percent of the overall message communicated, but they have a big impact on your results.

◼ The transition from experience to words

Language is a representation system and so is subject to the filtering process. Sometimes we hear what we want to hear, the result being an edited representation of actual events, recorded with our own words. This is how we make meaning of the world using language. Consider this example.

❖ example

Joe is a manager in a software company. He is alone at his desk contemplating a product launch. He is concerned that Helen, the Marketing Director, may not allocate the resources he wants for his campaign to be a success. Joe has never managed to secure Helen's approval before, and he remembers vividly how she declined his request for extra funds for a launch two years ago. As he thinks about this, he visualizes Helen in her office with a disapproving look on her face. He has seen this look before and he says to himself, "She's not interested in my launches. I'll not get what I want from her."

Later that week, at a pre-launch meeting with his peers, Charles, a business analyst, asks if the funding for the launch has been finalized, to which Joe responds, "No, but Helen is unlikely to sign off the additional amount we want, so we will have to go with how it stands now." At this, the next topic on the agenda is introduced and that's the end of that.

In this example, Joe has allowed his previous experience with Helen to ensure that he will consistently fall short of what he actually wants in similar future situations. He has done this by creating negative images and self-talk regarding his relationship with Helen. In fact, this is probably the movie he screens most of all when thinking about Helen. The continual re-runs make sure he's never going to succeed.

Now, in forming his representation, Joe has used his value and belief filters to predict an unsuccessful outcome. This is the *deep structure* to his experience. At the pre-launch meeting, however, he didn't provide the others with this deep structure; what they got was a *surface structure* of the experience. Joe's words were, "No, but Helen is unlikely to sign off the additional amount …", which contain no explicit information about his relationship with Helen or his feelings. If Joe were to have communicated his deep structure, it would have sounded more like this: "Two years ago I asked Helen for extra funding and she said no and, ever since then, I have not had the confidence to approach her. In fact, when I have thought about it, I hear her saying no and then I tell myself that there's no point even trying."

> We have developed our linguistic ability to communicate our experience using surface linguistic structures. There is always so much more behind the words.

Surface structure deletes so much from the real experience and the representation, perhaps because of our ego or because we adapt it to fit with different contexts. What we actually do is perform a series of transformations to derive surface structure from the deep structure. Whatever the reason, we have developed our linguistic ability to communicate our experience using surface linguistic structures. There is always so much more behind the words.

Surface structure deletes detail, allowing our conversations to be conducted in a brief, concise manner. If we all communicated our deep linguistic experiences, can you imagine how pedantic and drawn-out our meetings would be? So, we go around listening to other people's surface structures and filtering them to create our own deep structures, which are then transmitted back to others as surface structures.

So, what does all this mean and how can you use this to have more influence? Nelson Mandela worked with both. He knew how to get underneath the surface structure in the courtroom and find out what was really going on. He also knew that, to win people's hearts and minds, you have to let them form their own deep structures and not attempt to force yours on to them. So, at the highest level, for the purpose of influencing, we have two ways we can use language. One way engages people's emotions, develops rapport, paces their own deep structure experience and is empowering. This way has few details and has wide appeal, regardless of the filters individuals may apply. The alternative way is used to clarify and understand, to seek out precise accounts of experience, uncover facts, probe, and challenge the surface structure. This way is able to delve down into the smallest of details in its search for more useful resources.

There will be times when you want to motivate, inspire, and win hearts and minds. There will be other times when you want to get clarity and understanding, probe into the specifics of a situation, and uncover an important fact. There will be times when you want to do both. The complexity of human communication is such that you will want to alternate between each method fluently and elegantly, switching tracks smoothly in response to the progress you are making. Gregory Bateson[1] suggests that, much of the time, we focus like mongooses on single-purpose activity, thinking that this is the meaning of being alive, whereas the real meaning of being alive is to be able to handle highly multiple purposes using highly complicated thinking. First of all, we will deal with precision language – probing for the details – then the emphasis will turn to the opposite end of this continuum – exploring the use of artfully vague language patterns.

The metamodel

By learning the language forms that follow, you will develop a more intricate use of language that will help you gel together all the multiple purposes required to be successful. The forms come from transformational grammar, each form having a technical descriptor, which I have included, and a set of rules that for the purposes of this text are much too convoluted, so are omitted. You can find a technical representation of the rules, as used in therapy, in *The Structure of Magic*, volume 1, by Richard Bandler and John Grinder,[2] which I highly recommend for devout students of NLP.

The forms are known in NLP as the metamodel and learning them is a little like learning to use the alphabet. Take it a step at a time and explore ways of integrating them into your linguistic experience. Practice will help you to become proficient in their use. Each form is explained with simple examples to demon-strate its use and is followed by a scenario to help you get a wider understanding of practical application. Some of the forms will appear to you as common sense and may seem very simplistic. They are. It is the mix of simple generalization, deletion, and distortion in real-time conversation that so often leads to misunderstanding and inappropriate action.

> The more flexibility we have with language, the easier it is to bring about change.

As mentioned above, the metamodel is drawn from transformational grammar and was initially used as a tool for therapists to help their clients create change. In the business context it is just as effective at bringing about change in the ways people are thinking about their situations. The more flexi-bility we have with language, the easier it is to bring about change.

Presupposition

This form is responsible for many of the assumptions we make and can result in focus being put on inappropriate things.

> *Pete: "As we'll be working together, George, you'll need to understand more about how our group operates."*

This sentence presupposes that:

◆ Pete and George will be working together;

◆ George's understanding of how Pete's group operates is limited.

You might wonder about Pete's deep structure. Is Pete thinking about a past problem he has put down to "someone not understanding"? Is he assuming that George will create similar problems unless he understands more? How is George interpreting this presupposition? The answers, of course, depend on the non-verbal aspects of Pete's message and George's filtering process. Compare the sentence above with this variation:

> *Pete: "As we'll be working together, George, do you think we should start by understanding each other's operations?"*

This sentence presupposes that:

◆ Pete and George will be working together;

◆ neither Pete nor George understands each other's operations.

> *Anne: "The next time we are on a project together, Mike, you must keep me informed of all problems."*

This sentence presupposes that:

◆ Anne and Mike have been on a project together before;

◆ Mike has not informed Anne of all the problems in the past.

This may be interpreted by Mike as having been inadequate the last time and whatever feelings he has about that time could be carried over to the next project. Compare with:

> *Anne: "I would like to debrief this project, Mike. I feel that we could both improve our communication, what do you think?"*

This sentence presupposes that:

◆ there has been a project in the past;

◆ Anne has a feeling about improving communication;

◆ Mike can think.

Nominalization

You will recognize this form as a verb changed into a noun. It is responsible for distorting reality and putting limitations on progress.

Frank: "The IT department's blunders are getting worse."

In this example, the noun "blunder" is a nominalization of the word "blundering". The real experience in deep structure will contain much more information about the act of blundering, but Frank has nominalized this. To help this situation you might ask:

"In what ways have they been blundering exactly?"

or:

"Tell me about a specific blunder."

or:

"Give me an example of what you mean by blunders."

It is all too common for a person to blow up a problem and make it seem much bigger than it really is. Once a problem reaches a certain size, the response to it can become very personal. Checking out nominalizations in this way helps to clarify the issue more precisely, keeping things in proportion.

Mindreading

This form usually begins as a belief and comes out in linguistic form as a mindread.

Jo: "I know you are all worrying about the merger."

Jo has been thinking about how the merger will affect her people and she has formed the belief that they are all worried about it. You read earlier how beliefs are formed from very little evidence, so Jo might be completely wrong about some or even all her people. Whether this is so or not doesn't really matter. By speaking these words, Jo is suggesting that there is something to be worried about, so the self-fulfilling cycle completes. You can challenge a mindread like this by simply asking:

"How do you know we are all worrying?"

Quotes

With this form, another person's experience is brought into the present context.

Mike: "Mary said that the government team hasn't won one bid yet."

Are you going to make a decision based on Mike's account of what Mary said? Did Mary get this information from someone else? I wonder what the true experience is? Whether or not a decision is made, beliefs will be building in people's minds about the team's performance and this may have a worsening effect, as the expectation for losing bids grows. Challenge this with:

"Perhaps we could get the facts directly from the team."

Complex equivalence

There is an element of mindreading within this form, which can be recognized from the links made or meanings attached to behavior.

Peter: "Because I'm only a junior salesman, senior people won't want to listen to me."

Peter has taken his existing behavior as a salesman to form a conclusion that senior people don't want to listen to him. This is a mindread and will hinder Peter's performance as he will avoid contacting senior people. Challenge this form with counter-examples, such as:

"Susan is junior and she is listened to by senior people. What is different in your case?"

This will help to uncover the real reason behind Peter's performance block.

Cause effect

This is somewhat similar to the previous form except that it is often a way of avoiding responsibility for a problem or a limitation.

James: "Until the fulfillment section gets its act together, we can't improve the service we provide."

James has put the responsibility for improving service on the fulfillment section. His rationale is that it is causing the effect on service. This may be true, but, unless James accepts some responsibility for the problem, he will not be helping to resolve it. Challenge this form with:

"Is that the only department that has to get its act together?"

or:

"Are all the other departments' actions as together as they can be?"

or:

"Who else has an impact on service other than that department?"

Comparison

This form is used to compare against a standard. Sometimes the standard is missing or the one selected is not ideal.

Marge: "The alpha team's performance last month was dreadful."

In this example, the comparison is not explicit enough to be of any help. The fact that performance is the issue only suggests that there is a standard somewhere that has not been met. It often happens that performance standards are not properly specified, if they exist at all. The important point here is not to make the team feel bad about its performance, but to identify ways to help it improve. Remedial work is just as likely to consist of agreeing clear targets as it is the effort put in to achieving them. Challenge this form with:

"What specific aspect of its performance was dreadful and what are you measuring it against?"

or:

"Dreadful compared to what?"

Universal quantifier

You will recognize this form very easily as a limited experience generalized and applied to an entire category.

Julian: "Accountants never understand the vision."

I suspect that Julian has had some experience with at least one accountant who gave the impression of not understanding a vision. In surface structure conversation, he has applied this to *all* accountants – a very common process, but one that will backfire on you. Challenge quite simply with:

"All accountants?"

or:

"Has not even one accountant ever understood a vision?"

Referential index

This form excludes the source reference for the statement being made.

Angela: "This industry is suffering from technology myopia and we should be doing something about it."

This statement may be true, but how do you know? Angela may have the influencing skills to win people to her cause, but has she done her research accurately? Challenge this form with:

"Who says?"

or:

"What evidence do you have for this statement?"

Modal operators of necessity

Whenever you hear someone expressing a need, as this form suggests, you are listening to someone who has closed down their options and put a limitation on their choice. Typically, you will hear words such as "need", "must", "have to", "got to".

Sam: "We need to achieve this target by the end of this quarter."

Achieving the target may be very important to Sam and her team, but other things may crop up that have equal importance. It's not unusual in today's business environment for goals to become irrelevant with the passing of time. If you rigidly channel all your focus and effort into reaching one goal, you may miss other opportunities along the way. The point is not to do away with the goal, but to remain flexible and adapt if necessary. Challenge with:

"What will happen if we don't achieve it?"

or:

"What else could we be doing to contribute to the bigger vision?"

Modal operators of possibility

This form is used to keep options open and avoid being committed to one course of action.

> *Peter: "I'm really excited about this project – there are so many ways for me to get involved."*

Peter is clearly motivated by the possibilities this project presents for him. Variety offers scope, but unless Peter makes his choice and becomes committed to something that is not too diverse as to be unmanageable, he may procrastinate. Challenge this form with:

> *"How specifically do you want to get involved?"*

Unspecified verbs

Typically recognizable from words such as "going", "performing", "managing", "leading", this form gives very little away about the activity, which may not even exist in the deep structure.

> *Ross: "Bill has been leading his team down the wrong path for some time now."*

Ross has attributed the team's journey to Bill's leadership and there is nothing in the statement to even suggest how he did this. Challenge with:

> *"In what way has Bill been leading?"*

or:

> *"How has Bill been leading them specifically?"*

Ross may not have an answer to these questions, but probing the issue may uncover some accurate experience that is helpful in finding a solution.

Unspecified nouns

This is a similar deletion to the previous form and is recognizable from the absence of specific information about nouns, such as "him", "them", "the team", "people", "employees", "client".

Alice: "They never take my advice."

Alice has given advice to someone in the past and they have not taken it. We're not sure from this what the actual experience was and it might help Alice to form a more realistic statement by asking:

"Who, specifically, are you referring to when you say 'they'?"

The metamodel in practice

The 13 forms presented here do not always appear in pure form as portrayed in the examples. You are more likely to hear a number of forms in each piece of dialog. The objective is not to become a maniacal challenger of other people's language forms, which, I guarantee, will damage whatever rapport you have. Rather, it is to know which question to ask to help you meet your outcomes. If you know what you want from an interaction and you have the sensory acuity to recognize these forms, the most useful questions will become apparent to you. Here's a working example showing how the metamodel can be used in an everyday management situation.

❖ example

Mike gets some coaching

Dialog	Metamodel form
Mike: "I want to mention the *problems* we have had in meeting our delivery targets – particularly the lack of cooperation from production."	Nominalization
Estelle: "What problems specifically Mike?"	Challenge to the nominalization
Mike: "Well, last week, we missed the ABC order because *they* didn't sign off the batch in time. They do this *every time*."	Unspecified noun Universal quantifier
Estelle: "Who do you mean by "they" exactly?	Challenge to the unspecified noun
Mike: "Well, it's Bill – you know, the guy who transferred from Accounts."	

Estelle: "And you say Bill doesn't sign off batches every time? Has he ever managed to do it once?"	Challenge to the universal quantifier above
Sue: "Bill's always been OK with me."	Counter-example – Bill can get it right
Estelle: "So, it's not every time, then. What have you done about this Mike?"	
Mike: "*It's* not *up to* me is it? It's *their* responsibility."	Two unspecified nouns Unspecified verb
Estelle: "What's not up to you?"	Challenge to unspecified noun
Mike: "It's not my responsibility to fix this problem. Look, *you can tell* Bill doesn't give a damn *by his attitude* on the phone."	Complex equivalence Nominalization
Estelle: "What do you mean by 'attitude' exactly?"	Challenge to the nominalization
Mike: "He's short and aggressive."	
Estelle: "So, you have interpreted his voice as having an attitude of not caring, haven't you? What else could this voice mean?"	Challenge the complex equivalence
Mike: "I suppose it could mean lots of things."	
Estelle: "Well, Sue seems to get what she needs from Bill, what is stopping you from doing the same?"	Refer to counter-example
Mike: "Maybe I'm expecting him to fail me."	Accepting responsibility
Estelle: "So, what can you do to help Bill help you?"	Moving towards action

The metamodel is a valuable tool for working with language. It is a precision instrument, probing the surface structure to uncover more facts from a person's actual experience. Use it for yourself also. Teach it to your internal dialog and challenge your own impoverished language patterns. How are you limiting yourself? What presuppositions are you accepting as truth? Have you closed your options down with too many needs? Use your language as a way of developing flexibility in your thinking. Make a commitment to challenge your internal dialog and external speech using the metamodel every day.

Artfully vague language

We now come to the language used by Milton Erickson,[3] acclaimed as a leading practitioner of medical hypnosis. He said that: "Meaningful communication should replace repetitious verbigerations, direct suggestions, and authoritarian commands."

So, what relevance has this to the business environment? Am I suggesting that you learn hypnosis as an influencing tool? Well, in the way most people understand hypnosis, certainly not, yet we are all influenced by hypnosis every day, whether it be a subtle television advertisement or an enticing image of a tasty meal. We are drawn in by language and imagery appealing to our personal desires and dreams so that our inner energy is awakened to seek more about the products being sold to us in this way.

While it may be interesting to review Erickson's work in its entirety, some parts are more practical than others in the business context, so I have chosen the patterns that you will find of most use for motivating and influencing, particularly when addressing larger groups.

Whether you're in a meeting, giving a presentation or running a training seminar, artfully vague language – or the Milton model – will help you to connect at an emotional level with the group. Imagine a seminar with 50 people in attendance. What do they all want from the event? How is each person motivated? In any group, there are so many differences to cater for, including age, thinking styles, role maturity, profession, gender, motives, and egos. Remember what you learned about rapport and pacing – how can you get rapport with a group when there are so many differences?

Artfully vague language will help you to connect at an emotional level with the group.

Rapport is about making connections, so begin by acknowledging and including everyone. It is also useful to get people saying "yes", even to something irrelevant. Just the act of saying "yes" moves a person's energy in a positive direction. So, let's suppose that you are about to give a presentation to your company on a new plan for 2001. You might begin like this.

❖ example

Opening the presentation

"Good afternoon, I'm Jim Smith and I'm here to present plan 2001. As we're here today, with the week behind us, I am wondering how to begin the presentation. First of all, I know there are people here who have helped put the plan together, and others for whom this will be their first insight into the plan. I guess some of you will be looking closely at the financial details and some of you will be interested in the targets we have set. Whatever is on your mind, I will be pleased to take your questions at the end."

In this opening section, the speaker has stated some universal truths "as we're here today" and "with the week behind us" that the audience is unlikely to dispute. This gets agreement, although small, and their energy will begin to move in the right direction.

❖ example

Pacing

"On the way over here, I was thinking about the comics I read as a young boy. What comics did you read? In one title, I recall a test of problem-solving skills. You know how it goes – you are in the swamp and suddenly fall into quicksand up to your chest. There is an alligator at the other side of the swamp looking at you with a hungry eye – what do you do?"

So, the speaker has paced the experiences of the audience. Everyone will have read a comic as a child and you can bet everyone has, at one time, had a go at solving a problem scenario. The best topics for pacing will be found outside the context of what you are presenting – look to common human experience for your content here.

❖ example

Leading

"Sometimes I think the past year has been a little like that – feeling like I was sinking with hungry alligators waiting to pounce. I was never very good at problem solving as a young boy and I'm not sure that's changed, but what I do know is that plan 2001 will give me the best chance of making it through the coming year and emerging all the stronger for it. I'm sure that, like me, you all want to have success next year and that you will make use of whatever is there to help you on that journey. Plan 2001 was put together for that very purpose, so, what's it all about?"

Now the speaker has linked the audience's experience to the problem, and used the problem as a metaphor for work. This then moves elegantly on to the subject – plan 2001.

In the process, the speaker has brought in a little humor, using himself as the target – this is like saying "I'm human." There is also an embedded command: "like me", telling the audience to like him. Did you recognize the mindread – "you all want to have" – and the nominalization – "success"?

Nominalizations allow each person to draw their own meaning. The word "success" could mean something entirely different to each person in the audience. So, the speaker has worked with the audience's energy and led them into a receptive state before introducing the subject.

You may also have noticed in this example the use of conjunctions – words such as "as" and "so". These are used to keep a smooth flow and avoid giving direct commands. Other words you might use to achieve this effect are: "since", "when", "if", "then", "while", "because", "even".

Artfully vague Milton model language will help you to connect with people at an emotional level. It is the language for winning hearts and minds.

I will end this section with an excerpt from one of Nelson Mandela's speeches – a superb example of artfully vague language at work. Read it through once, looking for specific Milton model language, then read it a second time, identifying metamodel forms.

"Your majesties, your highnesses, distinguished guests, comrades, and friends.

Today, all of us do, by our presence here, and by our celebrations in other parts of our country and the world, confer glory and hope to newborn liberty.

> *Out of the experience of an extraordinary human disaster that lasted too long, must be born a society of which all humanity will be proud.*
>
> *Our daily deeds as ordinary South Africans must produce an actual South African reality that will reinforce humanity's belief in justice, strengthen its confidence in the nobility of the human soul, and sustain all our hopes for a glorious life for all.*
>
> *All this we owe both to ourselves and to the peoples of the world who are so well represented here today.*
>
> *To my compatriots, I have no hesitation in saying that each one of us is as intimately attached to the soil of this beautiful country as are the famous jacaranda trees of Pretoria and the mimosa trees of the bushveld.*
>
> *Each time one of us touches the soil of this land, we feel a sense of personal renewal."*

Enabling language

There are a few small words you will hear used often in your organization. Although small and seemingly insignificant, they can really hold you back, yet few people do anything to change this. The reason is sometimes because they are in such common use and it can seem too simple a thing to do. Surely change has to be complicated and hard work, doesn't it? Well, have a go over the next week at changing some of these words in your language.

◆ **Can't** This is all too often used when possibilities have been exhausted and you have given up looking for solutions, such as "I *can't* get people to listen" and "We *can't* get the resources we need." It's not that you can't, rather that you haven't yet found a way. Notice the difference here. "Can't" is final, it closes down. "Haven't yet" leaves the way open for a solution. Replace "can't" with "can". Talk about what you *can* do instead of what you *can't* do. This small change will have a significant impact on your attitude, state, and creativity.

Talk about what you can do instead of what you can't do. This small change will have a significant impact on your attitude, state, and creativity.

◆ **But** This tiny word has a clear function: it negates whatever precedes it. So, if you say, "I would really like to help you, but I have a meeting to go to", the message is received as, "you don't want to help me". Replace "but" with "and" or change around your sentence to make it more positive – for example, "I have a meeting today and, if I can get away in good time, I will be glad to help you." Sometimes "but" is useful for negating a negative and making it positive – "They have performed poorly in the past, but today they can change all that."

◆ **Try** There are too many people trying and not enough getting results. The very word "try" implies failure. If someone tells you they will "try" to make it to your meeting, will you expect them to be there? Probably not. "Try" is a word people use when they don't want to be committed to an action. It keeps the options open for failing and, in some cases, accepts failure as a legitimate outcome. The occur-rences of this word in your language will be proportionate to the outcomes you fail to achieve. Replacing it is easy – use "will" instead. This will force you to think more carefully about the things you commit yourself to, and you are likely to bring in the word "no" more often as a result. It is better to be clear about your commitment with a "yes" or "no" than to procrastinate and dither using "try". This is as relevant to your goals as it is to your interactions with other people.

> *It is better to be clear about your commitment with a "yes" or "no" than to procrastinate and dither using "try".*

In conclusion

This chapter has introduced you to three aspects of language: the metamodel, the Milton model, and enabling language. The words we use have such a strong influence on us – an influence that can hold us back from realizing our potential or help us to achieve more than we dare dream of. It is a complicated system of communicating and the effort you put in to developing your sensory acuity and linguistic ability will be a worthwhile investment for life.

Notes

1   Gregory Bateson (1991) *Sacred Unity: Further Steps to an Ecology of Mind*, edited by Rodney E. Donaldson, HarperCollins. Gregory Bateson had a major influence on the thinking of Richard Bandler and John Grinder, the originators and pioneers of NLP.

2   Richard Bandler and John Grinder (1975) *The Structure of Magic*, vol. 1, Science and Behavior Books, Inc.

3   Richard Bandler and John Grinder (1975) *Patterns of the Hypnotic Techniques of Milton H. Erickson, M.D.*, vol. 1, Meta Publications, Inc.

9

Metaprograms

If you have ever analyzed the reasons for people engaging in certain activities, you may have come up with answers such as money, security, self-development, belonging, enjoyment, and altruism. Values such as these are certainly reasons for committing time and energy to particular causes. We are motivated to fulfill physical, emotional, and spiritual needs, so, to understand the decisions we make in the pursuit of our needs, we must look deeper than values.

Metaprograms are deletion filters. They cause us to put our attention in certain places and not in others, resulting in habitual patterns of thinking, decision making and behaving. Metaprograms work at a deep, unconscious level, having a strong influence on our behavior and personality.

Metaprograms form a part of the unconscious communication message. They predict the "how" of behavior and, therefore, provide more information to facilitate pacing and leading. Mismatching a metaprogram is one of the easiest ways to break rapport and create misunderstanding. A good knowledge of metaprogram patterns will not only enhance your influencing ability, it will help fit people to the jobs they are more naturally suited to. Of course, all this applies to you also. Mismatches between job requirements and metaprogram patterns are major causes of poor performance and stress in the workplace.

> **Metaprograms form a part of the unconscious communication message. They predict the "how" of behavior.**

For each of the metaprogram patterns that follow, there are examples of how to recognize them in everyday conversation; some language examples for pacing and leading; and an insight into suitable and unsuitable jobs. My objective in this chapter is not to label a person as any particular "personality type", but to show the preferences people have for certain patterns, which can change over time and between contexts.

Information chunk size

This metaprogram describes a person's preference for the size of information chunk used in conversation. It may be represented as a continuum with "detail" at one extreme and "global" at the other (see Figure 9.1).

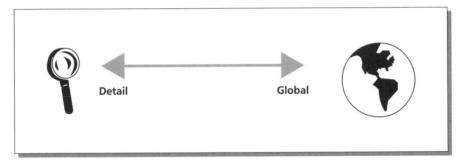

Fig 9.1 ◆ The metaprogram continuum for information chunk size

Compare the responses of Jill and Neil to the question "How did the project go?"

Jill: "Really well. I learned a lot from it. There were a few problems, but nothing we didn't manage to sort out. I wouldn't mind more projects like that one."

Neil: "Oh boy, it was great. There was this one day when the schedule got all screwed up because the computer lost its time. We had it checked, but the new program hasn't settled in yet. The new screens are a pain to work with; I have trouble reading them sometimes – the blue background doesn't help much."

The information chunks in Jill's answer are quite large compared with Neil's. Jill's response is about the project whereas Neil very quickly goes to a detail in a scheduling program used on the project. This is a much smaller chunk than "the project".

Job implications

Jill's preference for global chunks will help her to think in big picture terms. This will be useful if she has aspirations for a senior management position. Neil's preference for details is ideally suited to jobs requiring attention to these, such as engineering or accountancy. Neil will excel in a job where he can work with details, and this is where he will get the most job satisfaction. Jill may not do well in a job requiring lots of attention to detail. Thus, the important question to ask is, "How much of the job requires detail-level work?" If Jill is an extremely global-level person, she may avoid details as much as possible. She will dislike filling in forms, doing tax returns, and reading the small print. She may not notice small objects in her environment and perhaps be perceived as having her head in the clouds. Jill will enjoy discussing concepts and ideas, whereas Neil will want to rapidly get down to the details in a conversation. His focus on detail may cause him to overlook important higher-level ideas and concepts. Neil will find it very easy to keep busy with small things and leave the bigger things for when he has more time. Often the time to do this isn't set aside because the task of considering these big things has little appeal.

Should Neil be promoted to a position where he is managing people, he may find it difficult to let go of the work and delegate. He may be perceived as interfering in the detail of others' work. He will not adjust easily to communicating at a management level, wanting to get into the details of every agenda item at a meeting. His presentations will contain lots of slides showing facts and figures. In comparison, Jill's global style may cause her to miss important details in an agreement or initiative. It is often said that the devil is in the detail, which the global thinker is more likely to miss.

Pacing and leading

You can pace Jill with global language and Neil with detail. Here are some examples.

For Jill: "This new plan 2001 is based on the concept of success. It can help you guide your thinking and manage your resources. Here's a simple one-page description with a graphic to show you how it works. I would like to fix a meeting with you to show you around the system."

For Neil: "This new plan 2001 is big enough to handle all the tasks and subtasks for your projects. It can interlink resources and it keeps a real-time database of over 60,000 records for cross-reference. The amount of detail it can handle is incredible. Here's a full 60-page manual explaining its functionality with a complete reference index at the back. What's your diary like over the next couple of weeks? I would like to fix a meeting to take you through the system features and different functions."

Notice the different approaches used in each example. If you mismatch this metaprogram, you are likely to get an instant turn-off. A global person doesn't want a 60-page manual, whereas a detail person wants as much information as you can provide.

Motivational direction

This metaprogram describes the mix in a person's motivation between wanting something and wanting to avoid something. To "want" is future-oriented, looking ahead and being pulled by a desired goal. To "not want" is "away from"-oriented, looking in different directions, and being pushed by existing unpleasant experiences or the possibility of having them in the future (Figure 9.2).

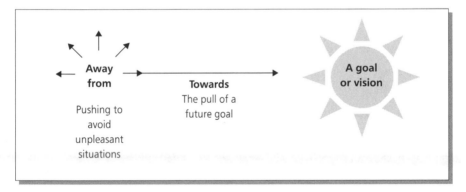

Fig 9.2 ◆ The metaprogram continuum for motivational direction

Here's another question for Jill and Neil: "What do you want in a job?"

Jill: "I want a job that has very little paperwork. I also want to cut down my travel time and I don't want a boss who puts unreasonable demands on me.

Oh, and I'm not interested in working overtime."

Neil: "I want a job with a challenge, something to stretch me creatively and intellectually. I also want to work in a team and to have lots of autonomy. I like to travel, so something with European connections would be ideal."

Jill is motivated to avoid unpleasant situations. She is talking about all the things she wants to move away from and there is nothing to suggest that she knows what she wants instead. In contrast to this, Neil is at the opposite end of the continuum, stating what he wants.

Job implications

The disadvantage for Jill of having a strong "moving away" pattern is that she may end up somewhere else that is not ideal for her. Until she begins to orient her thinking towards future goals and to put some detail into it, she may wander aimlessly between unsuitable jobs, driven by an avoidance strategy.

Neil is really thinking about what he wants and so he is more likely to get a job to suit his preferences than Jill.

However, the lack of an "away from" pattern could cause him to take a job with some unpleasant elements he hadn't considered. A "towards" pattern on its own may filter the things he would rather avoid, but even a well-matched job may end up containing some distasteful elements.

Pacing and leading

The language should match the motivation pattern you hear. Let us look at some examples.

For Jill: "I want to talk to you about a new leisure complex project that isn't going to be anything you can't handle. It's not going to require much traveling and the paperwork has been cut to a minimum. If you're interested, I would like to set some targets with you and talk to you about how this fits with your career development."

For Neil: "I have a new project that I think you will be excited about. It will be a challenge, and you'll be part of a multinational team we are putting together. If you're interested in finding out more, we could spend some time exploring the work you will be involved in and how it fits with your career development."

A balanced motivation pattern will help you to get more of what you want, and to avoid the things you would rather be without. When setting goals, the more specific you can be about what you want, and what you don't want, the better the outcome will be for you.

Options or procedures?

You will recognize these patterns quite easily as they are very clearly expressed in the things we do and say every day. People with a strong preference for options tend to talk about what they "can" or "could" do, while those with a strong procedures pattern are more prone to using words such as "must" and "have to". It's the difference between having a range of choices and having only one choice, which then becomes a procedure. A person motivated by options will seek out or create options for their choices in life, whereas a person motivated by procedures will look for sequence and, when faced with a choice, will quickly choose and align to a procedure (see Figure 9.3).

> *When setting goals, the more specific you can be about what you want, and what you don't want, the better.*

Fig 9.3 ◆ The metaprogram continuum for options and procedures

Time for another question for Jill and Neil, which is: "How do you want to run the teambuilding day?"

Jill: "Maybe we could spend the morning outside doing team games, then have the conference late afternoon. We could give people a variety of activities to choose from and there could be a flexible lunch period available for people as they complete their tasks, so you won't have to wait for every group to finish before taking lunch. Let's have some kind of debrief at the end to discover what people got from the day and ask them to give us some feedback."

Neil: "I think we should all get there early, at say 8am, and we can meet to go over the agenda. Everyone should be outside by 8.30am with a schedule of activities taking them through to 10.30 when we'll have a break for tea and coffee. Start again at 10.50 and rotate the tasks, finishing by 1pm for lunch. We'll start the conference at 2.30 with an afternoon break at 3.45. Everyone must be back in the conference hall by 4.15 for the Director's address. This will last about 45 minutes and will leave 30 minutes for questions and answers, plus some feedback. Everyone will get a feedback form with four questions on it asking for their comments on the day."

Notice how Jill is more concerned about the choices available than the agenda. While she has some idea of how the time will be spent, her interest is in variety and freedom of choice. Compared to this, Neil is very clear on his times and wants to make sure that things go according to plan. His first task is to make sure that everyone has seen and read the day's agenda. Neil wants to limit the choices available and arrange the day around a strict set of timings.

Job implications

The advantage of the options pattern is that it creates variety and choice. There is a spontaneity about options that is exploratory; there is little need for someone with a preference for options to consider the consequences of a new initiative – they will enjoy exploring the newness of the situation and reflect on the outcomes after the event. The disadvantage comes in the guise of procrastination and unfinished initiatives. In the example above, Jill wants to keep her options open as long as possible. Once she has closed them down and made a choice, she loses interest. She is motivated by choice and possibility and demotivated by their absence. She is particularly averse to procedures of any kind, which cause her to feel constrained and stressed. This reluctance to close options down often leads to procrastination. The motivation to seek out new possibilities means that Jill will lose interest in current assignments, moving her focus and energy towards fresh involvements. This ongoing pattern will cause her to create a trail of unfinished work.

Neil has a need to follow procedure. The advantage of this is that he will attend to the procedural details in any situation. Sequences and timings are really important and this brings consistency and routine into his life. He will consider the consequences of his actions and make decisions based on the procedural run of events. Neil's weakness is that, without a procedure, he will get stressed. Too many options bring mental torture and in a situation with no clear procedure, his priority will be to find or create a procedure. He will be motivated away from environments that lack procedure and towards those with a recognizable sequence of steps.

These patterns are particularly powerful in organizations. The procedures pattern does not work well at senior management level unless it is well balanced with the options pattern. Too much procedure can stifle creativity, while too many options can cause chaos. These patterns are complementary. They are like the Yin and Yang of organizational life: you require a good mix of both if you want to stay open to possibilities and have some clear steps for getting work done.

The problem, of course, is that organizations often suffer from the mismatches between options and procedures people. One can't fathom out the other. An options-oriented person gets stressed when forced to work to a strict procedure and a procedures-oriented person gets stressed when forced to work with too many choices.

> *Organizations often suffer from the mismatches between options and procedures people. One can't fathom out the other.*

The most peculiar aspect of these patterns is how new procedures are usually designed by options-oriented people to provide them with a new choice. This new choice soon becomes an old choice, however, and then the options person is the first to stop following the procedure.

Pacing and leading

Again, we will be pacing the language so that our communication fits the person's filtering process.

For Jill: "Are you interested in discovering some new software tools? There's a variety of brand new packages available, giving the developer many more design options. I think you'll enjoy using them and exploring their creative capabilities. What do you think? I want to give our partners a report comparing the features and benefits, can you create that for me?"

For Neil: "I need to talk to you about some new software – when will be convenient? First of all, I want you to take a look at a range of six new packages, then list the benefits of each one. Next, you will want to test their functionality and ease of use. When you're finished, I need a report for our partners comparing the features and benefits. Are you clear on what needs to be done? OK, when can I expect the report?"

Make a point of listening to these specific language patterns. Also, watch for physiological cues to the patterns. Options-oriented people tend to use more opening, outward gestures, suggesting possibilities. In contrast to this, procedures-oriented people will often mark out segments of time with their hands or use their fingers to suggest a sequence or procedure. Their gestures tend to imply closing down or moving down a fixed path. Remember to use these cues when pacing. If you want to influence a person who is talking in a procedural fashion, be procedural with your whole communication – the words and the body language.

■ Frame of reference

These patterns determine the sources of feedback we use to judge our actions. The feedback can come from two places: either external – from other people – or from internal thoughts and feelings (see Figure 9.4).

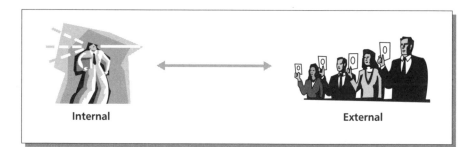

Fig 9.4 ◆ The metaprogram continuum for sources of feedback

Here's our question for Jill and Neil: "When you have completed a task, how do you know if you have done it well?"

Jill: "I just know. Other people may comment and give me feedback, but I usually know in myself that I've done it well. It's a waste of time getting feedback from people who don't understand my job."

Neil: "Other people usually tell me how well I have done a job. If they don't, I will probably ask them. There's nothing worse than getting no feedback on your performance."

The contrast is apparent in the filtering process Jill and Neil are using to form their judgments. Jill has a strong internal reference against which to judge her actions and she will filter feedback from other people to support her internal decision. If external feedback supports her own, she will accept it. If, on the other hand, external feedback mismatches her own, she is likely to fabricate all kinds of excuses to render it invalid. Reasons such as "What do they know?" "They don't understand!" and "You can't please everyone" are common filters on external feedback for internally referenced people.

In comparison to Jill, Neil will take the initiative to ask for external feedback if it is lacking. No external feedback will lead to stress. Even if he has a feeling of having done a good job, it will remain invalid until he can match it externally.

Job implications

Customer service roles require people who respond to external feedback. If you employ internally referenced people in these roles, they may not take customer feedback seriously. At best, they might go along with the processes you put in place, but their judgments are being made internally.

People with a strong internal reference frame require very little praise from external sources and, as managers, they think other people are the same. This can cause them to economize on giving people praise, encouragement, and feedback, with negative consequences on motivation.

Internally referenced people instigate actions themselves and they find it easy to make decisions when faced with a problem. Sometimes the decision, being sourced internally, may not be very well thought through. This may make them more of a challenge to manage because they often do what they think is best, rarely considering that others may have valuable input to their thinking. However, externally referenced people may put more demands on a manager's time because of their frequent need for feedback.

> Lots of data exists in the organizational environment and it will be the externally referenced people who track it down and turn it into feedback.

Training and personnel are other areas where external references are required. A trainer with an internal reference may rarely take on board the feedback from their delegates, but this is a vitally important component of ongoing training effectiveness. In some companies, personnel departments decide their policies and impose them on the workforce. As employees' needs and benefits increasingly become strategic to the success of an organization, so the ability to listen to employee feedback and act on it will require improvement.

Feedback is such an important part of organizational life, yet to rely on natural feedback processes is not enough. Lots of data exists in the organizational environment and it will be the externally referenced people who track it down and turn it into feedback. This is not a natural thing to do for internally referenced people.

Pacing and leading

You can match the language patterns and use appropriate phrases to pace and lead, as in these examples.

For Jill: "I'm sure you will enjoy the training course. We have lots of superb comments from past delegates, *but only you will know* if this is the best course for developing your skills in this area."

For Neil: "I'm sure you will enjoy the training course, but you don't have to take my word for it, we have lots of satisfied customers happy *to give you feedback* and help you make up your mind."

Conversational cues may require a little encouragement here. If your outcome can be heavily influenced by these patterns, you might prompt a cue by asking a few simple questions such as:

"How did you decide on your previous supplier?"

"Did you get any feedback from the last project you were on?"

"So, you've finished that job have you; how did you do?"

Remember that a person may not be *all* internal or *all* external. Most people will have a mix of both, with a stronger preference for one over the other. The mix will determine the weighting put to judgments made from internal thoughts and feelings and external sources.

▓ Attention direction

These patterns determine where a person's attention is directed on a continuum with "others" at one extreme and "self" at the other. Attention direction is not to be confused with the previous patterns for judgment on past action – the attention direction patterns say more about a person's focus in real time (see Figure 9.5).

It is not so easy to pick up cues from language for these patterns. You will recognize a self-focused person from their filtering of your non-verbal commu-

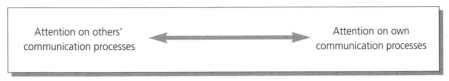

Fig 9.5 ◆ The metaprogram continuum for attention direction

nication. For example, you might let out a sigh or make some hand gesture connected to a concerning thought. The self-focused person will not even notice this, paying attention to the content of your communication only. The way you say something will have little effect on the self-focused person, who will be tuned in to their own processes, not yours.

"Others" types will let you out from a junction. "Self" types will close the gap.

A person with an "others" focus will read your process and respond to it, picking up non-verbal cues of your emotional state. The way you feel and think about something is important to them. Here are some ways to recognize these patterns from behavioral cues.

◆ **At the coffee machine**

"Others" types will serve you coffee first. If a person serves the entire group first, this is strong evidence for an "others" pattern. "Self" types will serve themselves first, and leave you to serve yourself also. They may not notice if they are obstructing the coffee dispenser.

◆ **At the restaurant**

"Others" types will ask what other people want to order first, deferring their order until at least one person has gone before them. "Self" types will just tell the waiter what they want regardless, except when "self" men are giving preference to women as a cultural gesture of courtesy, i.e. "ladies first".

◆ **At the wheel of a car**

"Others" types will let you out from a junction. "Self" types will close the gap and prevent you from getting out.

Job implications

People whose attention is mainly directed at self do well in jobs requiring little human interaction. They do not perform well as managers of people, sales executives or as trainers, but may do well in laboratory-based jobs as scientists, technicians or data researchers and workshop-based engineers. Rapport means very little to them, so they are often perceived as uncaring.

This is not necessarily the case – it's just that it may never occur to them to consider caring unless their attention is drawn to it verbally.

Pacing and leading

Match your language with phrases such as – for "others" types – "I can see how this new program will benefit everyone in the department" and – for "self" types – "When you have this new program in place, you will be able to manage other people's expectations better."

You can pace a "self"-oriented person by being self-sufficient in everyday domestic routines such as making coffee, door opening, lift door holding, coat hanging, and so on. Do for yourself first. With an "others"-oriented person, they are likely to do things for you, so accept their kindness and thank them, then reciprocate when you have an opportunity. When they thank you, acknowledge this with a polite remark.

▨ Relationship sort

These patterns are filters to our understanding and reasoning, determining the relationships we make when experiencing new data. Before reading further, take a look at these shapes and describe the relationship between them.

Sameness

If you noticed ways in which the shapes are similar, and nothing else, you may have a preference for sameness. In the work context, research by Roger Bailey[1] suggests that 5 percent of the workforce prefers this pattern. Wyatt Woodsmall[2] puts this figure at 10 percent of the US population.

People with this pattern see what is the same in things and dislike change, often staying in the same job for many years. They will resist change and are likely to have a great deal of sameness in their life. They will use the same bank, same holiday location, same type of car, same stores, and same routines day in and day out. Changing any of these things may create stress.

Examples of influencing language for people liking sameness include:

"You can count on us to give you *the same* quality of service that you expect from a professional company."

"This job contains *much of what you have been used to* and, in many ways, *is identical* to previous jobs you have had. Let's put some time aside to go over *the similarities* and see how it fits for you."

Sameness with exception

Did you notice differences in the shapes, then some exceptions? Perhaps you noticed they are all in a different location on the page? This pattern covers the majority, about 65 percent according to Roger Bailey, 50 percent for Wyatt Woodsmall. This matches my own experience of running exercises in our NLP classes, that most people notice similarities first, then some exceptions.

People with this pattern don't mind some change, but there is a limit. They prefer gradual change and will respond well to large step changes every five to seven years, which is also the length of time they will stay in a job before looking for alternative work.

Examples of influencing language for people with this pattern include:

"This new schedule is *pretty much the same* as the old one, *except* that it is easier to use."

"*We're alike in many ways*, and our *unique* skills complement each other."

Differences with exception

If you are in the 25 percent – according to Woodsmall – of population with this pattern, you may have spotted differences in the relationships between the shapes, then noticed some exceptions. Did you see the differences in juxtaposition between the same facing edges of each shape?

People with this pattern are likely to remain in the same job for between one and three years. They will tend to change routines regularly, choosing different holiday locations, different newspapers, different diets, and so on. They will upgrade their computer frequently and change their car often.

Examples of influencing language for those exhibiting this pattern include:

"This job is *different from* your current one in a number of ways and you will *have more* responsibility."

"This new system will bring *many changes* to the way you work and you will find it requires *less maintenance* than the old one."

Differences

Did you see only differences in the relationships between the shapes? If you did, you are among a smaller percentage of the population – 5 percent according to Woodsmall, 20 percent for Bailey. My own experience suggests the lower figure.

People with these patterns are mismatchers; they look for differences and are constantly reorganizing things, including their department or even the organization itself if they are the CEO. Don't expect these people to stay in a job for more than 18 months.

Influence using language that suggests the opposite of what you want them to do. For example:

"You wouldn't want to join this team, I don't think it's your kind of environment."

Their response is likely to be:

"Yes I would, and yes it is."

I remember an extreme differences person – I will call him Jes – who was on a team workshop with me some years ago. We were doing some juggling and I could see Jes wasn't joining in. I had noted his differences pattern the previous day, so it was only to be expected. I said, "Let's juggle," and Jes responded internally with "Let's not." I turned to Jes and said, "I'm glad you're not trying this Jes, you will probably never learn to juggle. In fact, you will only disappoint yourself by trying, so don't even think about it. Trust me, I have seen non-jugglers and you're one of them." In the time it took me to unleash this negative assault, Jes had picked up the balls and had learned to juggle adequately – in under a minute!

Primary interest

We know from everyday contact with our friends and colleagues that people have specific interests in life. What we often don't recognize is the larger pattern of interests or the category. At that level, you may notice how a person filters for certain categories of interest. Some people may filter for only one. There are five general categories of interests that we filter: things, places, people, information, and activity.

Things

This filter finds material objects of most interest, such as computers, machines, furniture, buildings, and clothes. A person with a strong filter for "things" is likely to have a job working with machines or other objects and will tend to associate with these objects more naturally and readily than with the contents of the other categories.

Places

This filter finds physical locations to be of most interest. A person with a strong filter for "places" will regard their working environment as a priority when considering a job. They will make choices in life based on location characteristics, such as climate, view, convenience, travel distance, and aesthetics. The office location and environment are extremely important factors in their job satisfaction. When arranging a meeting, the location will bc as important as the agenda.

People

This filter finds the connections with other people to be of most interest. Those with a strong filter for "people" will spend time with groups, in meetings, on the phone, and will enjoy a working environment where they can mix with people throughout the day. They work well in customer-facing roles and have a natural ability to create rapport. This is an important pattern for the service industry to observe when recruiting. My own research[3] in this area was carried out in the IT sector, modeling excellence in customer service skills. The results clearly showed a filter for people to be the most influential component in delivering consistent, high levels of customer satisfaction.

Information

This filter finds information to be of most interest. Researchers, academics, and people who work with ideas will typically sort for information. It is the actual information that is of interest, rather than the medium used to store, process, and transmit it. People with this filter will seek out sources of information including societies, journals, libraries, Internet sites, and news services. They are likely to have large stores of books and other reference media in their offices and at home.

Activity

The "activity" filter seeks out the action in a situation. How things are done, rather than why, what, and by whom, is of most interest. Decisions to visit locations, at work or on holiday, will be made on the basis of the activity going on there. You may recognize the existence of this filter from the action-oriented lifestyle of someone always on the move, and by the activity content of conversations with them.

Job implications

There are some obvious matches between these patterns and job suitability. While many people will have a spread of interests, the primary interest is the one that is most important to job suitability. In years gone by, it was considered acceptable to have people with primary interests of "information" or "things" employed in direct customer-facing roles. In today's customer-driven world, that is ceasing to be an option, as companies compete to deliver a superior customer experience. Consequently, more companies are putting rapport and interpersonal skills high on the list of requirements for employees in customer-facing roles.

Call centres are a typical example of an industry that is recruiting people to work with computers and telephones (things and information), and the customer, being remote and unseen, is becoming increasingly dissatisfied at the lack of human contact. The dilemma facing the modern call centre is that jobseekers with a "people" primary interest do not want to work with information and things, so you have a Catch-22 – the environment dissatisfies the customers and stresses the employees. A smart call centre will be taking on employees with a "people" primary interest and making their working environment more humane.

Pacing and leading

Pacing this pattern is simply a matter of matching your language to the primary interest, bringing in the relevant interest category wherever it makes sense to do so, and filtering your own primary interest if it is different. Imagine you were discussing a new computer system with someone whose primary interest is "things" and you want to talk about the information in the system. You might explain the information in thing terms – for example:

"Let me tell you about this screen. It has packets of data for each warehouse and each item is put in a separate box just here. The boxes will show you the status for each different type of product in each warehouse."

Here's the same topic modified to appeal to a person with a primary interest filter for information:

"Let me tell you about the data you can access with this screen. There's a six-digit number representing the status of each warehouse, and each data item has a unique alpha-numeric locator ID that refers to a product type."

Have a go at some of the other primary interest patterns yourself. Use your own work-related scenarios and practice modifying your language to appeal to each one.

Activity level

This metaprogram describes whether a person is *reactive* or *proactive*. There are linguistic cues to these patterns, but it is not so easy to pick them up from everyday conversation and behavior. It will be more noticeable over time, from the impact a person has on their environment. Reactive people have little impact on others compared with proactive people.

Proactive

These people enjoy being mobilized and doing things that make a difference in the world. They are not satisfied with just any type of activity – it has to have a purpose for them and be something with a measurable result. The type of activity itself is not so important as the end result.

In meetings, proactive people will become restless if discussion does not appear to be moving towards action. On training courses, these people want to move on to the next topic while others are still reflecting on an exercise. Forward body language, rhythmic tapping of a foot or finger, and concise speech are all symptoms of a proactive person. They will uses phrases such as:

"Let's get on with it."

"When do we begin?"

"What's the first thing we need to do?"

"We need to move on this."

Reactive

These people like to take their time and consider ideas before committing to action. In some cases, the period of consideration can extend beyond the time when action is relevant, and very little gets done. Consequently, they end up reacting to situations as they arise and become labeled as fire fighters. They make poor planners, preferring to sit and wait until the phone rings or some other external event forces them into action.

In meetings, they will continue to stream input to an idea until someone changes the topic. They are not good at chairing or facilitating meetings and rarely suggest a controversial idea for fear that they may be asked to champion it. Leaning back with a hand on the chin or cheek is a common body language sign for a reactive person. They will tend to use words that avoid commitment, such as:

"Maybe"

"Perhaps"

"I might do"

"Let me consider that"

"What do you think?"

Job implications

If you want fires putting out, hire a reactive person. If you want to bring some change to your organization, hire a proactive person. According to Bailey, 15–20 percent of the work population is reactive and the same percentage is proactive. The remaining 60–70 percent has an equal mix and will react in some situations and instigate action in others.

Pacing and leading

Match the language to the cues you pick up from verbal language and body language. Use action-oriented words and phrases with proactive people and reflective, considering language with reactive people, as in the previous examples.

▇ Using what you have learned

I have presented each of these metaprogram patterns to you in isolation from each other for the sake of understanding. In conversation, however, you will notice combinations of patterns from different parts of a person's communication. If you attempt to label people as just this or that type, you will get stuck because these patterns change over time and from one context to another. If you attempt to calibrate all the patterns that are going on, you are likely to have a breakdown!

> *Develop your sensory acuity so that you can notice patterns easily and work in real time with what is happening.*

The key is to develop your sensory acuity so that you can notice patterns easily and work in real time with what is happening. If you know what you want as an outcome of an interaction, you will learn to intuitively tune in to the patterns that are important for that outcome to be achieved. Remember, now *you know what the patterns are* and you have already identified *some of your own*, which ones do you want to *work on* to become even more flexible than you are *today*?

Notes

1   Shelle Rose Charvet (1996) *Words That Change Minds*, Kendall/Hunt Publishing. Also, Roger Bailey, *Hiring, Managing and Selling for Peak Performance*, Lab Profile Study Kit, Georgian Bay NLP Centre, Ontario, Canada.

2   Tad James and Wyatt Woodsmall (1988) *Time Line Therapy and the Basis of Personality*, Meta Publications, Inc.

3   David Molden (1999) "What NLP did for Computacenter", *IT Training*, November. Also David Molden (1997) "Communication and Change with NLP Technology", *Internal Communication Focus*, October. See media pages on www.quadrant1.co.uk

10

Alignment

So far in this section we have been dealing with relatively detailed patterns of communication and filters that make up an individual's unique model of the world. I am now going to change the emphasis from principles, processes, and functionality to organization and relationship. I'll explain by analogy.

Imagine you are on an ocean liner. You want to learn everything about this ocean liner, so you are shown around the engine room, navigation equipment, and the safety features are pointed out to you. Then you are given a presentation on hull construction and materials used to build the vessel. You read about all the different roles and tasks performed by the crew, how they communicate with each other, with other vessels, and with the shore. You learn about the functioning of the ocean liner, the principles on which it works, and the physical characteristics of the vessel – the materials, equipment, mechanics, power generation, communication, and navigation devices, the crew and what they do.

While your confidence regarding the workings of the vessel is growing, your learning is incomplete. You have yet to ask about the purpose of the ocean liner or why it is on its current journey. What about the benefits provided to the people who have a stake in the liner and the various contracts with the shipping company and travel agents? These are not functions, but relationships. The paper used to record a contract is functional, but what it contains is a description of a relationship between two or more stakeholders. Without this kind of information, you do not know what keeps it in commission. A liner can be in excellent functional condition, but it is the relationships it has with passengers and other stakeholders that will define its purpose.

The same is true for work. You need skilled people and resources to function, but if the relationships are neglected, like the ocean liner, your journey may come to a halt. When relationships are set up to succeed, functionality is maintained and so ongoing success relies on our ability to create and maintain winning relationships.

Organizations are very good at defining relationships between functions. We are less good at doing this for the relationships between people. Maybe this is because you can't actually see a relationship. You can do your best to describe it in words, but the real stuff of a relationship is in the emotion and energy, not in a description of the interaction. When things go wrong or don't go according to plan, it is usually the functional mechanisms that get the attention. What is needed is the ability to rise above function and view the world as a set of relationships. To help us with this, we have a universal model for aligning relationships to create success.

> *Organizations are very good at defining relationships between functions. We are less good at doing this for the relationships between people.*

NLP has drawn extensively from systems thinking and cybernetics to produce a universal model for aligning systems and, more specifically, aligning the relationships between components of human systems. The work on systems thinking by Dr. W. Ross Ashby[1] and Norbert Wiener[2] interested Gregory Bateson[3] whose ideas had a major influence on Richard Bandler and John Grinder and, subsequently, the forming of NLP. Robert Dilts[4] developed this particular area of NLP and has written extensively about hierarchies and logical levels of human systems.

The logical levels model

We grow and develop as people by means of the processes of learning, communication, and change. As individuals, we will apply a mix of these three elements to form our unique experience. When we are faced with difficult situations, conflict or challenges, we respond according to the patterns we have developed through our lives. The more significant the event we are presented with, the higher our level of response. We may develop new patterns as a result of high-impact events in our lives. The logical levels model (see Figure 10.1) is universal in that it applies to individuals, groups, and entire organizations. It is just as common for one person to experience inner conflict as it is for an organization. When we say that an organization has conflict, what we really mean is that some people in the organization are in conflict. From the diagram, you will see that there are six levels:

- ◆ purpose
- ◆ identity
- ◆ values and beliefs
- ◆ capability
- ◆ behavior
- ◆ environment.

A person may operate with a different logical level alignment in different contexts (where and when), so, in Figure 10.1, "Environment" is shown as a boundary for all levels, to remind us of this. Let me explain with the help of an example.

❖ example

James is a hard-working manager with responsibility for recruitment in a large organization. He enjoys his job and the recognition he gets for his innovative solutions to difficult recruitment problems. He has his sights set on a senior position where he can get involved with strategy formulation.

One day, his manager tells him, "You've done a good job, James. Recruitment has come a long way with your help. It is so strategic to our growth that we have decided to appoint a director to head this. I hope you will support the new head of recruitment when she arrives next week."

This was unexpected. James felt his future ambitions pulled from under him. He lost interest in the job and began to ask searching questions – "Why hadn't he been considered for the post?"

This example shows how easy it is to take something that is functioning, change the relationship, and damage the functionality. The insensitive way James' manager handled the situation inflicted massive damage on a set of relationships that were organized for success. We could consider the reasons for the manager's actions, but this would be a different example, so let's work with James' situation and use the logical levels model to understand what's going on.

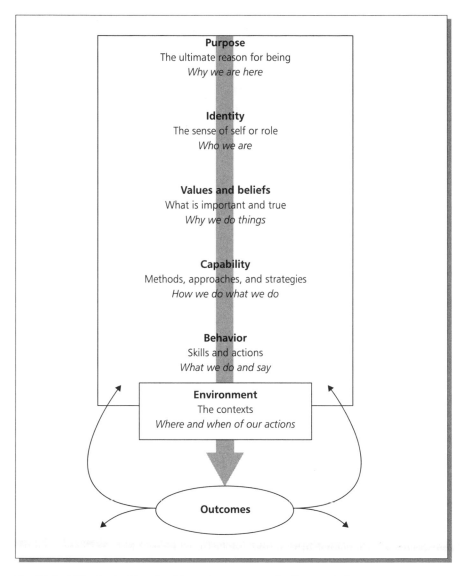

Fig 10.1 ◆ The logical levels of learning, communication, and change

Before the meeting with his manager

Purpose

James views his purpose in the organization as strategic, ensuring that the right people are selected and recruited into the organization. Without this, the business would suffer. James has a clear sense of why he is there.

Identity

He is an expert. He has done the job now for four years and knows his company's business and the recruitment market very well. He has a team of six people, all recruited by him, who are doing a good job for the managers in the company. He thinks of himself as a leader of people, an innovator in recruitment practice, a strategic thinker, and a professional in his chosen field.

Values and beliefs

James' work values can be shown as a hierarchy:

◆ working at a strategic level;

◆ delivering a superior service;

◆ being creative and innovative;

◆ keeping up with developments in the recruitment field;

◆ leading and developing people.

He believes in his potential for a senior management position, advising directors on recruitment policy, and contributing to strategy. He has received encouraging feedback from the management team and from his own boss, which has strengthened the belief that he will be promoted in the organization. He also believes that his values are what the organization wants from him, although no one has ever explicitly said this.

Capability

James' values and beliefs, sense of identity, and purpose are working in alignment with each other. His energy is positive and being put to productive and creative use. He has great potential and, if given the opportunity and appropriate development, his contribution will grow. His self-belief is a powerful driver, urging him to take new initiatives and have different experiences. James is clearly someone who likes to instigate. He is proactive and an effective manager of people.

Behavior

The higher levels determine what James will do and say. In meetings, he likes to talk about strategic aspects of recruitment. His ideas are different from conventional thinking and his initiatives are innovative. He spends a lot of time talking with other managers and asking for feedback about the service his team is providing. He is diligent, thorough, and speaks well of the organization.

Environment

At work, James is constantly on the move, attending meetings with department heads and arranging more informal liaisons with new managers. He lunches with his team and socializes with his peer group. He muscles in on seminars and other gatherings to promote best practice in recruitment, wherever and whenever the opportunity arises.

After the meeting with his manager

Purpose

James is now coming to terms with the realization that his manager does not share his career vision. His sense of purpose has been shaken and his energy has been blocked because any effort expended is unlikely to lead to his desired future. He has been emotionally hurt. The energy he was putting into the job is now directed inward to understand what has happened and what to do about it.

Identity

James is still the expert, but now thinks of himself as an unsung hero in the organization. He maintains his professional self-credibility and anticipates the worst of the new director, as yet not on the scene.

Values and beliefs

James' values haven't changed, but his belief system has taken a knock. Consequently, he strengthens his beliefs about his ability to work at a senior level on strategy, but now feels undervalued and believes that his career lies outside the organization.

Capability

Opportunities for him in his organization seem much more distant now, yet he believes he has the ability to achieve more. He sees his autonomy and strategic ability becoming constrained and is concerned that his development and career will suffer.

Behavior

James is now registering with employment agencies. He wants to test his marketability outside his organization. He will go for interviews seeking a job with strategic objectives. His focus and energy will be split between his current job and finding a new one. He will hold back on new initiatives because he can see only a short-term future in his current role.

Environment

He will go to fewer meetings and be less interested in meeting new managers. The uncertainty about his future role will cause him to withdraw from certain activities, spending time in reflection as he comes to terms with the new relationship he has with the organization and the people in it.

Using the model to analyze situations

The alignment between the higher logical levels determines behavior. Purpose, identity, values and beliefs, and capability have no physical form other than in thought and energy. You cannot see a belief; you can only see the behavior that results from holding the belief. This is significant, as most of the time we work with behavior, not recognizing the powerful influence we can have when we work at higher logical levels (knowingly or unknowingly). In James' case, his manager didn't have the foresight to consider the negative influence his news would have on him and his contribution to the organization. Perhaps he didn't care, but that would be another story.

> *Whether a perceived problem is one of conflict or change, those in positions of influence will often resort to changing behavior. This rarely gets the desired result.*

Whether a perceived problem is one of conflict or change, those in positions of influence will often resort to changing behavior. This rarely gets the desired result and may achieve a short-term truce or a begrudged agreement at best. You need to be persistent and prepared for a messy engagement when working at the behavioral level alone. The logical levels model offers this rule:

> *At whichever level you make a change, levels below will also change, but levels above may, or may not, change.*

So, the higher the level of the change, the more change you get.

The model is particularly useful for diagnosing situations before making an intervention. Here's an example.

A manager in a publishing company told me about a situation concerning three sections he was responsible for (see Figure 10.2). Most of the time things went smoothly, the work flow passing from design to print to finishing. However, the three sections would go to war whenever a major problem occurred, which happened about once a month. Each section's behavior to the others became aggressive and no one wanted to help anyone else. The manager would do his best to facilitate a solution, but he never got to the root of the problem. Each section blamed another for causing the problem and they did their best to highlight each other's weaknesses.

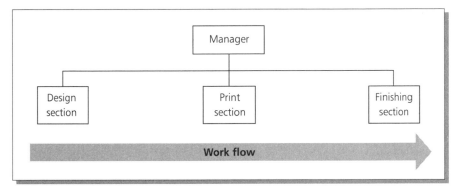

Fig 10.2 ◆ The structure of part of a publishing company

We used the logical levels model to ask questions about the situation and diagnose the cause. As we stepped up from behavior to capability, we asked, "Are the people capable of resolving these problems?" The answer was "Yes." Next, we asked value and belief questions and found that these were pretty well aligned with those of the organization.

Stepping up to identity, we discovered the misalignment. When we asked people in each section to describe how they felt about their identity, we found that the Print section had some negative energy stemming back to pre-merger days, when they were responsible for both design and finishing. New people had been brought in to work with new technology and the three sections were separated. They still considered themselves to be experts in the entire process and, because they had been badly treated during the merger, they were out to seek revenge. The opportunity for revenge came every time a problem occurred.

This particular problem was resolved at an open workshop where the real cause was confronted and dealt with head on.

Wherever a change is required, this model will help you to consider the change in a systemic way and find the real leverage for change or, as Gregory Bateson would say, the "difference that makes the difference". Sometimes people want to change, but they just don't know how, or they may not recognize that alternatives to what they are doing exist. Often the need for change is not considered important or people are just too comfortable in their existing grooves. Whatever the scenario, this model reminds us to check out the different levels and find the level of maximum leverage.

▨ Aligning for success

You need very little to grow and develop. You just need to acquire new skills, have an opportunity to practice the new skills so that you become more capable, and the motivation to do it. The model can help you to make the most of these three dimensions of development. First of all, if your personal growth is important to you, you will create opportunities for yourself. I have met many people who are content to stay with an employer because changing jobs seems like hard work. Yet, a number of these people also complain about the lack of opportunity and scope for development. This sounds like a painful existence.

> *If it is important enough you will find a way. Real change lies in your motivation, powered by the higher levels, particularly values and beliefs.*

If your employer is not prepared to make opportunities for you, find one that is. The same applies to skills development – if it is important enough you will find a way. Real change lies in your motivation, powered by the higher levels, particularly values and beliefs. Here are some questions to stimulate your thinking and motivation.

◎ exercise

Personal alignment

Before answering the following questions, choose a context – work, home, social, spiritual – and answer all the questions from that context. The questions seem very simple, but we rarely ask these types of questions, so the answers may require some extended inner searching. Take your time.

Purpose – *the source of motivation*

What purpose do you serve by what you do in this context?

Identity or role – *the expression of motivation*

How do you define your sense of who you are in pursuit of the above stated purpose?

Values – *the staying power of motivation*

What is important to you in fulfilling your role? Make a list of your values in this context and arrange them in a hierarchy.

Beliefs – *the energy of motivation*

What do you believe about your potential in this role? Do you have any limitations? If yes, list them, then think of at least two ways of overcoming each one. Get someone to help you with these questions or use one of the belief change techniques in Section 3.

Capability – *the application of motivation*

What skills do you want to develop? What do you want to be capable of as you pursue your purpose and deal with limitations? List the specific areas where you want to increase your capabilities.

Behavior – *the product of motivation*

What habitual patterns of behavior are preventing you from achieving your goals? What steps can you take today to start becoming a more capable person? What can you do to begin developing the skills identified above?

Environment – *the context for motivation*

Does your environment reflect the person you are? Think about the "where and the when" for this context. Do the places you go to support the pursuit of your purpose? What other places and times will help you to achieve your goals?

If you have any inner doubt about your current situation, step up the logical levels and ask some questions. If you become involved in a situation that ceases to offer you personal reward, these questions will set you on a new path of inner enquiry. If your actions are not getting you the results you want, changing those actions is easiest when you can modify the higher levels. Here are some further examples.

❖ example

An acquaintance of mine told me how he had changed his life's purpose by switching from being a business consultant to a caring professional. Instead of helping organizations that should be smart enough to help themselves, he found greater purpose in helping those less fortunate. Consequently, his identity, values, beliefs, capability, and behavior all made a shift to become aligned with his new purpose.

Another example involves an identity shift made by a young trainee manager who would become frustrated at his lack of influence among the management team in his organization. He thought of himself as an expert adviser and spent most of his time prescribing policy and procedure to an options-oriented management. After some coaching, he reframed his role to be a solution provider and began to listen more to managers' needs. His solutions were better tailored to their needs and he was respected more for this.

A senior manager had the job of making a large number of young people redundant and he was getting increasingly depressed about this. He thought of his role as being "the bringer of bad news". He made a shift at the level of his role after realizing that he could help these people think positively about their future. In his mind, he became a career mentor (his company was unaware of this) and he began to help people by putting them in touch with resources to widen their career horizons. This allowed him to carry out his duty in a way that benefited those made redundant and helped him to manage the entire process in a more resourceful way.

Misalignments are damaging. You don't always see the damage until it is big enough to be a major problem. In organizations, a misalignment left to fester can be disastrous. At Sellafield nuclear power station in Cumbria, England, a serious breach of safety was exposed. Here's a report from a local news service at the time:

> *The report found that workers had been so bored by the tedium of checks that they had not bothered to do them. Management's lack of safety culture had allowed this to happen from as long ago as 1996 and it had continued since.*

How could this occur in an organization that so strongly pronounced safety as its utmost priority? Even after the report was made public, a spokesperson for the plant insisted that safety had always been a high priority. Somewhere along the line a misalignment between values and behavior occurred and it was left to fester. For boredom to override safety, something must be seriously wrong. It is not enough to espouse value statements and trust that people will do what's necessary. A value such as safety only has an impact when it is used each day to question what people do and what they don't do. I frequently meet people who tell me that their team "awayday" resulted in a list of veritable work values on a flipchart, which changed nothing in the workplace.

Relationships govern function

Relationships at work are so important to the continuing effectiveness of any organization. If the relationship between workers and management at Sellafield had been better aligned, perhaps they would have identified the potential safety problem much earlier and been in a better position to do something about it. If their response to this particular situation focuses on function only, I predict more problems ahead.

When we talk about relationships, we often focus on such things as respect, cooperation, understanding, and empathy. We are often ignorant of the relationships between logical levels, yet these are so important for a successful alignment.

In forward-thinking organizations, there is a real move to harness the full potential of people. Emerging popular themes in the crusade for high-performance employees are leadership, teamworking, creativity, innovation, and continual improvement. The model can be used in all these areas to help align people to new roles, values, and behaviors.

How do you develop a creative workforce? How do you create effective leadership? The universality of the alignment model makes it a superb tool of great flexibility. Its effectiveness comes from the focus on the relationships between the logical levels and its simplicity, providing a robust framework for achieving success.

When used with other NLP techniques[5] you have a formidable set of tools for communication, learning, and change. By using this model in our development work with clients, we have been able to exceed expectations in every assignment.

◎ exercise

Here's an alignment audit you can use to gauge how well aligned your employees are to your organization's purpose. Copy it and ask each member of your team to complete it anonymously, then compare the results.

1 Do you consider yourself to be working at your optimum ability?

A Often		**B** Sometimes		**C** Rarely	

2 Do you agree with the values or principles inherent in your organization's culture?

A Yes, fully		**B** Partly		**C** Disagree	

3 Can you recognize a clear connection between the tasks you do and the objectives your company wants to achieve?

A Often		**B** Sometimes		**C** Rarely	

4 How much of what you do, when interacting with people at work, do you believe is the most appropriate way of contributing?

A Most		**B** Some		**C** Little	

5 Do you believe that what you read and hear about corporate mission, values, and principles is lived out by the originators?

A Mostly		**B** Some		**C** Little	

6 How clear are you about your role in the organization?

A 75–100%		**B** 50–75%		**C** 50% or less	

7 How much access do you have to available people and resources?

A Sufficient		**B** Some		**C** Restricted	

8 Rate your level of motivation to give your best, at this moment in time.

A High		**B** Ticking over		**C** Low	

9 Does the role you perform inspire you to want to do more for the organization?

A Often		**B** Sometimes		**C** Rarely	

10 When you hear someone talk about your company's mission or purpose, how much meaning does this have for you?

A Lots		**B** Some		**C** Little	

11 How much of what you do during a typical month do you consider to be effectively adding value to your organization?

A Most		**B** Some		**C** Little	

12 How much of what your organization is doing do you believe is contributing to its future success in the marketplace?

A Most		**B** Some		**C** Little	

13 When you think about your job today, how well connected are you to other roles in the organization where cooperation is required in order to get results?

A Greatly		**B** Partly		**C** Very little	

14 Does the technology you use help you to achieve your goals?

A Mostly		**B** Partly		**C** Not at all	

15 Do you believe that if you over-achieve it will be recognized and you will be rewarded for it?

A Most times		**B** Sometimes		**C** Rarely	

16 How much of your job is personally rewarding to you?

A 75–100%		**B** 50–75%		**C** 50% or less	

17 To what degree can you connect your company's business goals with your personal ambition and desires for your future?

A 75–100%		**B** 50–75%		**C** 50% or less	

18 How much of what you do during a typical month do you consider to be developing your ability as an individual?

| **A** 75–100% | | **B** 50–75% | | **C** 50% or less | |

19 How much of the contribution you make do you believe is valued and appreciated by the people who appraise and reward you?

| **A** 75–100% | | **B** 50–75% | | **C** 50% or less | |

20 How visible to others is the role you perform in the organization?

| **A** Highly | | **B** Partly | | **C** Hardly at all | |

21 To what degree do working practices support you in your role?

| **A** Highly | | **B** Partly | | **C** Hardly at all | |

Interpretation

Enter the scores in the boxes below as follows:

A = 5, B = 3, C = 1

Then add up the scores horizontally and shade in the appropriate "Total scores" boxes.

Question no: scores			Alignment levels	Total scores						
				3	**5**	**7**	**9**	**11**	**13**	**15**
3:	10:	17:	Purpose							
6:	13:	20:	Identity							
2:	9:	16:	Values							
5:	12:	19:	Beliefs							
1:	8:	15:	Capability							
4:	11:	18:	Behavior							
7:	14:	21:	Environment							

High scores 11–15

You are very well aligned with your organization. Your energy is channeled into meaningful tasks. A 100 percent alignment is an unlikely ideal as relationships evolve and change over time. This creates a dynamic tension and the challenge is to make it work for you in a positive way. Keep your eye on the ball.

Mid-range scores 7–9

The chart will show the level of intervention required to improve the alignment between yourself and the organization. Some energy is being lost doing meaningless work. If the score is typical among a high number of employees, consider how the organization might change in order to utilize more of what people have to offer.

Low scores 3–5

Serious alignment required. Lots of energy is being wasted on unproductive tasks. The chart will show at which level to begin making a difference to the relationship between you and the company. If this score is typical among a high number of employees, consider how the organization might change in order to utilize more of what people have to offer.

Copies of this instrument and others can be downloaded from www.quadrant1.co.uk

Notes

1   W. Ross Ashby (1952) *Design for a Brain*, Wiley.

2   Norbert Wiener (1989) "The Human Use of Human Beings", *Cybernetics and Society*, FAB.

3   Gregory Bateson (1972) *Steps to an Ecology of Mind*, Ballantine Books.

4   Robert Dilts (1983) *The Roots of NLP*, Meta Publications, Inc.

5   For an in-depth look at the model applied to a variety of organizational themes, see D. Molden and J. Symes (1999) *Realigning for Change*, FT Prentice Hall.

11

Time coding

There is no such thing as "time" – it cannot be seen and touched, like distance or weight can. It is not possible to look to the future in the way that you can look to the horizon, so we quantify time by representing events using a linear system called a calendar. You cannot hold time like you can hold a bag of potatoes. You think about it in your mind, see it with a diary, and use your wristwatch to inform you of the present by way of a number system. Time is not a "thing" but a concept or, perhaps more accurately, a metaphor, given the number of analogies we have to describe time, such as "killing time", "time to waste", "time on your side". It is questionable whether any creature, other than the human being, has a concept of time more complicated than noticing changes in the seasons or between night and day.

In Chapter 4, "time" was introduced as a psychological filter on our experience (see also Figure 5.3). Time is used conceptually as a measure of events, the modern clock having evolved from early machines designed to reproduce the movements of the planets. In any group of people, all with diaries and watches, it's a safe bet that some will be more effective at managing time than others and each will use their time in different ways. This will also be the case even after a time-management training course – there are several reasons for this, which I shall come to shortly.

Past, present, and future

If time is a concept, then so are the past and the future. The past consists of events we have recorded, in history. If a past event is not recorded, we have no way of thinking about it in the present. Libraries, museums, photo albums, videos, and stories keep past events alive. We also hold on to a store of our own experience in our memory, and use it as reference material to make decisions in the present. By remembering what we have done in the past, we will be better equipped to deal with the future – or will we? The answer to this question has more to do with our emotions than with the memory of the event itself.

When the mind stores an experience in memory, it doesn't just store the physical event, but also saves the emotion connected with it. The memory will consist of a captured internal representation after the experience has been filtered with the various types of generalization, distortion, and deletion. Memories are stored in our unconscious mind – that is, we are not aware of memories until we call one up and think about it with the conscious part of the mind. When we recall a past event in this way, we also recall the emotion attached to it. If the memory is unpleasant, then we have a similar unpleasant feeling and vice versa for pleasant memories. Think about the consequences of this process on learning ability and consider the following contrasting examples.

> *Memory will consist of a captured internal representation after the experience has been filtered with the various types of generalization, distortion, and deletion.*

❖ example

Ben worked in the central logistics office of a retail chain. His career was going well and the time came for him to give his first formal presentation to a group of store managers.

He had attended a one-day presentation skills course and had been given some tips by his manager on how to construct the presentation. He created a slide show and made some cue cards as prompts for what he wanted to say. His aim was to educate the store managers in a new system for dealing with returned stock. On the day, he performed reasonably well considering it was his first time. He was clear, perhaps a little hurried at times, but he succeeded in getting the message across.

When asked how he felt about it, he said, "It was awful. They didn't like what I was saying, and so I kept talking to leave no gaps for difficult questions. I knew they would be against it – you could see it in their eyes and body language. I'm glad it's over!"

In this example, Ben has filtered his experience in a way that creates an internal representation charged with negative emotion – even though most people thought he did rather well. Following this experience, Ben avoided presentations whenever he could. When the subject came up in conversation, he would respond by recalling his negative experience, creating an unresourceful state, which was how he felt at the time of giving his first presentation.

❖ example

Angela moved departments and location to become an assistant sales director. All went well until she had a run-in with Jeremy, the Marketing Director.

Jeremy was well known for his authoritative style and Angela felt the worst of this one day in a meeting about budget allocation. Jeremy was particularly sharp with figures and he was very influential with the other directors. His most cutting remark that day was, "If you haven't done your homework Angela, don't waste my time. I have far better things to do", which he delivered with a tone of voice and physiology Angela interpreted as "wolf-like".

The following day, Angela was asked how the budget meeting went, to which she replied, "I'm beginning to understand Jeremy. He likes to keep the emphasis on figures, and to have accurate reports to work with. He's like a wolf, hungry for a kill, and I wasn't prepared for that, but I will be next time."

Like Ben in the first example, Angela also filtered her experience, but in a way that left her with memories that will be a useful resource for the future. She is already thinking about the next encounter with Jeremy, considering it a challenge rather than a bad experience to be avoided. She is taking control of her situation and learning from it, not just stacking away a negatively charged emotional memory.

This is how it is possible to limit your potential as a result of the memories you use to store your experience. Memories are references for making future decisions, so the quality of your memories will determine the quality of your future. It follows, then, that emotions expressed in the present will influence the emotional content of your memories.

Conjecture

Roger, a middle manager in a small telecoms company, is an expert at conjecture. I sometimes think he has a crystal ball, such is his confidence in knowing his future. Just recently, we were talking about promotions and he mentioned a vacancy in his company that interested him. I asked if he was going to apply, to which he replied, "I don't think so. I doubt I would get it. It would be a good role for me, but I don't think the HR director will take my application seriously." Roger was qualified, experienced, and interested, so why would he put himself down like this and predict an unsuccessful outcome? The answer was in the references in his memory that he was using to decide whether or not to apply. You don't need too many negatively charged references of perceived unsuccessful experiences to create low self-esteem, then conjecture takes over to create the disempowering belief that is so damaging to potential. Your past is not your potential, but the negatively charged past experiences can make it seem that way.

> *You don't need too many negatively charged references of perceived unsuccessful experiences to create low self-esteem.*

Time and physical space

When we think about time, we represent it as a metaphor. Try this short exercise.

⊚ exercise

Remember the following instructions, then do the exercise with your eyes closed.

Recall three past enjoyable events from your life between two and five years apart. For each event in turn, concentrate on the very first thought that comes into your mind and notice the direction it comes from. Next, do the same thing for some pleasurable events that could happen to you in the future, perhaps special occasions such as birthdays or anniversaries. Close your eyes and spend a few minutes discovering the locations of past and future.

What did you discover? How much physical space was there between each thought? What is the relationship between past and future locations?

Drawing an imaginary line through each location will reveal your personal, metaphorical timeline, representing your personal concept of time.

So, what does this mean? Well, if there were no difference between these thoughts, how would you know whether a thought was from a past or future context? There must be a way of telling a vivid, imagined thought from a past event, otherwise our decision making would have very surreal outcomes. Timelines have a large influence on how you manage your goals, how you store your memories, and how you cope with programs, timetables, plans, and all the other devices created to fit events into limited blocks of time. Let's take a look at the planning aspect of time first.

Have you noticed how some people find personal organizers useful, while others give up on them shortly after returning from the time-management course? Why is it that some people seem to be late for meetings while others consistently arrive early?

The answer to these questions can be found in the timeline configuration, of which there are many. Any individual's personal timeline will be based on one of two types: in time and through time.

In time

People who code time in this way have their timeline going through their body. The point at which the line cuts through the body will be the present, while on either side will be the past and future. Figure 11.1 shows two examples of this type of configuration – A–B and X–Y.

The A–B style is common in people who are very future-focused (direction A), but with poor memories of the past (direction B). Each memory is stored in a direct line behind the body, making specific past events difficult to retrieve.

It is also possible to have the past and future reversed, as you might find with a person who sees the past more readily than the future. This particular configuration can cause resistance to change or a strong sense of "away from" motivation.

The X–Y style is better suited to recalling memories and planning future events, simply because the angle makes accessing a particular time period much easier than with the A–B style.

The common feature to both A–B and X–Y is the location of the present. Because the timeline actually cuts through the body at the present, someone with this style will typically be very associated with "in the moment". This means that, in a meeting, you get the person's full attention on the matter in hand. The disadvantage of this style is the tendency for

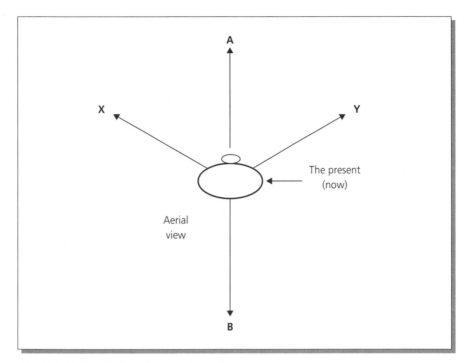

Fig 11.1 ◆ A typical in time configuration

meetings to run on and consume more time than had been allocated. Consequently, in time people are very often late for their appointments and can be
seen dashing to catch their train. They may also have a collection of unused
personal organizers in their desk drawer, preferring to use a simple pocket
diary to remind them of important events.

Through time

This style does not cut through the body. The present can be anywhere on the
line and the person dissociated from it, as in Figure 11.2.

The advantage of having this style is that you take to using planners
and schedules easily. Events are planned and timed to ensure everything gets
done. Beginnings and endings are very important to a person with a through
time configuration.

A disadvantage of this style is the tendency to be frequently distracted
by the need to reference future events. In a meeting, you will recognize this
when a person is clock-watching and their eyes are roaming.

A person with this style of timeline will be dissociated from the present and associated with their schedule. Through time people are rarely late and, in extreme cases, will organize their lives to be early for everything.

Figure 11.2 shows a common through time configuration, with the past moving out to the left and the future traveling out to the right in a curve. This is a very effective way in which to organize your timeline for a business context, except that it lacks the event-connectedness of the in time style.

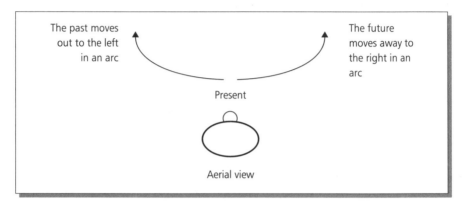

The past moves out to the left in an arc

The future moves away to the right in an arc

Present

Aerial view

Fig 11.2 ◆ A typical through time configuration

People have all kinds of peculiar timeline arrangements. These examples are typical configurations, of which there are many variations, and I have met people with fragmented timelines, spirals, concentric circles, and C-shapes, to mention a few.

This brings us to the practical application of the timeline concept, which here is that, if you have a poor memory or find time management difficult, you can change your timeline configuration and make some immediate improvements.

Changing timelines

The timeline has developed into an extremely powerful range of techniques, with a growing variety of exercises for creating personal change. Tad James and Wyatt Woodsmall[1] expanded on the original discoveries of Richard Bandler and developed a range of techniques under the name "Timeline Therapy".

As a simple introduction to the approach, I am going to show you how to change your timeline configuration, but with the understanding that, without a trained practitioner, success may be limited.

Emotions have a strong influence on the shape of a timeline and, in many cases, a person will resist change because of the fear of exposing past negatively charged events. If you have traumatic memories that cause you to feel bad when you think about them, I strongly advise against doing this next exercise and ask, instead, to contact a NLP practitioner who can help you with any change you want to make to your personal history.

If you are relatively comfortable with your past, you will find the procedure highly enjoyable, so find a quiet place to sit while you perform the exercise.

exercise

First of all, decide the configuration you want. Are you too much an in time person and want a better balance or is it the other way round? Do you want to improve your general memory or have a clearer future? When you know what you want, decide which configuration is best suited to the particular change you are seeking.

Next, commit the following instructions to memory, then perform the exercise in a quiet, comfortable area with your eyes closed.

Imagine you are floating up above your timeline as it takes on a form or shape. You float very high so that you can see the timeline extending back into the past and forward into the future. Notice the form it takes and change it to the one you have previously designed. Now, from this point on in the exercise, make sure that the qualities of the images you are creating are the same for past, present, and future (refer to Chapter 5, Figure 5.4 for a refresher on submodalities).

Focus on a series of enjoyable past events, and pull them, one at a time, from the timeline, up to where you are floating, so you can see them clearly. Make the image bright, clear, and colorful, then, after a few moments, place it back in your timeline at an appropriate chronological position, then do the same with the next one. Do this with about ten images from the past, ten images of the future, and a couple of images from the present. If your future images are unclear, this is a sign of an uncertain future, and you may find the exercise in Chapter 17 very useful.

When you have done this, float back down to a position either very close to the timeline (for a through time configuration) or on the timeline at the present (for an in time configuration).

Repeat the last two steps five or six times to burn in the new configuration. There you have it – a designer timeline.

The value of time

Some people regard time as extremely important, while others are less driven by the position of the hands on the clock. People with extreme through time configurations may be perceived as having an obsession with time, putting the timing of a task over and above the doing of the task. In roles such as project management and work scheduling, there is a danger that timing of tasks takes the focus away from the quality of the task and the benefits that completion of the task brings to the customer and other stakeholders. Putting a high value on time can take away pleasure and enjoyment from the present, and may lead to anxiety where unrealistic objectives have been set. There is a short rhyme reminding us of the importance of living in the present:

> *"Yesterday is history*
> *Tomorrow is a mystery*
> *Today is a gift*
> *That's why it's called the present."*

In contrast to this, a low value on time can cause others to perceive you as disrespectful each time you miss a meeting or turn up late. You may feel relaxed and comfortable in the moment, but others could perceive your state of ease to mean "unconcerned" or "uncaring".

The language of time

As you might expect, the strong emotional influence of time is reflected in the way we use language to talk about the past, present, and future. This is important when we want to have an influence with someone or tidy up our own thinking, and there are two basic rules to observe. The first of these is:

> *Emotions are fixed to memories, but can be recalled and changed using submodalities.*

Compare the feelings you get as you read each of the following two phrases:

> *"I am pleased you have seen the benefits in our proposal of last week."*

> *"It is encouraging that you see the benefits in our proposal so clearly now."*

The first example begs the response, "Yes, we saw the benefits last week", and serves to leave the emotion buried in the memory.

The second example begs the response, "Yes, we are seeing the benefits now", and continues to build on the submodalities of the internal representation and, thus, the emotion attached to it.

Present events are stored with present emotions.

This is the second rule.

When you meet a person for the first time, they will form an opinion of you. There is a saying, "You only get one chance to make a first impression", so don't you want to make it a positive one?

The stronger the emotion you can create, the more memorable you will be. This is where your rapport skills come in, connecting on as many levels as possible, to give the other person a positive reference for your visit. If you talk about past problems during a client meeting, the client is likely to store away a negative record of your visit. Positive emotions can be created by accessing past enjoyable events, then helping the client to intensify the submodalities – such as "It must have been so exhilarating to have succeeded like that" or "That's a fascinating scene you've just painted, what was the high point for you?"

You can also facilitate a positive association to a product or project. For example:

"Imagine having succeeded with this project. What are the positive benefits for you?"

"This product will cut out half the time you currently take to complete orders. Imagine the benefits that will bring you."

Being aware of how you code time can help you to identify some of the patterns that are working against you. Being too much of an in time person, for example, may cause you to be late for other people's important events. Using negative linguistic metaphors for time, such as "time is against me", can cause stress and lead to tasks not being finished. If you are heavily oriented towards the past, speaking in the past tense can dampen enthusiasm and draw out too many negative experiences.

> Being aware of how you code time can help you to identify some of the patterns that are working against you.

Timeline is a very powerful technique for fixing many of the unsuccessful patterns in a person's life and you will notice it in a number of the exercises in Section 3.

Note

1   Tad James and Wyatt Woodsmall (1988) *Time Line Therapy and the Basis of Personality*, Meta Publications, Inc.

Section 3

Tools, techniques, and skills:
creating change

Introduction

If you have opened the book at this section first for rapid access to the many techniques inside, you are to be commended for your pragmatism. However, if you don't have the NLP principles and patterns to underpin the techniques, go back to Chapter 1 and read them before attempting the exercises in this section.

The material in Sections 3 and 4 has been edited from the collective contributions of ten people with diverse backgrounds and roles. There are two fellow authors, two managers, two directors of personal development companies, and some independent consultants. While their backgrounds and roles may differ widely, they all share an experience of using NLP to create change in commercial organizations. The ways in which they have done this are also varied and, together, show you many ways in which NLP is being used in business. The result is a compendium of advanced change techniques drawing on the NLP material you have covered in Sections 1 and 2.

You will find examples for use on training courses, facilitating change, managing meetings, coaching others, and, of course, your own personal development. Some of the techniques will be easier to use than others and I recommend enlisting the help of an experienced NLP master practitioner if you are not trained to that level yourself. The contributors' contact details are listed at the end of the book, should you wish to approach any one of them directly.

12

Corporate and competitive envisioning

Marcus Muir

This exercise was used in the early stages of an organizational change project to get a more in-depth understanding of how the company and its competitors were being viewed by customers. It was a benchmarking exercise, but one that would put a lot of flesh on to the bones of the internal reports that had been prepared thus far. Comparing turnover ratios, lead time to installation, customer satisfaction scores (and often these weren't available) only gave a partial picture. By eliciting subjective views, we were able to gain a richer insight into the situation and use much of the material to further communicate the change process to the organization.

The current situation

The client was a large, multinational telecommunications organization – we'll call it Company X – that was facing increasing competition in previously secure markets. There was much complacency throughout the organization and a great deal of resistance to change. Although there had been several attempts at communicating the severity of the situation, because no major customers had actually migrated to another provider, there was disbelief that the changing marketplace would affect the company.

Company X traditionally relied on providing tailored technology to its customers, which was an effective barrier to entry for its competitors. There was also a very strong technical mindset running through the company, causing people to focus on problem fixes or bigger and better technical solutions. However, the telecommunications marketplace was changing rapidly. Older, legacy, tailor-made systems were increasingly becoming obsolete as the customers' systems were required to communicate with newer, more advanced equipment, the trend being for common or easily connected platforms. A further change of major significance was the filtering through of customer demands to Company X, driving a requirement for increased customer focus.

As part of the situation analysis, many different comparisons had been made to provide a benchmark for how Company X compared with its competitors. Although the figures in the reports showed a significant gap in terms of the softer issues, such as customer service and account management, there was a certain amount of consolation that, from a technical perspective, Company X faired relatively well. In keeping with the technical mindset, the focus naturally tended towards the more positive technical elements of the reports, supporting the apathetic "business as normal" culture.

In order to counteract this very dangerous situation, the company commissioned a survey that would give customers the opportunity to provide direct feedback on the company and its competitors. The thinking behind this was that it would be a way of not only generating a further comparison, but also creating a powerful way of communicating the situation as perceived by the customers themselves.

Desired outcomes

The intention was to have a number of discussion forums, which would be videoed from behind a double mirror so as to avoid distraction. These would then be used to build up a profile about Company X and the ways in which it needed to change. A secondary key output was to have video clips of customers expressing their opinions about Company X and its competitors, which could be used as an internal communication vehicle.

The exercise

The sales account teams for the top 20 customers were asked to nominate individuals they thought would not only be likely to volunteer for such an exercise, but would also be outspoken in their views. The selection of customers was essential, as it was important that they were sufficiently senior to have dealt with a number of different telecoms providers and yet junior enough to want to take part in the exercise (the positioning by the external research company was important to reflect the balance). The whole exercise was to be done without the customers knowing the research sponsor, so the account teams were fully briefed as to the importance of keeping the research a secret until after the forums had been held. Anonymity was important to avoid bias, either way, because it was a competitive comparison.

The external research company invited groups of five or six customers to each forum and balanced the groups based on the profiles provided by the account teams. The account teams were kept briefed at each stage and asked to check the makeup of proposed groups to avoid any potential conflicts. The forums would be filmed and observed, with the participants' knowledge, from behind a double-sided mirror. This was to make the filming as unobtrusive as possible and so lead to more open discussions, but also so that the researchers could watch the dynamics of the group in real time.

Each session was to be run in the same way and last two hours, with refreshments available in the room. There was a single facilitator to run each group and carry out a number of roles:

◆ leading the discussion by asking a set of predetermined questions;

◆ providing explanations where required;

◆ allowing the discussion to be led by the group.

In the event of the dialog drying up, there were several additional subquestions that would be asked. The facilitator was also there to ensure participation by all members of the group and keep the focus on the question in hand.

After the introductions had been made, the facilitator thanked the participants for their time and reviewed the purpose of the forum. It was explained that it was researching a number of competitors in the telecoms field and that the sponsor would not be revealed so as to avoid any potential bias. The objective for the day was to elicit the subjective impressions that the participants had of each competitor, so it was important to remember that there were no right or wrong answers, only differing points of view. It was also asked that the participants be particularly aware of the first things that came into their head and to try to avoid editing their thoughts before sharing them. These last few points were stressed in order to put the participants at ease and allow them to have access to as many of their unconscious thoughts as possible.

The experience

The participants were told they would be taking a "virtual" walk in their minds through a number of different competitors' sites, one site at a time.

They were to note what occurred to them and what their impressions were at each site.

The facilitator started by inviting them to imagine that they were on their way to a meeting at the first of the four competitors' sites. This often provoked thoughts of the kind of journey that had to be made – was it by car or train? Was the site easy to get to? What kind of area was it in and what did that say about the company's prosperity? Was customer awareness affected by being sited in an obscure place?

The facilitator then moved on to arriving at the site and walking towards the building. What did they notice? There were comments about the number of expensive cars in the car park and the similarity of the cars, perhaps reflecting a restrictive car policy. There were comments about the appearance of the building and how that reflected the wider perception of the company. They also considered the impression given to visiting customers by smokers huddling outside the building.

The participants were asked to then walk into the reception areas and notice what they heard. Some were busy and frantic; others quiet and calm. One didn't even have a reception, which caused some amusement in the group. The participants started to get the hang of the exercise now and began talking about how one company always had beautiful, fragrant flowers in reception or how the receptionists would be smiling, if they remembered their name or not and whether or not they were calm and in control. There was quite often discussion about the size of the reception, the quality of the seating, the artwork on the walls or the company information that was available.

The participants were then asked to imagine being met or escorted (and what difference that made) to the meeting room. They were asked to talk about what they noticed on the way, with comments about the general level of activity, the open door policy or open office layout, the general state of décor of the building, the piles of technical equipment in the corridors or on corners, any overflowing bins, and the general state of tidiness.

The participants were next led into the virtual meeting. By this time, there was usually no need to even ask the questions, as the group started to talk about the style of the meeting room (if there was a meeting room at all, as some meetings took place at desks in an open plan office due to a lack of designated meeting space), if the desks all matched, if the chairs all had four legs (one particular company had a reputation for broken, cheap furniture). The conversation was guided on to the subject of how the people in the meeting were dressed, ranging from smart business attire to jeans and T-shirts. Was the meeting organized and run to time? Were refreshments provided? Were they of a good quality?

The facilitator would then call a close to the session, although there was a tendency for the sessions to run over time, as there was such active conversation going on. Because of the elements of fun and creativity, none of the participants found the exercise strenuous and, in the post-session questionnaires, the feedback was consistently positive. There were also very few comments about the filming or double-sided mirror; the feedback indicated that within a few minutes everyone had relaxed and got into the flow of the session.

Each of the groups had a different dynamic, mainly due to the characters of the participants. Although different material came out of each group, some very strong themes started to emerge. A great deal of analysis was done to condense all of the material into a manageable format, and a number of video highlights were made as a way of capturing the essence of the forums. These were received exceptionally well and included balanced views of each of the competitors, with a lot of humor coming through in the ways in which the groups had perceived each company, and lots of groans of recognition as customers identified issues everyone knew were problems but nothing had been done about them.

The results

Although the exercise was only a part of the overall change program, it turned out to be significant. Creating virtual "caricatures" of the company and its competitors, as seen through customers' eyes, was a way of bringing the message home. It also gave rise to a whole host of change initiatives that people could relate to as they could see the significance because of what the customer groups had said.

The exercise itself was used very effectively as part of a change process using customer input. This process of "facilitated envisioning" can be very effective for other purposes also. It can be used by internal teams to flesh out the vision of a company by talking about the tangible elements that surround the business case. This could make it really come alive for a team – what the company will look like, where it will be located, what other

> *Creating virtual "caricatures" of the company and its competitors gave rise to a whole host of change initiatives that people could relate to.*

differences will be noticeable. Alternatively, it could be used to create a profile of specific companies, competitors or customers by using the resources within a team. This kind of visualization exercise is very effective for utilizing the brain's natural creativity and gives greater access to information stored in the customers' deep structures that is rarely offered in more conventional benchmarking approaches.

13

My perception becomes your experience

Jane Revell

Exercise 1 sitting in the passenger seat

Purpose

To encourage participants to think about the beliefs they have about their clients and give them the opportunity to reassess those attitudes and the behavior that inevitably stems from them.

     This exercise has obvious applications for anyone who deals with the public as part of their job, but, in fact, it might also be extended to anyone in a professional relationship where there is some kind of difficulty or conflict: manager/employee, colleague/colleague, members of a team, and so on.

Context

This simple exercise was part of a one-day workshop for the crew of a large catering company responsible for service on high-speed trains in Europe. The aim was to help them become more attentive, proactive, and flexible towards their passengers. This particular exercise evolved out of an introductory activity in which each member of the group was given three cards and asked to write a major problem in their work on each one. When the cards were combined and categorized, "difficult passengers" figured very highly as a problem.

NLP content

- ◆ NLP presuppositions:
  - the map can become the territory – what you believe either is true or becomes true;

- the meaning of my communication is the response that I get.

◆ Perceptual positions, specifically regarding the second.

Procedure

1 Group members individually write sentences beginning, "The passengers are … ."

2 Ideas are shared, written up on a flipchart, and comments invited.

Here are just a few of the suggestions I received: "The passengers are …
- rude
- demanding
- sexist
- greedy
- inconsiderate
- good and bad
- nice
- passengers
- people
- what you expect them to be!"

Note how, interestingly, the last one in this list anticipates the theme of the exercise.

While there was a certain amount of agreement, there was also quite a lot of disagreement and discussion, with cries of "But they're not all like that!" often responded to with "No, but a lot of them are!" and so on.

3 Each member of the group describes, briefly, how powerful our beliefs are and how they determine our behavior, even unconsciously, giving some personal or second-hand examples. (One of my more dramatic examples is the newspaper story of the man who was locked inside a refrigeration lorry overnight. It was actually switched off, but he was convinced it was switched on and he died of hypothermia.) The group members are invited to share some of their own examples of self-fulfilling prophecies. Finally, they are asked to think how the beliefs about the passengers they expressed earlier may actually be influencing how they behave towards them and how the passengers, in turn, respond to them.

4 The group members draw "Mexican on a bicycle"-type drawings, as in Figure 13.1, without saying what they are, and ask the group to suggest what they could be. They can be something from the front, above, underneath or from the side.

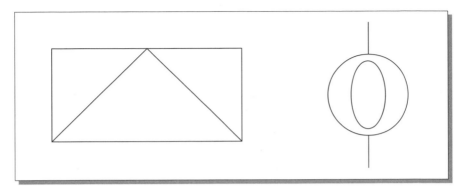

Fig 13.1 ◆ Some simple "Guess what it is" drawings

Here are some suggestions for the drawing on the left:
- from the front, a mountain peak, witch's hat, curtains in a window, road or railway going into the distance;
- from above/below, the nose of a plane, prow of a ship, bird's beak, toe of a shoe, an envelope;
- from the side, the roof of a house, apex of a fishing rod and line, box or parcel.

This shows that when you look at something from a different angle or point of view, it changes or rather, *it* doesn't change but *our perception* of it does and we get some new information about it. With this idea in mind, the group next thinks about the passengers from a different point of view: the passengers' point of view. They will sit for a moment in a passenger seat to find out if and how that changes anything about the way in which they perceive the passengers.

> When you look at something from a different angle or point of view, our perception of it changes and we get some new information about it.

5   The group is asked to close their eyes for a moment: "Imagine you are a passenger sitting on a train traveling on one of your busiest routes. It is the evening and it has been a long, hot, exhausting day in the city. You were up at dawn to catch the early train and now you're on your way home. How do you feel? What do you want during this journey? What is important to you?"

6   The group members individually write down their thoughts.

7   Their ideas are shared and written up on a flipchart. Here are some of the things they said they, as passengers, wanted:
   - to be left in peace;
   - arrive on time;

- given information if they needed it;
- treated with courtesy;
- greeted warmly;
- helped if they had a problem.

8   The two flipchart sheets (from steps 2 and 7) are put up side by side and the group looks at them for a moment. They are asked if, having gone through this process, anything has changed at all in the way the crew members feel about the passengers? If so, how is it changing things? In what ways will it affect how they interact with passengers on a train? Here are some of the things they said:

- "I didn't realize how influential our beliefs are. I can see that we sometimes bring things on ourselves."
- "I've been expecting passengers to behave unreasonably … and they have. I need to be open to the possibility that they're OK … so that they will be."
- "They're only human. And so am I."
- "I think I've often responded to any complaints as a personal criticism of me. I'm beginning to see that that's not necessarily true."
- "I still think some of our passengers are really awful, but perhaps I need to remember that that doesn't mean all of them are."
- "Maybe I tend to scowl at them too readily. I'll try to be a bit friendlier and see what happens."

Results

It is impossible to judge the results of this exercise in isolation, given that it was part of a series of different exercises taking a whole day. However, feedback on this section from participants at the end of the day was very positive, with many of them saying that it was something they had not really thought about before, that they had found it both a fascinating and very useful way of thinking about things, and they felt that it could make a significant difference in their personal as well as their professional life.

In terms of the whole day, managers who traveled on trains after the training noticed a big improvement in the crews' attitude, attentiveness, cordiality, and flexibility. My colleague and I traveled on trains before the training took place, in order to guage the kind of input that would be most useful on the course, and found the service generally very efficient, but rather cold. We have yet to embark on our post-training train journeys, but we are looking forward to the experience.

Alternative procedure

Split the task by dividing the group into two subgroups – one focusing on beliefs about the passengers, the other imagining they are passengers. Members of the two different groups then form pairs or foursomes to exchange ideas.

Exercise 2 walking in management's moccasins

Another major issue, which emerged during the introductory activity, was the crew members' relationship with management. They felt there was a lack of acknowledgment and appreciation of their work in various ways. This led to a second exercise, which, in many ways, mirrored the first one described above, but had its own purpose.

Later on in the day, we asked them to put on management's shoes, imagine things from their point of view, and come up with at least ten solutions to address some of the problems they had described in the morning. They did this in groups and then presented their proposals to the whole group. With their consent, we later fed their proposals back to management, and several of them have since been implemented.

A final note

The activities outlined above were designed for a specific group at a specific point in time and the content was very much dictated by the participants. I do believe, however, that such an activity may well prove useful in a very wide variety of contexts.

14

The tiger and the rose garden

Exercises for developing sensory acuity

Imagine a tiger in the wild – a strong beast, fearing nothing, hunting to provide meat for its family. Now, take your mind away from the jungle and enter a rose garden – tranquil and vibrant with delicate blooms and fragrances. Now, put the two scenarios together and imagine what it would be like to have the courage, confidence, determination, and strength of the tiger combined with the sensory acuity to appreciate the subtle sensations of the rose garden.

In almost ten years of running manager development programs, one of the more common blocks that has prevented managers from getting the best out of their people has been a habitual directive style of communicating. Even when the manager has wanted to develop a more flexible, developmental, open style, past habits have made progress in this area challenging. It is hardly surprising, as the accelerating pace of change encourages managers to become predominantly action-oriented and task-focused. The CEO of a large computer services company likened a period of extremely high sales and fast growth to "riding the tiger", because of the intensity of task focus required to satisfy customers. The danger with this mode of operating is the impact it has on communication – when time is at a premium, the default of giving instructions and telling people what to do often prevails.

A sales director spent in excess of $175,000 sending all his sales executives on a two-day coaching skills course. When I mentioned to him that I saw little evidence of people using the skills in the workplace, he replied, "I'm not surprised – around here we only have time to tell people what to do." What a waste.

The point I am making here is how habit, working environment, and attitude are barriers to developing communication skills. If you are unresponsive to the non-verbal cues people are giving out, how will you know when things are not going well? You know from experience that people do not offer bad news readily. Even when you ask for it, the reply can hide the reality. The key is to bring the senses and attitude of the tiger to the learning process – to have the courage to do things differently and learn to recognize when all is not well from non-verbal communication cues. So, how can you become a tiger and develop the sensory acuity so crucial to the act of influencing?

The skill of sensory acuity will develop in a mind that is open, curious, and wants to understand other people. So, if you practice sensory acuity and, at the same time, maintain your personal agendas for other people, your learning will be arduous and ineffective. It's

> *The key is to have the courage to do things differently and learn to recognize when all is not well from non-verbal communication cues.*

like the moments before opening presents on your birthday or on Christmas morning – you can either be curious to see if someone has bought you the thing you really want or to find out what is in the wrapping paper, with no thought of what you would like to find inside. Similarly, you can either enter into an interaction with someone curious to know how you can get the other person to do what you want them to do or to find out about the person – what they think, what they want – with no preconceived ideas, then decide how best to structure the relationship for a win–win outcome.

The key elements for learning sensory acuity are:

◆ testing your intentions;

◆ describing your outcomes for an interaction;

◆ being in a receptive state of mind;

◆ being curious to know about the other person;

◆ practicing detection skills in visual, auditory, and kinaesthetic channels.

Testing your intentions

How many times have you heard someone say, in the midst of a personal conflict, "It didn't turn out the way I intended." The reason this happens is often due to an intention being formed within a win–lose frame and a lack of behavioral flexibility. In seeking a win–win, your flexibility will be a major factor in determining your results. If you have only one strategy for influencing people, don't be surprised if a good percentage of your attempts fail to get the results you want. So, think before acting.

How much do you know about the person you want to influence? What are they motivated by? What do they enjoy doing? What does your project have to offer them? Avoid the trap of answering these questions for yourself, then acting from the assumptions you make. Keep an open mind during the interaction and find the answers you want from real-time conversation. Whatever the outcome, learn from the experience and increase the range of behavioral options you have for influencing this person, and others, in the future.

Consider this linguistic example. Suppose you want to enlist a colleague to your cause and your intention is "to get their commitment to attend your presentation". The attitude implied by the language is close to coercion – the word "get" is a win for you, but a lose for them, so, in the long run, this is also a lose for you. Contrast this with "find out how to win their commitment to go to the presentation". This implies that you will first seek a way to motivate them to want to come to your presentation, which is more likely to end in a win–win. If you fail to motivate them, you can rethink your decision to ask them – rather than coerce them into compliance – or try an alternative approach.

Describing your outcomes

It makes sense to have an outcome for your interaction with the person you want to influence. If you don't have an outcome, you are leaving things to chance and losing control. Some outcomes will net you better results than others, the more successful ones being those that give the other person a choice. Here are some examples of, first, a poorly stated outcome (A), then an improved outcome (B):

A I want to tell Person X how to do this job.
B I want to motivate Person X to do this job willingly.

A Person X must do Y to help me finish this task.
B I want to find out if there's anything Person X can do to help me finish this task.

A I am going to put Person X clearly in the picture on this situation.
B I want to understand how Person X sees this situation.

A I will insist that Person X is loyal and committed.

B I want to know how to earn Person X's loyalty and commitment.

A I'm going to tell Person X just how difficult they are being with everyone.

B I want to find out what's behind Person X's puzzling behavior and let them know how their behavior is affecting the team's performance.

Being in a receptive state of mind

There are two ways to direct your conscious attention – inside and outside. When you are processing information, you have your attention focused on the inside – the time you spend in this state of mind is called being in "down-time". The contrasting state is called being in "uptime", having all your faculties alert and tuned in to the external environment. It is not easy to do both at the same time, which is why we are generally poor listeners. The cleaner you can make the change between uptime and downtime and the more conscious control you have over flipping between the two states, the better your sensory acuity will become.

> *When you have your attention focused on the inside, this is called being in "downtime". The contrasting state is called being in "uptime".*

A common block to developing sensory acuity is the tendency for internal dialog to cut in as the other person is speaking, blocking off the listening channel. The simple rule here is "when the other person is communicating, be in uptime". This may take a little getting used to, as it will force you to think on your feet and make informed decisions during conversations, rather than in isolation of other people. Practice this exercise for the next week or so.

⊚ exercise

◆ **Before a conversation**
Adopt the tiger and the rose garden state of mind. Be curious to know what's in the birthday parcel.

◆ **When listening**
Suppress internal dialog. Watch, listen, sense – notice state changes.

◆ **When responding**

Confirm what you heard, specifically where you noticed a state change – for example, "You said that the last project was a disaster for you and that Tim really helped you."

◆ **When replying**

Ask for more specific details surrounding the subject corresponding to a state change – for instance, "What exactly was it about the project that made it a disaster for you?"

 Be curious to know about the other person

Refresh your memory of states and calibration by rereading Chapters 5–9. When you are in uptime, you will be looking and listening for:

◆ state changes

◆ the preferred communication channel

◆ metaprograms

◆ values

◆ beliefs

◆ language patterns.

These are the things you want to know about a person to be able to influence with integrity and sincerity.

If you are thinking that there is an awful lot to pay attention to, you are right – there is. These aspects of a person's communication are so often overlooked or missed, usually out of ignorance or preoccupation with self, things, other people, information or the task. Learning how to recognize these classes of information takes effort. It's called learning to communicate and it's done in uptime. Take it one chunk at a time, focusing on state change for a week, then listening for language patterns for a week, then moving on to metaprograms, and so on. Remember that whatever you are tuning in to, be curious to understand the person you are communicating with. A useful technique is to recall an experience where you were intensely curious and work on the submodalities. Use this past event to get into a heightened state of curiosity before entering into an interaction. Daily practice will refine your sense receptors and give you all-round improved sensory acuity.

■ Detection skills

Here are some exercises to help you practice with another person or in a group.

◉ exercise

Contrasting states

Objective
To practice calibrating two contrasting states.

Procedure

1   Person A will calibrate as Person B recounts a past unpleasant experience (internalize only).

2   Person A will find ways of describing Person B's state using physiological distinctions, such as:
   - *body*: posture, gesture, breathing, movement;
   - *skin*: tone, texture, tightness, lines;
   - *voice*: tone, pitch, volume, speed, modulation.

3   Person B will break out of the current state, stand or sit in a different location, and begin to recount a highly pleasant experience (internalize only).

4   Person A will calibrate Person B's state as in step 2.

5   Person A describes the differences between the highly pleasant state and the unpleasant state.

Coins

Objective
To develop sensory acuity in the auditory channel.

Procedure

1   Collect a number of coins of different sizes, weights, and denominations.

2   Person A is to stand behind Person B, then drop one coin on to a table.

3   Person B is to guess the denomination of the coin by sound only. How many distinctions can B make in the auditory channel?

4   Person A continues to drop coins, one at a time, while Person B guesses the denomination.

5   When Person A has dropped all the coins, do the exercise again, twice over. Person B will learn to make distinctions between the different coins.

6   Describe the differences.

What's in a voice?

Objective
To recognize differences in a person's voice when they are in contrasting states.

Procedure

1   Person A and Person B are to sit back to back. Person C observes. Person A thinks of an unpleasant experience while counting out loud, slowly, from one to ten.

2   Person B listens to the qualities of the voice (pitch, volume, speed, modulation, and so on), and describes it to Person C.

3   Person A breaks state. A and B swap seats.

4   Person A thinks of a highly pleasant experience while counting out loud, slowly, from one to ten.

5   Person B listens to the qualities of the voice (pitch, volume, speed, modulation, and so on), and describes it to Person C.

6   Person B describes the contrast between the two, noting some key differences.

Truth or lie?

Objective
To recognize the differences in physiology between contrasting *truth* and *lie* states.

Procedure

1   Person A describes two personal experiences – the first will be true, the second will be a lie.

2   Person B calibrates the physiology for each experience, noting key differences in body, voice, and skin qualities, such as:
   ◆ *body*: posture, gesture, breathing, movement;
   ◆ *skin*:   tone, texture, tightness, lines;
   ◆ *voice*: tone, pitch, volume, speed, modulation.

3   Person A describes two more personal experiences – again, one will be true and the other a lie, this time without announcing the category in advance – that is, whether it is true or a lie.

4   Person B has to guess whether it is the truth or a lie.

5   Repeat from step 1 a further four to five times.

6 Person B describes the distinctions made, and the differences in physiology, between "truth" and "lie" for Person A.

Congruity test

Objective
To recognize a signal of incongruence in another person.

Procedure
1 Person A writes down ten things that they enjoy and gives the list to Person B.

2 Person A must answer "yes" as B asks if A enjoys each of the items on their list, such as "Do you like skiing?" As Person A answers, Person B is calibrating their physiology, paying particular attention to the voice.

3 After five to six questions, Person B will throw in an item they know A dislikes, such as, "Do you enjoy watching darts on TV?" Person B will calibrate the state change as Person A lies with the answer "Yes".

4 Describe the differences between "truth" and "lie" states.

This exercise works best when done with an element of surprise – that is, your subject does not know the purpose and procedure of the exercise. That way you are likely to calibrate strong cues and notice the differences quite easily. If the exercise is done overtly, it will force you to look and listen for much finer contrasts between distinctions as Person A will try to catch you out.

Sensory acuity is the most fundamental of all NLP skills, and to develop it requires daily practice. But this is easy, as every interaction you have with another person presents an opportunity to improve. It is the key to enhancing not only your work-related relationships, but those in your personal life too. The more in-tune you become to the states of others, the better communicator you will become. Be the tiger, and have the sensory acuity to appreciate the rose garden.

15

Choices in time management

Graham Yemm

■ The exercise and its purpose

This activity is useful for a variety of contexts, and this particular variation is set within a frame of time management. The purpose is to create the understanding that we make choices, albeit unconsciously, about what we do with our time, and these choices are led by our beliefs and values.

Conventional time management training tends to put the emphasis on skills and behaviors – an approach that often has a limited effect because existing beliefs and values will still control the use of these behaviors and skills. This method, however, invites you to explore your limiting beliefs attached to your metaphor of time and develop more choices.

Explore your limiting beliefs attached to your metaphor of time and develop more choices.

You will then examine your values for both work and home contexts and consider the degree to which you are living these values with reference to your goals. The overall purpose is to move from understanding the influence beliefs and values have on your personal metaphor for time management to the position of having made changes that will result in a better balance in life.

The exercise can be used at an individual level or for teams to identify shared beliefs and values. I have used it extensively with multinationals, small organizations, management levels, and staff levels, in Europe and the Middle East. It has applications for anyone who is open to personal change and is particularly useful for sales and customer service staff.

■ The outcomes

As a result of completing this activity, you will understand the concept of limiting and empowering beliefs and have identified your own limiting beliefs in this context. You will be aware of the consequences of holding your beliefs and will have made choices to develop beliefs that are more empowering for you. You will have thought about and listed your main values, assessed their priority, considered how well you are satisfying them at present and what you can do to achieve an improved life balance.

◉ exercises

The procedure

This procedure is set out based on the assumption that you are running the activity with a group.

1 Get a rapport going with the group and pace their experience of time management, asking for personal examples of effective and ineffective behavior. Ask each group member to state what they want to have instead of the ineffective behavior, and list these as outcomes on a flipchart. When ready, lead the group to be motivated to want to achieve their outcomes.

2 Explain the alignment model and how it will help the group to achieve their outcomes. Ask the members of the group to work individually and write down their life goals spanning the next five to ten years. (This goal list will be referred to later in the exercise.)

3 Explain the concept of beliefs, that they are generalizations of our experience and influence us by empowering or limiting our capability. Stress that the creation of limiting beliefs is a deliberate choice – they are not necessarily negative! First, give examples of how beliefs are originally acquired from "adult" figures in our lives and then we build our own, based on a variety of life experiences. Ask for examples, of who thinks, for instance, they can't sing, draw, be creative, and so on, then ask them to recall the beliefs they held at about four years of age. This leads into how language expresses our beliefs – "I'm hopeless at writing reports" or "I'll never get to grips with finance", for example. Discuss why we have limiting beliefs, explaining that all beliefs have a positive intention for us, and how we can, and do, change our beliefs throughout life.

4 Refer to the "Beliefs" work sheets (at the end of this chapter) and begin by exploring beliefs they have changed. This is done individually, identifying key limiting beliefs that impact their use of time. Examples might be "I must always do what my boss wants", "I have to clear my desk every day", "I have to help everyone."

5 Get the group to work, individually, through the next series of questions about consequences and benefits or payoffs from their beliefs.

6 The next step is to choose beliefs that would be more useful to have, while retaining the benefits of the limiting ones. Emphasize the fact that these beliefs are extras and choices. The limiting beliefs can still be used if appropriate.

7 In groups or pairs, share these results and discuss what to do to bring the new beliefs alive and how to handle potential blocks.

8 Next, move on to the "Values" work sheets (see the end of this chapter) and explain how the degree of success in bringing new belief choices alive will depend on whether or not they are supporting personal values. Also, consider how the personal values hierarchy directly influences commitment to both work and life goals.

9 In small groups, have the participants explore what the values on their list mean and arrange them in priority order, rating each in terms of how well they are satisfying it currently. The next step is to link the values to their beliefs and decide what they can do differently to achieve a better balance in their time management and in their lives in order to better satisfy their values.

10 The outputs from this exercise help to identify better ways of dealing with time stealers and interruptions, to have a stronger basis for prioritizing tasks and activities, and identify what they can do differently to achieve more satisfaction from the way they spend their time.

Some sort of ongoing support, after the training, such as the formation of learning sets, often helps people to burn-in new belief systems, eliminate unwanted beliefs, and adopt appropriate behavior.

▨ Work sheet 1   Beliefs

Write down a list of things you once thought to be true in your life, for which you now have a different belief. For example, *"The tooth fairy leaves money under my pillow."* Think about beliefs you have changed in your adult life also.

_____

_____

_____

_____

_____

_____

_____

_____

Now write down a list of beliefs you have that you feel prevent you managing yourself and your time more effectively.

_____

_____

_____

_____

_____

_____

_____

_____

_____

Work sheet 2 Beliefs

What are the consequences of holding on to these beliefs?

_____

_____

_____

_____

_____

_____

_____

_____

_____

What are the benefits of having them?

_____

_____

_____

_____

_____

_____

_____

_____

_____

_____

Work sheet 3 Beliefs

What would it be more useful to believe?

_____

_____

_____

_____

_____

_____

_____

_____

_____

What can you do to start to "live" these beliefs?

_____

_____

_____

_____

_____

_____

_____

_____

_____

_____

What might stop you from living them?

_____

_____

_____

_____

_____

_____

_____

_____

_____

_____

_____

_____

_____

_____

_____

_____

_____

_____

_____

_____

_____

■ Work sheet 4 Beliefs

Linguistic clues to beliefs

Reactive language	Proactive language
There's nothing I can do	Let's consider the options
That's the way I always …	I can choose a different way
They/he/she makes me angry	I control my …
They won't allow …	I can decide …
I have to …	I will choose to …
I can't…	I can choose …
I must …	I will …
If only …	I want to …
How often do you use these words?	Who do you know who uses phrases like these?

■ Work sheet 5 Values

Compile a list of your current top ten values. As you think of each one, ask yourself: *"What is important about having this?"* Repeat the question until you are sure you have identified the underlying value.

1 _____

2 _____

3 _____

4 _____

5 _____

6 _____

7 _____

8 _____

9 _____

10 _____

Are there any conflicts between two or more values? If so, ask yourself, *"By having this, what will it mean for me?"* Repeat this several times for each conflicting value until you find a higher value that is applicable to both.

Choose one of your goals and consider what values in your current hierarchy will be satisfied by achieving the goal. If one or more can be identified, then the goal is worth striving for; if none, then it is unlikely that you will achieve the goal and you can choose to discard it.

■ Work sheet 6 Values

1 **Think about some of your interests, desires and ambitions.**

Consider the goals you are pursuing now, even if they have not been formally outlined. Think to the future and see yourself achieving them. Pick the most important ones that come to mind – there may be two, three or more.

2 **Determine your values and principles.**

Take each goal in turn and imagine achieving it. Turn up the submodalities of the image you have created and fully associate with it. You can do this by bringing the image closer to you. Try it slowly first, then bring it in quickly and compare the feeling you get. Intensify the image and the experience until you get a strong kinaesthetic feeling. Run the movie past the point of having achieved the goal to a future time where you are looking back and reflecting on the outcomes. Think systematically about this, checking the consequences for other people in your life. When you have done this, ask yourself, "What do I value about having this goal?" If the goal is to travel, the answer might be "learning" or "fun". If it is to be promoted or get a new job, the answer to what you value might be "challenge", "development" or "excitement". The answer may be one value or several. Usually, they will be single words or phrases.

3 **List your values and principles.**

Now perform step 2 for each of your goals, asking, "What do I value about this goal?" List your answers.

4 **Find your deepest values.**

When you have reached this point, you will have a list of deep values and principles. Now ask yourself, "What is important to me about *all* of these values?" The answer will be a deep value that is even more important. These values have been motivating and influencing all of your actions and achievements in your life.

Slow Dance

Have you ever watched kids on a merry-go-round
Or listened to the rain slapping on the ground?
Ever followed a butterfly's erratic flight
Or gazed at the sun into the fading night?

You'd better slow down
Don't dance so fast
Time is short
The music won't last.

Do you run through each day on the fly
When you ask "How are you?", do you hear the reply?
When the day is done, do you lie in your bed
With the next hundred chores running through your head?

You'd better slow down
Don't dance so fast
Time is short
The music won't last.

Ever told your child, "We'll do it tomorrow"
And in your haste, not see his sorrow?
Ever lost touch, let a good friendship die
'Cause you never had time to call and say "Hi"?

You'd better slow down
Don't dance so fast
Time is short
The music won't last.

When you run so fast to get somewhere
You miss half the fun of getting there.
When you worry and hurry through your day,
It is like an unopened gift … thrown away …

Life is not a race.
Do take it slower
Hear the music
Before the song is over.

(Source unknown)

16

Resource sphere

Marcus Muir

This exercise is a development of an already powerful tool called the "circle of excellence", one of the earlier NLP applications devised by the founders of NLP, John Grinder and Richard Bandler. This variation integrates other elements of NLP to expand and enhance its effectiveness.

The original exercise (the circle of excellence) is widely used in many different situations – preparing for a meeting or presentation or dealing with a particularly difficult situation, for example. The aim of the exercise is to enable people to have access to a resourceful state when they need it, and have the ability to change, and thus manage their state regardless of the context.

There are three underlying principles involved in the exercise.

- Our state, or mood, affects our behavior and, therefore, our performance. Most people can relate to the change in state one would have if asked to sing or perform in front of a large audience (for some, just thinking about it is sufficient to effect significant state changes).

- Our thoughts affect our state, so focusing our attention on different things will produce a state change.

- We can consciously control our state by controlling what we focus our thoughts on. This principle has wide-ranging implications and places the onus and locus of control with the individual. This can therefore require a significant shift in belief for people who may have thought that life was being "done" to them and that there was little that they could do to influence this dynamic. The kind of language that is used reflects this, such as "I feel awful today because the weather is so miserable" or "You always make me feel unhappy when you do that."

Although I am not asking you to agree with these principles, I ask that you consider them to be true in order to get the most out of the exercise.

■ The context

The exercise was developed as part of an NLP training course, so has been tried and evaluated by other NLP trainers and master practitioners. I have since used it a number of times with people as part of coaching sessions when working with them on their mission statements and core values.

■ The outcomes

The exercise is designed to provide the participant with a sensory awareness of their core sense of being – the place where there is peace, harmony, and an inner congruence. People refer to this in different ways, and it is important to match the language each person uses. For the purpose of this explanation, I will refer to it as one's "centre". Because the exercise is working with the unconscious mind as well as the conscious, it is not necessary for someone to have an understanding, in a physical sense, of their personal centre.

The experience of becoming consciously aware of one's centre can have a very profound impact in life contexts other than the one selected for the exercise. For example, I have used it with clients who wanted to have a better sense of direction, helped by a better understanding of what drives them. In addition to this exercise, personal mission, values, and belief work has also been instrumental in achieving that outcome. I have also used it with clients who wanted a sense of calm, almost a meditation, on which to focus and get a better sense of balance and clarity of mind.

■ The exercise

The nature of the exercise requires a very strong level of rapport and trust between the person leading the exercise (the practitioner) and the person taking part (the client). If you want to do this exercise for yourself, read and memorize the procedure first, so you can complete it without interruption.

However, it will be much easier to find a skilled NLP practitioner to facilitate it for you. You may find it useful to revise the material in Chapter 5 referring to submodalities and state management.

exercise

1 Describe the state when you feel most in touch with your inner self. (This can be done with the eyes open or closed. Most people have found it easier with their eyes closed. As a practitioner, it is important to use the precise language the client uses and not to abbreviate or translate.)

2 What would you call that state?

3 Remember a time when you felt this way. Choose a particularly strong or intense experience.

4 Recall the details of what you saw, what you heard, what you felt (possibly even taste and smell), so that the experience becomes even more real to you.

5 Become fully associated into the experience and be aware of the energy that is flowing from your body. When you are able to identify the energy flow, locate the source of that energy and mark that point by placing a hand over it (anchoring the state).

6 While keeping your hand on that place, be aware of the color of the energy, then intensify the color and brightness of the energy.

7 Be aware of your breathing and notice how, with each breath you take, the energy and the color flow throughout your body. Continue to notice as the energy and color expand to form a sphere around your body. Allow it to expand until you can sense it has expanded enough; it will feel just right.

8 As you experience this sphere around you, be aware of the words that you hear describing you as the person you are being when you are truly centered. Let these words resonate around the sphere at just the right volume and at just the right pitch. Keep reinforcing the color, the energy, and the sound to enhance the experience.

9 When you have reached the peak of the experience (which a practitioner will be able to tell from practice and from being in close rapport with the client), then press down the hand that was marking the place where the energy emanated from, and keep it pressed for three seconds (reinforcing the anchor) before releasing. Slowly open your eyes and feel free to share any observations that you have made.

It is worthwhile reinforcing the process by going over the same steps, so that the anchor becomes stronger and stronger. As a possible test, talk about something else for a few minutes, then press your hand in the same place and notice if any of the feelings you generated during the exercise return.

The results

Like much of NLP, the results are very experiential and often depend on the level of trust and rapport that has been built up, and the skill of the practitioner. The results from this exercise can be profound as it gives the person a tangible and multisensory experience of a very personal element of their psyche. It has been found to be very useful in progressing an individual's personal development and creating an anchored state that can be accessed when needed.

17

How to achieve anything

Did you ever fail to achieve a goal? What caused you not to achieve this goal? Did you procrastinate over a decision? Did your interest in the goal diminish? Perhaps other people let you down? There are all kinds of reasons for our not achieving things for ourselves. In this chapter, you will learn how to set goals that are compelling and find out what you can do to make more of your goals happen.

Setting goals is a natural function of being human, yet some people seem to have better success at it than others. This is good news for all of us, because, if one person can achieve a goal, the rest of us can learn from this success. Over

> *If one person can achieve a goal, the rest of us can learn from this success.*

2,000 years ago, Aristotle is quoted as saying, "All men seek one goal; success or happiness. The only way to achieve true success is to express yourself completely in service to society. First have a definite, clear, practical ideal – a goal, an objective. Second, have the necessary means to achieve your ends – wisdom, money, methods, and materials. Third, adjust your means to that end." Notable advice for anyone seeking success, I'm sure you agree. As NLP is all about being successful, it has done the hard work of modeling successful people for you. All you have to do is learn to adopt the "success strategies" contained in NLP and you can achieve anything you want. So, what do you want?

◼ The key elements of success

The exercise in this chapter offers you a structure and method for achieving anything you want. It is probably the most powerful section in the book, and it relies on you learning all the NLP principles, models, and skills covered in Sections 1 and 2. So, having these firmly under your belt, you can put your energy into the key elements of being successful at anything, which are:

◆ deciding what you want and don't want – defining the goal;

◆ a means to an end – getting motivated;

◆ aligning goals with your personal mission – creating a fit;

◆ metaprogram influences – patterns to help, not hinder;

◆ belief power – mustering determination, energy, and commitment;

◆ the journey – what you are learning.

The exercise is comprehensive, so you certainly would not use the entire procedure for every goal you want to achieve. It is designed to help you achieve your bigger goals and you can also experiment using steps 1, 2, 5 and 6 on some of your smaller goals.

To demonstrate how to work with these six elements on a big goal, I have used the example "I want to be promoted". All the questions in this exercise have been answered using this example. As you read through, you may find it useful to have a goal of your own in mind and come up with your own answers.

◎ exercise

1: Deciding what you want and what you don't want

This may sound very simple, yet it is probably one of the most common hurdles at which to fall when activity towards achieving a goal goes off track. Without a clear and well-formed set of outcomes for your goal, the target you will be channeling your personal energy towards will be fuzzy and ill defined.

To help you with this stage, you can use the acronym "PRIEST" to set well-formed outcomes for your goals. We'll begin with the "P" of PRIEST.

P positively stated

Define the outcomes in positive terms – that is, what do you want? I know many people who can tell you what they don't want, but struggle to define what they do want. If you have a strong need to express what you don't want, that's OK. For each separate "don't want", ask yourself "So, what do I want instead?" The reason this is so important is to do with your energy and focus. In order to think about what you don't want, you have to think in past terms to a time when you were unhappy in that particular situation. This does not energize a future-oriented goal.

Now, answer the following simple questions:

Q What exactly do you want?

A *I want to be promoted.*

Q Is there anything you don't want?

A *I don't want to be constrained by decision making.*
I don't want to do too much traveling.
I don't want an administration job.

Q What do you want instead of these things?

A *I want to be free to make my own decisions.*
I want to be close to home, at least for three weeks out of each month.
I want a job where my results come mainly from face-to-face communication.

R resourced

What resources will you need to achieve your outcomes? Consider internal resources, such as energy, confidence, capability, knowledge, and thinking strategies, as well as external resources, such as materials, information, support from other people, training, and time.

This is a particularly creative part of the process, generating ideas to support your outcomes. Use the following questions to stimulate your brainstorming.

Internal

Q What do you want in terms of knowledge, skills, and attitude?

A *I would like to feel more confident, communicate more effectively, and manage time better.*

Q Which parts of this book will help you?

A *Section 2 and Chapters 14, 15, and 16.*

Q How can you get longer-term support?

A *Find a coach or mentor to guide my thinking.*

External

Q Where can you look for external resources?

A *Books, the Internet, courses, seminars, government departments.*

Q Who can help you?

A *My manager, a coach, my friends, my professional group, my family.*

Q How will you find sufficient time in your schedule?

A *I'll cut out redundant tasks and delegate some things.*

Q What material resources will you require?

A *Learning materials. Nothing else.*

I initiated and maintained by you

Are you going to take the first step or will you wait for someone else to act first?

If you wait, you will end up reacting. There are, fundamentally, two places to be in this life – one is being at *cause*, the other at *effect*. The former puts you in the driving seat while the latter makes you a passenger in someone else's vehicle. Be proactive – take action to make your goal happen.

> *There are, fundamentally, two places to be in this life – one is being at cause, the other at effect. The former puts you in the driving seat while the latter makes you a passenger.*

Once you have begun working towards your goal, the more you hand over control to others, the greater is the possibility of being let down. This doesn't mean that you must work alone – on the contrary, you are likely to interact with any number of people in the achievement of your goal – but the key controlling and decision-making functions should remain with you. If you let go of these functions, you also let go of responsibility. Remember, you can involve other people, but you must be the one responsible for making critical decisions.

E ecological

Not all goals are well thought through. Sometimes the achievement of a goal in one part of your life can produce problems in another. I am reminded of a female client who realized an ambition to become a senior manager in her organization, but, in the process, she acquired the male-dominated stereotypes of her role models and, as a consequence, she became alienated from her family.

How will achievement of your goal affect other parts of your life and other people around you? Take a systemic, or ecological, perspective on the consequences of achieving your goal. Answer the following questions.

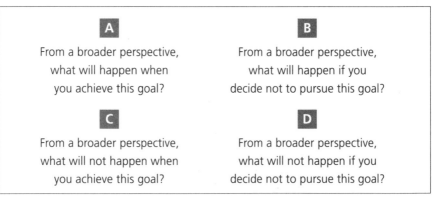

A	**B**
From a broader perspective, what will happen when you achieve this goal?	From a broader perspective, what will happen if you decide not to pursue this goal?
C	**D**
From a broader perspective, what will not happen when you achieve this goal?	From a broader perspective, what will not happen if you decide not to pursue this goal?

Here are some examples of possible answers to these questions.

A *I will earn more money. I will work longer hours. I will learn to communicate at a higher level. My family will see less of me. I will lose touch with some of my peers. I will have less time to visit my parents.*

B *My salary will remain about the same. Life will be much the same as in the past few years. Work will have less meaning for me. I will retain my peer friendships. I will not require many new skills. I will become less marketable.*

C *I will not be able to maintain my regular sessions at the local college. My family will not be able to rely on me being home at a regular time.*

D *We will not be able to afford a bigger house. My savings will not grow very much. My long-term ambitions will not be met. My family will not benefit in a number of ways.*

S sensory-based evidence to chart your progress

It's all very well having a good feeling about your progress, but what you need is hard evidence, things you can see and hear. You can see a bank balance and you can see how much mail you are getting. You can hear what people are saying and you can ask for their feedback. Whatever your goal, if you don't measure your progress, you could end up anywhere.

A young manager was given a promotion, becoming Customer Services Manager. So pleased was he with this appointment that he didn't get an agreement on authority, responsibility, and remuneration. He trusted his manager to do the right thing. Six months later, he left the company after a succession of broken promises and problems due to a lack of authority to make decisions.

Answer these questions. I have included some examples.

Q How will you know when you have achieved your goal?

A *I will see an announcement of my promotion.*
   I will receive more pay.
   I will be given higher-level goals to pursue.

Q What sensory evidence will you use to measure your progress?

A *I will ask my boss for a progress report.*
   I will ask senior people to give me feedback on my performance.
   I will ask senior managers how I am doing.
   I will keep in contact with the Human Resources Director for comment and feedback.

T time phased

When do you want this goal to be achieved? Consider all the things you will be doing to make this goal happen and plan a realistic timeline, taking you from now to then. An effective way to do this is to pace it out physically on the floor. Here's how to do this (see also Figure 17.1).

1   First of all, place a marker on the floor to represent "now".

2   Next, consider how long you think it will take you to achieve your goal and pace the amount of time between "now" and "goal achieved" on the floor in a straight line. The distance could be anything between 3 feet and 133 feet; just make it what seems right to you, and place a marker there as the "goal achieved" spot.

3   Now, project on to the "goal achieved" spot a visualization of what your success will look like. Intensify the submodalities (see Chapter 5) and make it an image that gives you a good feeling inside.

4   Next, walk along the timeline and stand on the "goal achieved" spot. Linger there for a few moments and associate with the feeling of being successful.

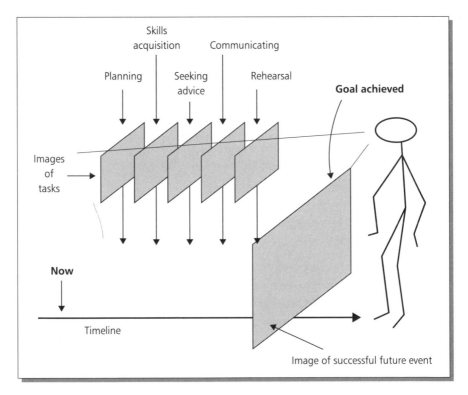

Fig 17.1 ◆ Timeline

5 Now, walk past this spot even further into the future, turn around, and look back at the journey you made from "now" to "goal achieved". What did you have to do to achieve that goal? Visualize each task on the timeline. If you run out of space, perhaps you need to allow more time. If there are a lot of blank areas on the timeline, maybe you could shorten the time you need.

I have used this technique many times with project teams, and it has always produced excellent results.

2: A means to an end – getting motivated

How important is this goal to you? Does it have sufficient importance for you to be fully committed to achieving it?

Answer these questions. I have included some examples of possible answers.

Q When you have achieved this goal, what higher values will it serve for you?

A *A more varied lifestyle.*
More disposable income.
More challenging tasks to do.
New things to learn.
Different people to meet and work with.

Q How important to you are these higher values?

A *Very important – the only values above these are health and well-being for my family and me.*

Q Does your goal also meet the criteria of your highest-level values?

A *Yes, all of them.*

It is worth spending some quality time on this values section, looking for compatibility between different values. Refer to the values exercise in Chapter 4 and combine it with this one for extra thoroughness. When you have clearly identified the highest-level values, make them prominent in your mind using the visualization techniques you have learned. Make your future come alive with color, stereo sound, and great feelings.

3: Aligning goals with your personal mission

Create a fit with your general sense of life mission. Answer these questions. Again, there are some sample answers.

Q How would you describe your purpose in the context of this particular goal?

A *To get results using leadership and influencing skills.*
To be a suitable role model for others.
To become better at learning from experience.

Q In what ways does achieving your goal align with your purpose as described above?

A *As a senior manager, I will have more opportunities to develop influencing skills, more exposure to new learning experiences, and I will be observed by more employees.*

4: Metaprogram influences

It may be useful to review Chapter 9 at this stage.

Will your metaprogram patterns help or hinder you as you work towards achieving your goal? It can take some time to understand your patterns fully,[1] but persistent curiosity will pay off. If you have desires to be a leader, you will need to be able to communicate in big picture terms. Likewise, other goals may require specific skills that you may find difficult to learn because of your metaprogram patterns. However, do not despair – you can change your patterns to suit your goal and this may be one of the most significant changes you make to increase your flexibility. As a general rule, practicing the exercises in this book will help you to operate from a broader base of metaprograms. You will also want to identify the patterns you want to develop the most – that is, the ones that will serve your achievement of the goal the best.

You can do this by working on two key areas: external behavior and internal state. The same example will be used to show how to change a metaprogram. In this case, let's suppose I have a strong preference for procedures and I want to develop strengths for options patterns.

External behavior

I will recognize all the occasions where my behavior is subject to a clear procedure. I will also be conscious of the procedural language I am using and my gestures. Having made myself aware of these patterns, I will begin to feed in alternative choices using options-oriented language, such as:

◆ "What if…?"

◆ "What other choices are there?"

◆ "How else might we do this?"

◆ "Let's keep our options open for a while."

I will observe and copy the gestures used by people with a preference for options and build more of these into my everyday communication. I will also begin to break habitual procedural patterns, such as taking a different route to work, varying breaktimes, and being more flexible with my diary. Wherever there is a pattern, I will look to build in some options.

Internal state

My metaprogram is filtering the external environment using a procedures filter. This is forming my internal representation, from which I will respond. I can change this using submodalities quite easily. Here's how.

1 Think of a time when you were enjoying doing a procedural task and take note of the submodalities of your internal representation. When you have identified one, intensify each submodality until you locate the critical one that changes your experience.

2 Break state.

3 Think back to a time when you were working in an options pattern and take note of the submodalities. If you don't have one of these reference experiences, imagine enjoying a procedure that is designed to give you more options, such as brainstorming or a lateral thinking technique.

4 Compare the differences between the two representations.

5 Now, bring back the options pattern representation and impose the submodalities of the procedural representation. Intensify the image and trigger the critical submodality.

6 Repeat the last step another five or six times and notice any change in the way you feel about doing the options task.

Use this procedure for other metaprograms. It will be useful to have a skilled NLP practitioner to help you with this exercise. Also, see Tad James and Wyatt Woodsmall's book *Time Line Therapy and the Basis of Personality* (Meta Publications, Inc., 1988) for more ways in which to change metaprograms. Also, observe people who operate successfully using the metaprogram you want to have and copy their techniques. For some of the less observable metaprograms, you will need to use a more thorough modeling process. Refer to Section 4 for guidelines on modeling.

5: Belief power

This is the really vital component of your compelling future goal. Your beliefs alone have the power to determine success or failure. They are behind your determination, energy, and commitment.

This part of the process will deal with any limitations you may have (perhaps unconscious) about your ability, identity, and any doubts at all about your success. The following questions will help deal with these things. As before, there are some sample answers.

Belief power – dealing with your objections to success

Q Is anything stopping you from achieving this goal?

A *I may not be seen as senior manager material.*

Q If you were to have any doubts in addition to this, what would they be?

A *I may not be able to influence at a senior level.*
What if I fail?

Q In what ways are these objections ridiculous or absurd?

A *I have been given positive feedback about my communication skills from senior managers.*
I will not fail because I have a well-formed outcome, strategy, and belief in myself, and I am continually learning new skills.

Q What counter-evidence can you find to show that the objections above have no validity for you?

A *I have been successful up to now, so why should this change?*
I am already a good communicator and am improving this skill every day.

Q What would be more empowering and compelling beliefs to hold?

A *I am a successful person and I will continue to succeed.*
I will achieve my goal by continued personal development and determination.
Other people are there to help me achieve my goal.

Take some time to answer these questions for yourself. The process will help you to remove any limiting beliefs you may be holding, and create more empowering beliefs to help you achieve your goals. If the answers don't come easily, ask a friend or colleague to help you. The time taken to work through these questions will pay significant rewards.

The journey

The main block to future success is your learning potential and the act of blaming or finding excuses for failing. If everything you do goes the way you want it to, you are probably super-human. Be prepared for surprises and for some of your plans delivering less than you want. The most important aspect of all is the way you deal with these situations. If you maintain a state of determination and self-belief, treating every situation as an opportunity to learn and improve, you will achieve success. If you blame others for your shortfalls, you will fail.

So, take responsibility for your thinking and actions. Use the journey to your goals as a personal development vehicle. With this attitude, is there anything outside your reach?

Note

1   You will find a metaprogram questionnaire free to download at www.quadrant1.co.uk to help you identify your personal metaprogram profile.

18

Coaching the presenter

Jon Symes

Coaching businesspeople in the art of giving presentations has provided me with some very interesting challenges and is an area where a wide range of NLP ideas have immediate application. I am going to describe three coaching assignments where I have used NLP techniques to help clients break through thinking patterns that were previously limiting their performances in very different ways. The three techniques[1] are:

◆ reframing

◆ the six-step reframe

◆ language location pattern.

Presenters can usually make some quick, relatively easy, and very audible improvements to their spoken message by the introduction of clear outcome thinking ("What do I want to happen as a result of this presentation?"), some second positioning ("If I were in the audience's shoes, what would I want, how would I react?"), and some chunking of ideas, from big picture through a small number of key points to an appropriate amount of detail.

The visual presentation can also be quickly affected by some coaching on the use of body language. As we know that 55 percent of our communication impact is via the unspoken (see Chapter 6) – our posture and gestures – we know it is worth rehearsing these vital parts of the overall message.

Each of these ideas is reasonably simple, uncontentious if clearly explained, and can be practiced easily. The coaching becomes more interesting and more challenging when presenters are unable or unwilling to incorporate into actions the ideas they intellectually accept as valid and necessary for their improvement.

The techniques

Reframing

Reframing is a way of helping people to change the way in which they interpret the world. The concept of framing – which lies behind the activity of reframing – is that we make meaning of information according to the frame within which we consider it. For example, the sound of a police siren behind me as I drive my car causes an anxious reaction for as long as the frame I use is one in which I might be the guilty party. If I change the frame – perhaps seeing the police car is nearby, but framing the event with a feeling of reassurance – my reaction is completely different.

> *The concept of framing is that we make meaning of information according to the frame within which we consider it.*

Reframing as a coaching technique is useful when the coach can sense that the client is unable to perceive a problem situation differently because of the particular frame within which they are making sense of that situation. Reframing then helps them to see another frame within which they might more usefully view the situation. This is usually achieved by making comments or posing questions. Whether or not a particular intervention succeeds in reframing a person's thinking cannot be predicted. It can only be sensed by close observation of the person – normally there will be some physiological signs of a change of thinking.

Here is an example of the technique in action.

❖ example

The client

My client – let's call him Derek – Divisional Managing Director of a large blue-chip retail chain, had been experiencing problems in preparing himself fully for presentations, particularly those he made to his senior management team of 50 or so.

Intellectually, Derek understood the need for preparation, but he felt sufficiently capable and confident that he could say to himself, without any trace of arrogance, that he didn't need to prepare for a fairly informal presentation to his team. Afterwards, he would berate himself for the missed opportunity, knowing that preparation would have helped him use it to better effect. He was a willing coaching client, genuinely wanting to improve this aspect of his professional skill.

The outcome

My broadest outcome was to help Derek to improve the impact of his presentations. My specific outcome, in this part of the process, was to help him begin to prepare thoroughly. He knew how to prepare and he knew the importance of preparation at an intellectual level, but he had yet to incorporate it into his behavior. Success would be measurable only after the event, in Derek's subsequent approach to presentations.

The coaching

I had been able to build a good rapport with Derek over a series of meetings, both with other people and just the two of us. Derek had identified the preparation issue as the highest leverage change he could make to his presentation style and a change that had consistently eluded him.

We were in session, just two of us, in his office, discussing his approach to preparation for these top team meetings. He again repeated how easy it was for him to speak "off the cuff" to his team, without preparation.

I decided to try to reframe this comfortable way of viewing the situation. "Could you get better business performance from your people if you prepared for the meeting?" was attempt number one. Derek agreed, but there was no evidence from his response, spoken and unspoken, that this had helped him to change his view of the matter.

My second attempt was, "Maybe you don't respect your people sufficiently to do them the courtesy of preparation." This hit the spot. Derek immediately and very visibly paled, and pointing to the door of his office, he said, "I could have you thrown out of here ... but I don't think I will." The scale of his reaction told me his view of the world had been destabilized – for the better, I hoped.

The results

Derek was, by his own admission at a subsequent meeting, unable to approach his top team meetings again in such a relaxed manner. The outcome of preparing thoroughly had been met, as were the broader outcomes of helping him to present with more impact in the future.

The six-step reframe

The six-step reframe is an intervention that, like the last, is also designed to change the way in which a person makes sense of their experience – in this case, we wish to alter an unwanted behavior by seeing it in a different light. It is based on the premise that our behavior, even when unwanted, self-sabotaging or inappropriate, is ultimately driven by a high-level and worthwhile intention. The new perspective is taken from this higher intention and, by substituting this goal in our thinking, we are then able to create alternative choices that avoid the drawbacks of the unwanted behavior.

The following is an example of this technique

❖ example

The client

My client was a research scientist I shall call Jane whose problem was a tendency to speak extremely fast in presentations. She worked in a multinational environment, the daily language of business and of her presentations was English, but for many of her audience this was not their native tongue. Despite repeated feedback and a stated desire to solve the problem, Jane was unable to do so alone. She was a willing client for coaching.

The outcome

My outcome was to provide Jane with the help she needed to change this behavior. Initially I was interested in understanding why she was driven to repeat the pattern of speaking too fast.

The coaching

After understanding the broad context of the issue, establishing a working rapport, and clarifying Jane's objective, we were able to proceed to a deeper understanding. Eventually, in response to my questions, Jane was able to articulate for the first time the purpose of her irrational behavior. I asked her, "What is your purpose in continuing this pattern of behavior?" "What will you gain from this behavior?", and "How does it serve you to repeat this behavior?"

Gentle but persistent enquiry in this vein helped Jane to unlock reasoning of which she had previously been unconscious. In this case, it involved a desire not to be intellectually outstanding among the group. The higher reasoning for this was the avoidance of rejection, a risk she was sure existed because of school-day episodes where she had perceived the loss of friendship was based on envy of her academic prowess. Beyond that, the higher purpose still, was to have and retain strong relationships with friends and colleagues.

Once this reasoning was exposed to examination, Jane became very motivated to find alternative ways of retaining friendship without sabotaging her professional standing and repeating the rapid speech pattern in her presentations.

The results

Jane attributed her complete resolution of the presenting problem to this intervention and also reported some unexpected but valuable benefits – her overall level of confidence improved.

Language location pattern

I heard from a Dutch NLP trainer about a pattern he had been experimenting with whereby people speaking more than one language can avoid confusion between their different languages and speak each better and more fluently.

The basis of the pattern, which I believe he had devised himself, was that we could attribute to each language a specific location within or adjacent to our physical body. A native tongue might typically be stored in or near the voice box, the throat or the chest area. Foreign languages often seemed to be stored somewhere different, typically in the head. Language proficiency comes from being able to temporarily replace the native tongue in its normal location with the desired foreign tongue.

Here is an example to clarify the technique.

❖ example

The client

Shortly after learning about this pattern, I was coaching a senior executive in a financial services company in presentation skills. I'll use the alias Rupert for this client. While he was a seasoned presenter and confident man, he frequently became muddled or tongue-tied when presenting.

The outcome

My broad outcome was to help him raise his presenting to a higher level, measured by his Managing Director's feedback and his own sense of capability. Once I had heard about the temporary speech difficulty, my specific objective was to help Rupert to resolve it.

The coaching

There were no foreign languages involved in this case, but I decided to see whether or not the language location pattern could help. I asked Rupert where he kept his words. Clearly, there needs to be a high level of rapport and a willingness to explore unconventional avenues for a client to be able to enter into such an unusual metaphor. Rupert was very willing to examine his thinking patterns and agreed to explore them in this way.

His reflection on this question led him to discover that he didn't have possession of his words while presenting. Indeed, he indicated that they were hovering some ten feet in front of him, about five feet off the ground. I walked to the spot he pointed at and, gesturing as if I were gathering up a four foot-diameter beach ball, I asked him if these were his words. "Yes, you've got them," he replied. I asked him if he wanted them back and proceeded to appear to squash the beach ball down to tennis ball size and slowly placed the imagined ball of words on his outstretched hands.

A physical reaction could be seen as Rupert became reacquainted with "his words", eventually deciding to keep them in his left little toe for safekeeping.

The results

Rupert enjoyed the metaphor of the words and experimented with it in the following weeks. He was initially unwilling to start his presentations in direct possession of his words, preferring to keep them in sight in front of him. His strategy, on beginning a presentation, was to imagine taking the words in through his mouth and keeping them inside until the end of the presentation.

The standard of Rupert's presentations was seen to rise along with his confidence, due in large part to having developed a strategy he could manage himself to deal with his language proficiency and fluency.

Note

1   For further reading, see Richard Bandler and John Grinder (1982) Reframing, Real People Press.

19

The risk wheel

Mark Underwood

This is a simple tool developed for an entrepreneur who was concerned that the innovation and creativity responsible for fueling his company's growth were becoming stifled. His concern was a response to the increasing discipline, systems, and accounting practices that were creating internal tensions, a lack of communication, and friction among employees.

There were two reasons for choosing to focus on risk rather than innovation and creativity. The first was that interviews with members of staff showed they clearly had a risk-averse approach to their work. The second was the way in which the entrepreneur used a mixture of language when talking about risk, creativity, and innovation, yet made very little distinction between them. His internal state remained the same when switching from using risk, creativity, and innovation. The evidence was mounting for a misalignment of attitudes towards risk, and different meanings for creativity and innovation existing for the entrepreneur and his management team.

The purpose of the exercise

The purpose of this exercise is to:

◆ explore the elements that we think contribute to situations when we are at risk;

◆ determine which of those elements we feel we can influence and which we think we cannot;

◆ assess each element and decide whether we would like more or less risk in those situations.

The exercise leads on to an open discussion on attitudes towards risk and the beliefs held about it.

Outcomes

My outcomes were to assist people in understanding their attitudes to risk and highlight the variations across a management group, including the founder director/entrepreneur. I also wanted to stimulate their thinking about the purpose of the business, if it was not, indeed, to take risks, particularly in discussions about return on investment, return on capital employed, and the balance between risk and reward.

The exercise procedure

The exercise begins with a series of questions, followed by a mapping of some of the answers on a risk wheel. The result of comparing the differences between individuals' wheels is to show the misalignments of attitudes and beliefs in the company.

◉ exercise

1 The first question is, "What does risk mean to you?" Take 20 minutes in small groups of three or four (to stimulate discussion) and come up with your personal meaning. Gather the answers and list them on a flipchart for later reference.

2 The second question is, "What do you want to be able to take away from this session and use tomorrow?" The answers are also put on a flipchart for later reference.

3 Next, identify a situation when you were at risk and notice, for separate discussion, whether you knew before, during or after the event that you were at risk. Then start to identify the factors that contributed to that risk (this is a variation on a values exercise).

4 Next, separate out the factors that you can and cannot control. Your perceived controllable factors will be the spokes on your wheel.

5 Draw five concentric circles, where the centre is zero (no risk) and the outermost circumference is ten (maximum risk). Each successive circle will represent two more points on the scale.

6 Plot the controllable factors as spokes from the "zero hub" and self-score each factor for the reference situation identified earlier, then join up the dots to form your "wheel" (see Figures 19.1 and 19.2).

7 Work in groups of two or three to discuss similarities and differences between the wheels, and consider how comfortable you are with your current perceptions of risk.

8 What questions were asked in the group about each other's wheels? Do you want to increase or decrease your score on any of the factors?

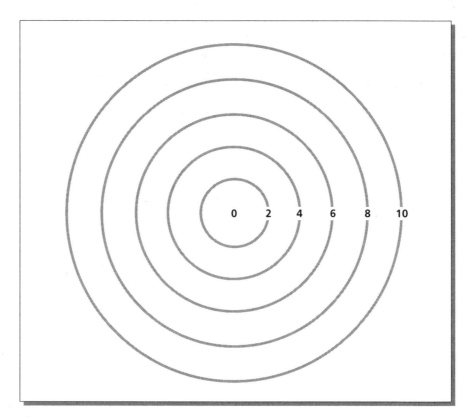

Fig 19.1 ◆ The risk wheel

9 Discuss feedback on what the group has noticed.

10 Repeat the exercise with the "uncontrollable" factors and notice whether or not your perspectives shift. You can choose to create a new wheel or map these factors on to the same wheel using a different color.

■ Results

The feedback showed that everyone got enormous value from recognition of the different situations that people find risky and, further, that different members of the team have widely differing attitudes to risk in general. This had not been obvious before the workshop.

The entrepreneur identified how he was happy to take some risks as a matter of course – that is, he considered them low risk, but became more nervous if someone else was taking risks on his behalf, and on the company's behalf. This varied from employee to employee, depending on how he rated their abilities.

The systems people and the financial controller were employed specifically to introduce systems and controls, respectively, to contain many of the company's risks. However, they regarded their own situations as fairly low in risk, and preferred to minimize the scores on most factors/spokes, which could lead to friction if, ultimately, these factors were more under his control than theirs.

The sales team was closer to his views on risks, with one or two differences. Several salespeople were prepared to increase their scores on some points, thus increasing the "buzz" factor, until asked "What if it were your money/company?" There was some backtracking at this point. Risk means different things to different people, and even different things to the same people in different situations or contexts. Some of the answers to the first question, "What does risk mean to you?", were most illuminating. Among the employees, there were many underlying beliefs that risk was bad and, therefore, to be managed, minimized or avoided. This was expressed by words such as "scary", "doing something new", "doing something we don't know we can do", "to be controlled", "exposed", and "unexpected".

This was where the management team was having difficulty, particularly as the entrepreneur had noticeably different beliefs about risk to most of his staff. Even where salespeople shared his beliefs, many of them would score lower when asked "What if it were your money or company?"

Answers to "What do you want from this session?" were diverse, with most of the participants wanting to find ways to reduce the risk in their jobs (with one explicit request about job security), while both the entrepreneur and sales staff wanted to know more about how to balance the risk with the potential reward.

■ Effective questions

A number of questions have arisen in the various groups I have used this simple tool with. Here are some of those that were most effective in helping the group to work towards a team solution:

"What if it were your money or company?"

"Where are you in relation to your wheel?"

"Whose risk is it?"

"Overall, how does the risk feel?"

"Are you happy with that?"

"Do you want to change anything on your wheel?"

"How many times do you need to take the risk before it is no longer a risk?"

"Have your scores changed over time?"

"What would happen if the scores changed, up ... or down?"

"When did you notice the risk, before, during or after the event?"

"What specifically, at that moment, made you go for it?"

■ Observations

The risk wheel technique was further refined as a result of feedback received in workshops with two networking groups in London – the Exploring Learning Group[1] and the NLP Business Group.[2] The attendees were a mix of business managers, independent consultants, and personal development trainers.

Participants from the Exploring Learning Group found it difficult to identify a reference experience for when they were at risk, so confident had they become of their abilities in training design and delivery. However, when asked about the first time they had ever delivered a course, they were able to recognize that they were at risk more often than they thought, but had become confident and competent in developing solutions within minutes, usually without noticing the risk until afterwards, if at all.

For most of the independent consultants, the underlying beliefs were very similar to the entrepreneur's – that risk is good – and, in some cases, they were happy to explore ways to increase their scores. Their beliefs were expressed as "exploring learning", "high gain", "can be exciting", "possibility", "personal stretch", and "going outside boundaries". This group was open to having fun, sharing ideas, being challenged, and picking up tips, techniques and tactics – a contrast to the more business-oriented groups.

The entrepreneur and the more experienced independent consultants knew that they had all the resources they needed and had very strong self-belief. Some of the factors related to the differing logical levels, even though people varied in whether they believed they could control them, e.g. the environment or the influence of others' behavior. The more experienced, resourceful participants were constantly reframing. Some of the controllable and uncontrollable factors were a function of the filters that people were using to create their internal representations of risk.

"I can now be more creative without risking too much for my company."

Feedback

Here are some of the comments I received in response to following up each workshop.

"I now have a better idea of how to balance the risk and creativity for myself and my colleagues."   *Managing Director*

"I realize that I manage risk for my clients – that's what they pay me for."
                                                                      Independent Trainer

"I now understand what my role is in providing adequate, not restrictive, controls."
                                                                      Financial Controller

"The thing that stuck in my head … is the combinations of things 'away from' and things of 'going to'."   *Independent Trainer*

"I can now be more creative without risking too much for my company."
                                                                      Sales Manager

"I have some insight into how to sell development plans to my risk-averse colleagues."
                                                                      Independent Trainer

"I think the very fact that people have such varied responses was a personal eye-opener. I am putting together a training program for experienced trainers and it gave me an insight for the risk element."   *Independent Trainer*

"A very useful tool, as it encouraged me to have thoughts and discussions that I otherwise wouldn't have had."   *Internal Trainer*

Additional insight from David Molden

Mark's approach using the risk wheel has an interesting dimension, reminding us that, whenever we look to create change, the ideas you begin with will have a determining influence on the process and outcomes. The catalog of failed change initiatives is well documented in the business press. Often it is not the intention that causes failure, but the initial perspectives of the change agents.

What I find intriguing about the risk wheel is the focus on something that has very few presuppositions at the start. If you refer to the stated purpose and outcomes at the beginning of this chapter, you might find the following presuppositions:

◆ people can be at risk;

◆ we can influence risk;

◆ we can choose the degree of risk we want;

◆ attitudes to risk vary;

◆ risk can be a purposeful activity;

◆ risk and reward can balance.

When you consider this list of presuppositions, it is difficult to find a point of disagreement, so securing employees' buy-in to a development or change process using this perspective should be relatively easy. In contrast to this, many change programs begin by presupposing that some people will resist change and even seek to sabotage it – a perspective that serves to alienate and distance people from the change initiative.

I like the elegance of Mark's approach and believe there is scope for developing this concept further to help companies design change workshops that work for all their people. It might be called "beginning with a neutral perspective".

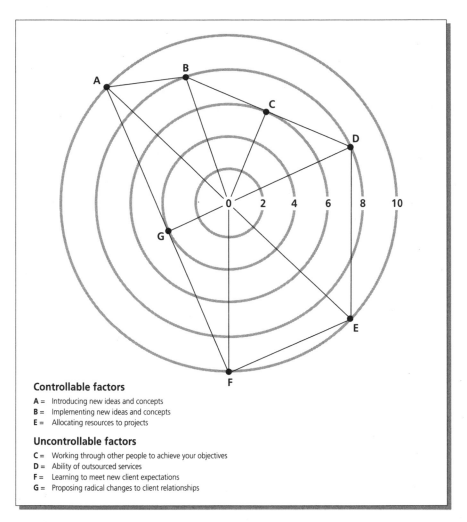

Controllable factors

A =   Introducing new ideas and concepts
B =   Implementing new ideas and concepts
E =   Allocating resources to projects

Uncontrollable factors

C =   Working through other people to achieve your objectives
D =   Ability of outsourced services
F =   Learning to meet new client expectations
G =   Proposing radical changes to client relationships

Fig 19.2 ◆ Example of a manager's completed risk wheel

Notes

1   Exploring Learning Group, London – contact Bridget Strong on +44 (0)20 8355 0496.

2   NLP Business Group, London – contact Mark Underwood on +44 (0)7074 269 843.

20

Information frames for meetings

A client had come from a difficult meeting with a project group and was feeling exhausted. I noticed her in the cafeteria, slumping over her coffee cup as her shoulders sank with a sigh of release. She looked in need of a sympathetic ear, so I walked over and sat beside her.

"Hi Linda, mind if I join you?"

"Oh, Hi Dave. No, please sit down, but, I must warn you, I'm not in a very good mood at present."

"What's happening?" I asked.

"I'm managing a project to develop new marketing strategies, and it's just so tiring dealing with the issues people bring out in the project meetings. You wouldn't believe some of the things I'm having to put up with."

"What kinds of things?" I asked.

"Well, we had just got the meeting started and I had asked for an update on stage 1, when Jerry started going on about the lack of communication from the project office. Mike got defensive and took us right off track."

"It sounds like you could do with some help. Have you come across information frames before?"

"No, how can they help me?"

"Well, they will help you to facilitate meetings so that you can get the best contribution from all the attendees."

"Now that would be worth having, but would it help me to handle people like Jerry and Mike?"

"Well, the best way to manage that type of behavior is to exclude it by putting a frame around the entire meeting. But first you must think about the individuals and the personal agendas they bring to meetings. You see, the written agenda for a meeting only covers the business need."

"Well, that's what the meeting's for, isn't it?" Linda remarked.

"Yes, of course it is, but, as you know, people also bring their personal needs with them, and if you don't pay attention to these, they will find their own way into the proceedings, and you end up with a Jerry and Mike problem to deal with."

"That's what happens all the time. So, what should I do?"

"You recognize personal needs by asking every person what they want to get out of the meeting. This is called the outcome frame. Do it straight after introducing the agenda, and begin by stating your outcomes so the others can follow your example. The most important thing is to put everyone's outcomes on to a flipchart and stick it on the wall in full view. Then you can refer to the outcomes during the meeting if someone attempts to take the meeting off track. Let me summarize this for you ... ."

Outcome frame

◆ Welcome attendees and introduce the business agenda.

◆ Explain that you would like to know what everyone's personal outcomes are for the meeting and begin by stating yours.

◆ As each person expresses their outcomes, write them up on a flipchart and stick it on the wall.

◆ Refer to these stated outcomes when dealing with diversions.

I could tell Linda was taking all this in, but the expression on her face told me she wasn't entirely convinced.

"Hmm. It sounds good, Dave, but what if their outcomes differ from the agenda. Then what do I do? I have my priorities to meet on this project."

"Of course you have your priorities and you will be guided by them. You can challenge a personal outcome with a relevancy frame before writing it on the flipchart. Just ask the person to explain how the outcome is relevant to the business objectives. If the outcome proves to be irrelevant to the immediate business in hand, but has some implications, you can decide to address it off-line at another time. The important thing here is to respect the validity of the outcome to the individual concerned."

"I like that one, Dave. It would have come in handy at the last meeting."

"Use it with care, Linda. Too many relevancy challenges may indicate a major flaw in the business agenda or that more work needs to be done to get buy-in. You can use the relevancy frame at any point in the meeting to make sure contributions are actually moving the agenda forward. To summarize that … ."

Relevancy frame

◆ Summarize what the person has said – for example, "You are concerned that budgets may be inadequate."

◆ Restate the business objective and the person's personal outcomes.

◆ Ask the person to explain how the contribution is relevant to the outcomes or objectives.

◆ If the topic is not immediately relevant, take the issue off-line and address it at another time.

Linda's eyes began to sparkle, and I noticed she was sitting much more upright now as she said:

"I'm getting the hang of these frames now. They would seem to help the flow of a meeting."

"Yes, that's exactly what they're used for. They help you to manage the process of the meeting and ensure that the content has a value for the business agenda and stated outcomes. By putting a frame around the entire meeting, you are introducing a discipline that allows individuals to express their personal needs, while you remain in control of the process. Any difficulties you experience during the meeting can be dealt with using one of the seven information frames."

"OK, Dave, so what are the other five frames?"

"The next one I'll tell you about is the backtrack frame. This is also useful at the beginning of a meeting and is used to pace and lead the attendees' thinking."

"How?"

"Well, you begin by backtracking over the past activities that got you all to the meeting. It reminds people of the process they are in and of decisions made. It also makes you the focal point and establishes your role as facilitator of the proceedings."

"So, it's a bit like summarizing?"

"It can be used to summarize, but its main function is to keep the flow going in a range of activities. Let me give you an example. I was once asked to facilitate a project to create job grades for 3,000 employees. One of the problems I had to deal with was new people getting involved at various stages. To make sure everyone was up to speed on the current state of progress, I would begin every meeting with a backtrack frame that went something like this: 'Welcome everyone. Before I ask for your personal outcomes, let me cover the key events leading up to today's agenda. The initial steering group decided to involve the CEMA region and they have successfully completed stage 1. The project leaders met to design stage 2 ... ' Of course, like the other frames, you can also use this one at any point during the meeting to clarify earlier points. Here's a summary for you ... ."

Backtrack frame

◆ Keeps the flow going between any number of past events and the current one.

◆ Use it to pace and lead attendees' thinking.

◆ Can be used to summarize during a meeting.

◆ Establishes you as facilitator.

◆ Reminds people of past decisions.

"OK, Dave, so now I understand outcomes, relevancy and backtrack frames. What about the other four?"

"Let's cover the ecology frame next."

"That sounds like something an environmentalist might use."

"Yes it does and, similarly to an environmentalist considering the wider implications of an action, in an ecology frame we consider the consequences on the business of our decisions."

"That doesn't happen often enough in my experience."

"I agree with you, Linda. Often, a small change in one part of a company can have a major effect on another part. Like the time I changed the authorization procedure for training in my last company. I thought I had communicated it to everyone, but one department didn't get the message and missed out on some major new product training. We lost an account because of that action, and I have since learned to do an 'ecology check' on all my decisions!"

"What do you mean by an 'ecology check', Dave?"

"You identify all the possible people who may be affected by your decision – let's call them stakeholders – and then you adopt their perspectives on your decision. Where possible, it is best to involve as many stakeholders as you can and keep them informed of your intentions along the way. This not only covers you against surprises later, but pre-empts any resistance to change, giving you time to deal with it. So, in summary, use an ecology frame for the following reasons ... ."

Ecology frame

◆ Considers the wider consequences of your decisions.

◆ Involves all the stakeholders in a project.

◆ Pre-empts resistance to change.

◆ Prevents unwelcome surprises.

◆ Keeps people outside the project informed of progress and future intentions.

"Three to go, Dave – what's next?"

"Have you ever been in a meeting when someone has made a statement that blocks progress and leads to a messy debate?"

"I'm not sure I know what you mean, Dave."

"Well, the other day I was in a meeting with a client and we were evaluating the results of an earlier brainstorming session. It was going well until James, one of the client participants, objected to my idea for getting input from customer research groups. He said they were unlikely to provide any worthwhile information. I introduced an evidence frame to clarify the validity of this dismissive statement. I asked James what evidence he had to support his statement."

"Wasn't this confrontational, Dave?"

"Yes, and that's the intention. You see, people are very good at generalizing from past experiences and using them to evaluate future ideas and plans. It's far better to learn from experience and improve how things are done in the future, rather than dismiss ideas as non-starters. Ideas often fail because of the ways in which they are implemented, not because they are wrong ideas. Just think about the problems experienced by companies introducing quality programs. In the early years, there were many more failures than successes. Coming up with ideas is easy, successful implementation is the real challenge – but you know all about this, being a project manager. In my case, James could only answer by saying that previous attempts to work with customer groups had failed. So, I asked him what he had learned from that experience. He found this difficult to answer because learning was not part of his company's culture. If something doesn't work, you dump it and look for another way to achieve your goal."

"So, Dave, did you convince James to give it a go?"

"Yes. I said that if he had evidence of finding alternative ways of working with customer groups, then perhaps he had a valid point, but that I had evidence of where customer groups had worked well for other companies."

"Can you use this frame in other ways?"

"You can use it wherever evidence will bring clarity. For example, suppose you want to agree some objectives with your team. How will you know when you have achieved your objectives? Some evidence would be useful, wouldn't it? So, introduce an evidence frame and imagine having achieved the objectives. What evidence shows the objectives have been met? Here's a summary of the evidence frame ... ."

Evidence frame

◆ Challenges generalizations.

◆ Defines how you know when goals are achieved.

Linda was taking it all in. I think she was comparing how her recent meeting had gone with how much more productive it might have been if she had known about information frames.

"Tell me about the contrast frame next, Dave. Is it about comparing different situations?"

"Yes, it is about comparing, and it can help to put things into perspective when they get difficult."

"I think I understand. It would have been useful at the meeting this morning when Jerry and Mike were both complaining about the time they were giving to the project. Perhaps I could have pointed out how much time they would save in the long term by investing time now."

"That sounds like a good use of a contrast frame. How would you put it across, Linda?"

"I would ask them to calculate, as accurately as they could, how much time they were actually giving up. It can't be much more than seven days each in total. Then, I would contrast that with the anticipated time savings the new marketing systems will bring and the benefits to the business in profit terms, then ask them to assess the importance of their current contribution of time. There really is very little room for arguing against that logic."

"That would convince me. So, let's summarize the contrast frame ... ."

Contrast frame

◆ Clarifies the objection or difficulty in quantifiable terms.

◆ Chooses a suitable scenario to use as a contrast.

◆ Describes the contrasting example in simple terms.

◆ Relates the contrasting example to the original objection or difficulty.

"I'm feeling much better about future project meetings now, Dave, but I have a question. What do you do when someone makes a suggestion and you are unsure if the idea is any good? If you have no experience in this area, what do you use to evaluate the idea?"

"Your question brings us to the last of the information frames, the as if frame. This can be used to judge the merits of an idea before committing to an action. It will also help you to identify any potential problems and areas requiring special attention."

"How does it work?"

"You use your imagination and visualize the idea in action. It's like you are constructing a storyboard of likely events required to make the idea work. It can be quite fun to do it with a group. Do you have an example we could use?"

"Well, in the last meeting, Mike said we should run a parallel project with some well-established marketing approaches and compare the two."

"A contrast, that's not a bad idea."

"Yes, but I'm concerned that it might distract us from the main project and we may end up confusing the sales teams."

"So, you can see some potential problems – that's good. Let's imagine you have decided to run a parallel project. What's the first thing you would have to do?"

"Involve the sales teams and communicate with the project group."

"What's the next step?"

"Setting up a project schedule and agreeing specifications with the steering group."

"OK, sounds straightforward so far. What's next?"

"Putting measures in place to compare the results of the different approaches. This may be difficult because the feedback mechanisms may not be fully in place for the new project."

"So, Linda, you have identified the first potential problem area."

"Yes, I see what you mean now about using an as if frame – it puts a kind of reality around an idea to make its feasibility easier to assess. I think I'll be using this one a lot! Aren't you going to summarize it for me?"

"Why don't you do it?"

"OK, the as if frame in summary ... ."

As if frame

◆ Used to assess the feasibility of an idea or proposal where little evidence exists to support it.

◆ Begins a storyboard of the likely events involved with implementing the idea or proposal.

◆ Takes it step by step, visualizing the process and interactions between people.

◆ Identifies potential problems and areas for special attention.

"Thanks, Dave. Now I'm ready for the next meeting."

"I wish you every success, Linda, but there's another technique you might like to consider using with your information frames."

"If you think it will help."

"You can decide that. It's to do with the sizes of the chunks of information people use to communicate their ideas."

"Sizes of chunks? You mean like a chunk of chocolate?"

"In a way, yes. Let me explain by telling you about two colleagues of mine. Peter is what I call a 'big chunker'. He likes to talk in big picture terms and will avoid details wherever possible. In fact, his attention wanders when the conversation gets detailed, or 'small chunk'. Kent, on the other hand, is what I call a 'small chunker'. He likes to get involved in the details and loses interest if a conversation is conducted at a high level for too long."

"Sounds like some people I know."

"I'm sure it does. You see, we all have a preference for the sizes of the the chunks of information we use to communicate ideas. There is no one best chunk size; it's better to develop flexibility to communicate effectively using any size, but it rarely occurs to many people to do that."

"Don't I know it? Jerry is the worst stickler for detail you can imagine. When he gets going, it's difficult to stop him, and most of the details are irrelevant."

"You are absolutely right, Linda. Most details, in a meeting context, are unnecessary. The details are usually sorted out in the actions following a meeting. It may be appropriate to bring in details now and again as evidence to support an idea, and knowing just how much is appropriate is the job of the facilitator. Too much time spent on details will make your meeting unproductive. Let me draw you a diagram to clarify chunk size (see Figure 20.1)."

"When we communicate, we can choose how much detail to give. The more detail, the more time is needed. The less detail, the less knowledge is imparted. The key is to move up, down, and across with your communication, like in the diagram I have drawn, to suit the required need. Many people are unaware of the way they communicate and so, as a facilitator, you will have to help them with this."

"So, are you suggesting I stop Jerry mid-sentence when he gets into too much detail?"

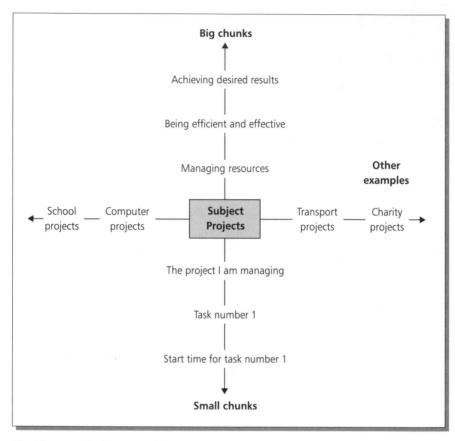

Fig 20.1 ◆ Relative sizes of chunks of information

"You could use one of the frames."

"Yes, I could use the relevancy frame or the outcome frame. Now I am seeing more ways to use frames. In fact, I can imagine running the next meeting just using information frames, and keeping out of the actual content."

"Now that's what I call facilitation. Here's a picture to remind you of the seven information frames (see Figure 20.2)."

"… and remember chunking!"

"Good luck, Linda, and let me know how you get on at your next project meeting."

"I will, but before you go, tell me, can I use information frames in other situations?"

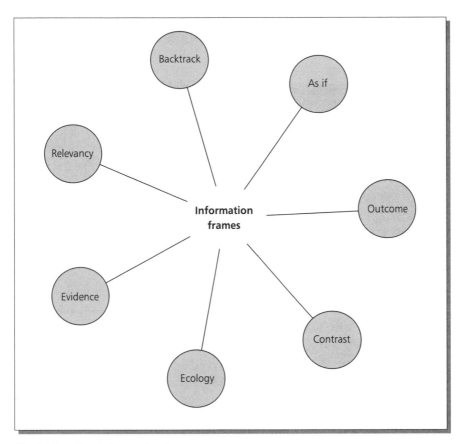

Fig 20.2 ◆ The information frames

"Do you have something in mind?"

"Next week I have a meeting with my team. Perhaps I might encourage them to be more disciplined using information frames."

"Sounds like a good idea to me. Keep me posted."

"I will, bye Dave."

21

The Walt Disney strategy for creativity

Walt Disney is regarded as one of the most creative thinkers of our time. He established a successful business empire by creating fantasy characters with the ability to express human feelings so vividly that they tug at the very root of the emotions. Jiminy Cricket's role as Pinocchio's conscience is a classic example of the mix of metaphor, morality, and emotion built in to the Disney characters. For any individual, team or organization seeking a strategy for creating ideas that work, Walt Disney is an ideal paragon. Robert Dilts[1] has written extensively on the creativity strategy used by Walt Disney, which became an essential part of the culture in the Walt Disney Company. Today's CEO, Michael Eisner,[2] continues to blend a creative and fun climate with realism and common sense.

For any individual, team or organization seeking a strategy for creating ideas that work, Walt Disney is an ideal paragon.

The strategy

Walt Disney had three clear stages for taking an idea through to a marketable product: dreamer, realist and critic. Mickey Mouse was created in this way, as were many of the other characters we have come to know so well.

Dreamer

This is a state of dreaming and visioning, of imagining the ridiculous and absurd, superimposing contexts to create bizarre associations. More than anything, this stage is free from real-world constraints and limitations. It uses a process where fun, enjoyment, spontaneity, and color are the mechanisms for producing ideas.

Realist

This stage is firmly rooted to the ground, taking the output from the dreamer stage and immersing it in a vat of real-world principles. For example, it may be crazy to imagine a cricket as the conscience for a puppet boy, but give the cricket a personality, build in one or two elements reflecting human frailty, and suddenly it becomes a character we can connect with very easily.

Critic

The critic stage checks for the accuracy of details. It is not criticising in a negative way, but, rather, making the idea more robust and complete. If Jiminy Cricket is supposed to have wisdom, which is often associated with an older person – that is, "old" goes with "wise" – what if we give him a walking stick and a gentleman's hat and coat?

The exercise

The following exercise utilizes this three-stage strategy, using NLP to intensify each of the three very different states. This is but one variation I have used as a method of helping groups to create new options for their cultural dilemmas. Here it is offered in a simple form you can use with any group.

The purpose of the exercise

To provide an experience where a group can recognize and respect the different ways people think and value the creative strategy as a process to help them be more cooperative and successful as a group. The exercise presupposes that the group you will be working with wants to be more creative.

Outcomes for the exercise

The members of the group will recognize three distinct ways in which people think – dreamer, realist, critic – identify their own preferred style of thinking, and observe the different preferences of others in the group. They will also experience the effectiveness of having respect for others' preferences and cooperating as a group. Further, they will recognize the value of each person's contribution to the process of creativity, realize how each style is valid, and that a creative process requires all three styles if it is to be effective. The group will also create a solution for an existing real problem situation.

Preparation

Give the group time to think of a current problem or issue that would benefit from some quality creative thinking. Make sure they choose something within their sphere of influence and of real value to them as individuals. Use a room large enough to create three separate zones for "dreamer", "realist", and "critic", with space between them and an area in the centre to be used for "break state" activities, such as juggling, diabolo and other fun, physical games (see Figure 21.1). You will need plenty of flipchart paper, colored pens or poster paints, and a music system. The exercise will take between 2½ hours and half a day, depending on the number of participants.

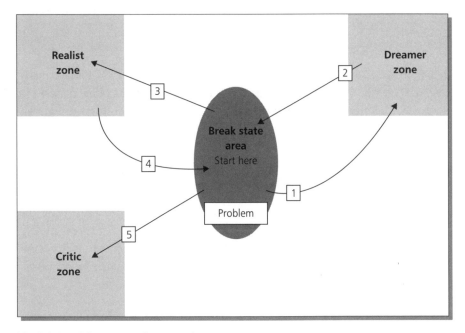

Fig 21.1 ◆ Disney exercise room layout

⊙ exercise

Procedure

1 Pace the group's experience of creative processes in their organization and ask what is preventing them from being more creative as a group. Next, discover what they want instead. Do they want to be more creative? Why? What will this get for them? Inform the group that the Walt Disney strategy can help, and link the benefits to the group's stated desires.

2 Describe the strategy and invite the group to help create a Disney studio in the room. Designate the three zones as in Figure 21.1, then describe each zone using an appropriate communication style – that is, for dreamer, head up, eyes up, using open, upward gestures and words such as "explore", "discover", "imagine" and "dream"; for realist, be more leveling with body posture and gestures, using words and phrases such as "practical", "in the real world", "here and now", "pragmatic", "things that will work"; for critic, use small gestures, close to the body, and be very precise with your words and your body language, gesturing with your fingers and following with your eyes, using words and language such as "details", "examine", "test", and "inspect". When you have described each zone, invite the group members to go and stand in the zone they feel most comfortable with. This self-selection approach reveals the differences between people's thinking preferences, and clearly demonstrates the need for all three styles in a creative process.

3 When you have people in each zone, ask them to decorate the zone with flipcharts, using words, pictures or symbols to represent their zone. You can even ask them to make up a group "sound" to go with the mood of their zone. Comparing the styles of decorating for the different zones is often fascinating. Ask each group to comment on the other zones, and ask if anyone would like to change zones at this point. It is rare for anyone to move, which shows just how strong the differences can be between the styles of thinking.

4 Gather everyone in the break state area and run through the exercise procedure. Explain that the reason for breaking state between each zone is to ensure states are not carried over between zones, and that a clean state can be created and maintained while processing in each zone. It is difficult to create a state for realist and critic if you have not broken your Dreamer state. Also explain the importance of keeping to the strategy, resisting any urges to evaluate while in the dreamer zone. Ask the group to define their problem or issue with a simple and concise statement. Keep this on view in the break state area.

5 Follow the sequence shown in Figure 21.1 – everyone moving first of all into the dreamer zone. Stay with the group and lead them into a visual dreaming state with body language, eye movements, gestures, words, and music to help visualization. Ask them to just represent their thoughts on flipcharts in any way they want to. No talking is allowed at this stage, just putting ideas on the flipchart. There are no rules here – ideas can be connected, built on, and changed by anyone in the group. The objective here is to create an expression of the group's ideas.

6 Move the group into the break state area and get them to spend five to ten minutes doing physical activities. This will break them out of their dreamer state and prepare them for the next stage.

7 Move everyone into the realist zone and lead the group into a realist state using appropriate kinaesthetic language and words. Explain that their task in this zone is to choose the most popular idea from the dreamer zone, by vote if necessary, and ask the question, "What does this idea need to make it work?" Lead the group into a reality where the idea is in place and having an impact. The group can discuss their answers, and represent their conclusions on the flipchart.

8 Back to the break state area again for more juggling and other physical games for five to ten minutes.

9 Move everyone into the critic zone and lead the group into a critic state using appropriate auditory body language and words. Explain that their task in this zone is to strengthen the solution they created in the realist zone by discussing all the ways it might not work and fixing it. They will be working in smaller groups of two or three here, dividing up the different parts of the solution between the groups. They can consider the detail of the solution, and think of exaggerated scenarios to identify weak areas. A useful statement to set the group going is, "This will never work because … ", followed by, "So, what it needs is … ."

10 Back to the break state area again for five to ten minutes of physical games.

11 Remain in the break state area and debrief the exercise. The following questions will help the group to draw new learning from the exercise.

◆ Did you find any particular zone easier than the others?

◆ What surprised you about the strategy?

◆ Did you observe others thinking differently to you?

◆ Did you experience frustration or other emotions?

◆ How do you feel about your final solution?

◆ What strikes you most about what you have just done?

◆ Can you imagine using a strategy like this as a recognized way of problem solving?

Results

Having used Walt Disney's strategy in a variety of formats with a high degree of success, I encourage any organization that is looking to be more creative to experience it. You will discover the tremendous impact it can have, not only on creativity, but also on communication and cooperation. Used with the right attitude of mind and with purpose, it is incredibly energizing, simple, and effective. Also, what could be more natural in any organization than for colleagues to co-opt each other's help to solve problems because of their particular preference for one of these thinking styles? Dreamers, realists, and critics can be very different people, but they need each other's strengths in order to create innovative and workable solutions.

> *Dreamers, realists, and critics can be very different people, but they need each other's strengths in order to create innovative and workable solutions.*

Notes

1   Robert B. Dilts (1994) *Strategies of Genius*, Meta Publications, Inc.

2   Suzy Wetlaufer (2000) "Common Sense and Conflict: An interview with Disney's Michael Eisner", *Harvard Business Review*, January–February.

22

High impact presenting

Alan Black

Over the years, I have observed excellent presenters and wondered how they were able to quickly capture the attention of an audience, keep them engaged, create enthusiasm, and get the message across simply. I have observed this skill of presenting in trainers, teachers, facilitators, and effective leaders. One day, I decided that I wanted to learn this skill also. The exercise I describe in this chapter is the result of a modeling project[1] to discover how the best presenters achieve excellent results. It uses the common elements of the top performers' strategies to form a universal strategy for high impact presenting.

Features of excellent presentations

I initially noticed the following common behaviors among the presenters I had been observing:

- surprise at the beginning;
- continuous eye contact with the whole audience;
- use of space available by walking around;
- use of hands to "place words" in time with accompanying language;
- incorporation of interruptions from the audience and outside;
- asking questions of the audience;
- use of humor;
- making requests for action from the audience;

- varying voice tones;
- upright or solid stance.

Purpose of the exercise

This exercise is designed to enable you to have the ability to catch the attention of an audience during a meeting, lesson, assembly or a presentation, then get your ideas and opinions across clearly and quickly.

The strategy on which the exercise is based I call "the act of distillation and absorption", as a metaphor of my identity as a chemical engineer. A different metaphor could be used to suit a particular user of the strategy.

Outcome

This exercise will give you skills to inspire an audience to listen attentively, understand what is being said or requested, and want to take action. You can use it as a tool to enrol others to your cause and get the best out of your staff. You will hear a lot more from the audience (whether one person or 1,000) about new ideas, more conversations about possibilities, and much less about history, constraints, and limitations.

Exercise procedure

Description

Imagine that you have been asked to give a presentation, teach a lesson or address an assembly of people about an important subject. Proceed in two clear stages:

- rehearsal (distillation);
- production (absorption).

⊙ exercise

Rehearsal – the act of distillation

1 First, think of yourself as a metaphor of distillation – as whisky is distilled from a mixture of liquids, so your talk will be a distillation of the ideas about your subject. Ask yourself, using your internal dialog (moving your eyes down and to your left or right, whichever gets the best results), the following questions to select your subject and its related ideas.

◆ What do they need to know?

◆ What will they be interested in?

◆ Have I considered different angles and questions that could be asked?

◆ Are the subject and related ideas something new or interesting?

◆ Can I think of a new angle?

◆ Are the subject and its related ideas important and true enough for me to talk with passion and enthusiasm?

◆ Are the subject and its related parts simple to understand? How can I make it so?

◆ What surprise from my existing repertoire do I want to start with that is relevant to the subject or even not relevant but amusing?

2 Note the feelings associated with each question as you ask it. If your association with the subject does not fire you up emotionally, you are unlikely to rouse your audience either. Enthusiasm is infectious, but you have to have it in the first place! Your answers to these questions are your criteria for selecting your subject and its related ideas. If your subject or any idea doesn't match your criteria, then discard it. You will now have a subject, a surprise idea for a beginning, and a set of related ideas (no more than, say, six).

> *If the subject does not fire you up emotionally, you are unlikely to rouse your audience either. Enthusiasm is infectious, but you have to have it in the first place!*

3 Next, don the "cloak of the leader" – be an actor or an actress in this part. Recall a time when you were in charge of a situation. If you don't have a memory reference for "being in charge", choose a character (real or mythical), someone who is always in charge of things, and adopt the attitudes and personality characteristics of that character.

4 Search your mind for occasions when you were able to really surprise your listeners – by topical humor, a joke relevant to your subject, a shock, say. Access these memories by moving your eyes upward to the right or left for visual recall and from

side to side for auditory recall, downward for the associated feelings. Select the one with the biggest element of surprise, and represent it in your mind with one word and a small picture. Make the picture very clear and colorful. This will form part of an art gallery in your mind's eye, where you will add similar small pictures with associated title words.

5 Surround your "surprise" picture and word with a set of pictures and associated single-word descriptions. Each picture will represent one part of your main subject and anything connected to it. Construct these pictures with associated words by moving your eyes upward to the right and left for visual recall and construction and from side to side for auditory recall and construction, downward for associated feelings.

6 Now you can see a veritable art gallery of pictures with associated single words in front of you, reach out with your hands and place them in some sort of positional order around your "surprise" picture, which will be in the middle somewhere.

7 Starting with the "surprise" picture and its label, make it larger in size, as if you were blowing it up with a photographic enlarger. Step inside this picture, at the same time saying the associated word to yourself. Color the picture, turn it into a movie of its subject matter, and make its sound loud with an echo. Now articulate what you want to say.

8 Still inside your picture, locate yourself in the audience, hearing and seeing yourself on the stage in front of you. Be "with" your audience as you are talking on the stage in front of you.

9 In seeing and hearing yourself articulating your idea, do you get a feeling of comfort because it is easy to understand for you, enthusiasm because its passion and conviction moves you, fascination because it is interesting or new to you or warmth because it amuses or surprises you? If "yes", then go back to step 6 using another picture and word from your gallery. If "no", then eliminate that picture from your gallery.

10 Carry on with your rehearsal in this way until each picture and word has been "lived" and either articulated or rejected.

Production – the act of absorption

You are now ready for the "real thing" – your production. Just as whisky is absorbed by your body to give you pleasure, so the audience will absorb your message.

◉ exercise

1 Recall your picture gallery and associate with each picture/word in turn, starting with your surprise picture/word. Don the cloak of the leader again and prepare to act, as you articulate what you remembered from your rehearsal of listening to yourself successfully from the perspective of the audience.

2 After articulating each picture/word, observe the audience by looking around at the sea of faces. Blur the edges of your area of focus. If the eyes are staring straight at you each time and no words or movements are detected, then move on to the next picture/word. If you detect any eyes not looking at you or movement in any area as you sweep the audience, keep looking at this area and repeat the previous picture/word, increasing the picture/word submodalities (size, movement, color, volume, and so on). If you still detect disengaged eyes, relax and move on to the next picture/word to keep the flow going. Carry on in the same manner until all the pictures/words have gone from your gallery.

3 Finally, ask for questions and answer them truthfully and enthusiastically. If you get questions that you think and feel are congruent with you, you've done it! Congratulate yourself.

4 Thank the audience for their time and attention.

▦ TOTE – the difference that makes a difference

The research contrasted my performance with the superior performance of my exemplars, discovering "the difference that made a difference". First, they are all "in charge" of the audience. They believe they can teach and lead. What they say is of value to them and the audience. The subject will be thoroughly researched and the presentation will kick off with a surprise.

A key operating TOTE (test–operate–test–exit; see Figure 22.1) in the strategy is during rehearsal, when they are testing how they feel when listening and looking at themselves from the audience's perspective. If it feels right (comfort, enthusiasm, fascination or warmth), then that idea/subject being talked about by their imagined self is worth keeping and important and/or new enough for the production. If it doesn't feel right, then the TOTE is exited and the picture/word representation of that idea/subject is discarded. The next picture/word is selected and the process repeated.

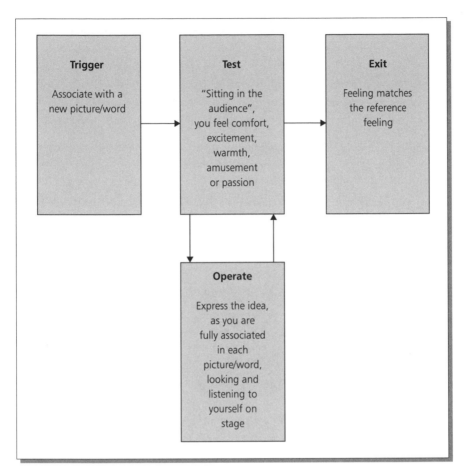

Fig 22.1 ◆ The "feeling" TOTE

Another important TOTE (see Figure 22.2) is during production, when the exemplars are looking for feedback signals indicating audience attention levels (observed in body and/or eye movements). If they see movement indicating a lack of attention (such as wandering or closed eyes and fidgeting), the operation is repeated again, but this time the presenter will directly address the person or people showing a lack of attention. The TOTE is exited on one of two conditions:

◆ if, after two to three repetitions, there is no change, they decide to move on;

◆ attention improves.

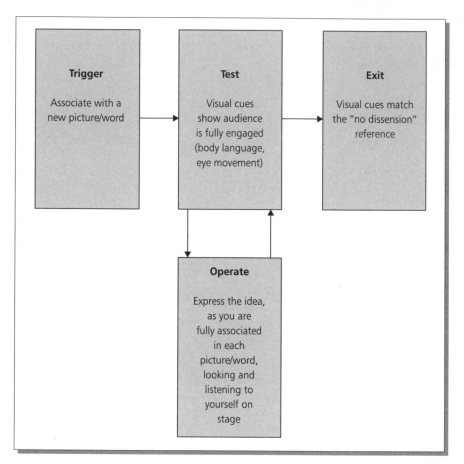

Fig 22.2 ◆ THE "operating" TOTE

■ The results

Since using this strategy, I have been asked more frequently to give presentations, and I have received lots of positive feedback, interest, and questions from my audiences. I look forward with enthusiasm to future opportunities to use the strategy in other contexts – meetings and seminars, for example. Other people who have used the strategy have also said how they are enjoying their communication much more and that they are able to really connect with their audiences.

Note

1   This strategy was created as a modeling project in the final stage of an NLP master
     practitioner course run by PPD Personal Development, London.

23

Anchoring – accessing all the resources you need

Denise Parker

An anchor is a stimulus that triggers a response, in you or in others, and it may involve any of the five senses – sight, sound, touch, smell, and taste. For example, the sound of an alarm bell or the sight of a red traffic light both lead us to respond automatically. An anchor is also something with which we associate a particular feeling or state. This might be a piece of music, a word or a place that brings back memories and emotions connected with it.

Anchoring is a natural phenomenon of communication that we can use with intention in many contexts, as a way of creating more positive feelings for yourself and others, changing negative or unwanted associations, and influencing people to respond in certain ways. Can you imagine being able to create a strong feeling of confidence just before giving a presentation, or calmness and focus before an important meeting? How useful would it be to influence the level of enthusiasm or commitment of a client or an audience?

> *An anchor is a stimulus that triggers a response, in you or in others, and it may involve any of the five senses.*

You may already be creating anchors all around you without recognizing how they link to the responses you are getting from other people. An understanding of the technique and process of anchoring will give you much more control over your feelings and more flexibility when influencing others. Before going any further, it is worth mentioning that your success depends on the technique being used ethically to achieve win–win outcomes. If used in a manipulative way to achieve something that is not desired by the other person, they are likely to sense this and resist your attempt to influence.

What is anchoring?

Anchoring is a technique for creating and changing the associated feelings experienced in response to a stimulus.

A stimulus or anchor can be almost anything, appealing to any of the five senses, and examples exist all around us. For instance, as you think now about a certain song or piece of music, it may automatically trigger a memory or emotion associated with it. Similarly, a picture or photograph, the smell of a certain perfume or the taste of a particular food can all have an impact.

> Anchoring is a technique for creating and changing the associated feelings experienced in response to a stimulus.

The cry of a baby stimulating its mother to respond to its needs is nature's way of ensuring the baby receives nourishment and care until it can fend for itself. The mother's response is anchored to her baby's crying. Some Vietnam War veterans developed responses to the sound of gunfire and have been observed diving into hedgerows in response to backfiring motorcars.

We can also develop anchored responses to people. So when we consistently see someone in a certain role or situation at work, we may respond automatically in a particular way without really knowing very much about the person. The response could be a smile or a nod of acknowledgment or, perhaps, a tut or a feeling of irritation.

The workplace is awash with automatic responses. How often do you hear the phrase "his reputation precedes him"? How common is it for someone's suggestion or idea to be dismissed out of hand? Does everyone get a fair hearing in a meeting or are certain individuals' ideas consistently favored over others'? These situations may be the consequence of colleagues experiencing a conditioned or anchored response associated with a previous situation where that person may have made a poor impression.

❖ example

Several years ago, I was in a role where I had taken over responsibility for a team of specialist salespeople. Each member of the team was based in a particular region of the country and was responsible for supporting the salesforce and generating new business.

Within one week of taking up the role, I was approached by two regional sales managers who demanded that I sack a member of the team. They could supply me with no evidence on which to make this judgment, other than unsubstantiated comments about how this particular person was "useless", "none of the sales team wanted to work with him" and "he added no value"!

Naturally, I refused to take any action without making a full investigation and establishing some facts. My findings showed that, far from being useless, this particular person had assisted a number of the sales team to complete some significant sales, all the salespeople I contacted were very complimentary about him, and valued his support. It also transpired that the managers who wanted him dismissed had, unfortunately, experienced a situation where this person was, through no fault of his own, unable to secure a very large piece of business for them, which would have earned them a considerable commission payment!

Needless to say, I retained the person as a valued member of the team and shared the positive evidence with the two managers. This clearly outweighed their own negative experience and, in time, working relationships between them improved.

In this example, the managers' initial behavior was a direct consequence of a negative response anchored to my team member rather than an objective consideration of the facts. We were also able to collapse this negative anchor by producing more positive evidence and creating a number of positive experiences to counterbalance this.

Such automatic responses are all conditioned or learned and may not always be the most helpful or desirable. Anchored responses of stress or frustration may serve to limit effectiveness when communicating with others and can also hinder results. An extreme example of a negative anchor is a phobia, where an individual experiences an overwhelming negative response to a stimulus. NLP offers techniques for creating, changing, and collapsing anchors to give more choice in how we respond and so help us achieve our outcomes more effectively.

> *Anchored responses of stress or frustration may serve to limit effectiveness when communicating with others and can also hinder results.*

Creating anchors can be a very quick and simple process, and it is worth becoming aware of the anchors that you may set unknowingly, which create an undesirable response in yourself or in others. For instance, have you ever noticed the overuse of words such as "failure" and "problem" in someone's presentation? These words anchor negative feelings in the audience, exactly the opposite of the state the presenter wants the audience to have.

❖ example

I was invited to give a presentation, along with a number of other guest speakers, to a large group of businesspeople as part of a one-day meeting. The meeting was run in a very traditional and procedural way, with the Chairman introducing and guiding each speaker in turn to the same place on the stage, behind a lectern.

One by one, each of the speakers stepped up, but, despite having expertise in their particular topics, their presentation skills were of a low standard. To make things worse, the two speakers before me made a particularly poor job of their delivery. Finally, it was my turn to speak, by which time the audience was beginning to lose interest and become distracted.

The Chairman led me to the same spot on the stage, which by now had some fairly negative experiences and feelings anchored to it! So, making a deliberate choice to move the lectern out of the way and stand in a different position on the stage, I broke the state of the audience and also broke any association with what had gone before. I am pleased to say, the audience gave me full attention and interacted with enthusiasm!

Anchoring exercises

The following examples illustrate situations in which you can use anchors, describe the process involved, and offer some simple hints and tips. For each of the exercises, you may find it easier to read through and memorize the procedure first, to avoid breaking your concentration by trying to do it and read the steps at the same time.

Managing your resourcefulness

This technique is useful for creating positive and resourceful states or feelings for yourself, which you can then access whenever you choose.

The outcomes

With increased choice and flexibility, imagine how much more effective you can be in situations such as delivering a presentation, attending an interview, running a meeting, leading a training course, dealing with customers, using the telephone, and, indeed, any other task when using more of your resources will have a positive impact on your results.

⊚ exercise

Procedure

1 Choose a resourceful state or feeling that you have had and would like to access whenever you choose – something that you really want. It might be confidence, enthusiasm, motivation, energy, relaxation, calmness or excitement, for example.

2 Choose an anchor that you can use easily and discreetly – perhaps a gesture, such as a fist or pressing your finger and thumb together. Make sure your anchor is something specific and unique, rather than something you already do frequently, so that you can choose when to use it and avoid accidentally setting it off at inopportune moments.

3 Recall a time when you experienced this state or feeling at its strongest. Imagine being there now, looking through your own eyes, and notice all that you see, hear, and feel. Make sure that you don't see yourself in the picture, and notice all the qualities, or submodalities, of the image, including any sounds. Allow yourself to really associate with that feeling and, when it becomes even stronger, anchor it by making your chosen gesture.

4 Hold this gesture for a few seconds and remove it before the feeling subsides (see Figure 23.1).

5 Break the state by moving around or thinking about something else.

6 Test the anchor by making the gesture again as you think about something else and notice the response you have now. This is called "firing" the anchor.

7 Repeat steps two to five at least five times to strengthen the connection between the anchor and the feeling that you want.

8 Think about an event in the future where you would like to access this state and, as you imagine this time, fire your anchor and notice how you feel.

Congratulations! You now have access to this resourceful state whenever you choose. Remember, anchors can also be words, things you see, in fact, anything you feel is appropriate. Experiment with different anchors or cues and find what works best for you.

Stacking anchors

If you want to be even more adventurous, you can repeat the process using the same anchor with a different state to associate an appropriate combination of resources to the anchor.

Additional tips for anchoring

To ensure that you create a powerful and lasting anchor, remember the following important tips:

◆ **Intensity of state**

When recalling a previously experienced state, make sure it is a really vivid experience and one in which you were fully connected with the feelings that you now want to recreate. You could create an anchor that triggers a state of feeling only slightly confident rather than really confident! Also, be fully associated in the experience. In other words, be there now, looking through your own eyes rather than seeing an image of yourself, and really intensify the feelings.

◆ **Uniqueness of the anchor**

Use a cue that is distinctive, easily used, and not something that can be randomly triggered. You might not want to access deep relaxation every time someone shakes your hand!

◆ **Timing of the anchor**

Set the anchor just prior to reaching the most intense part of the experience, hold for a few seconds, then remove it before the feeling subsides (see Figure 23.1).

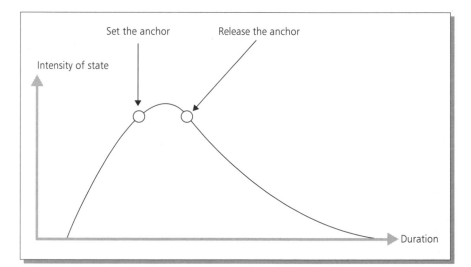

Fig 23.1 ◆ Setting and releasing an anchor

◆ **Accuracy of duplication**
When testing the anchor and when using it to recall your desired state, be precise.

Sales meetings with customers

Anchoring can be useful in meetings to elicit resourceful states in your clients and positively influence their responses so that they become more receptive to you and your proposals. Use this technique in meetings with customers or anyone you want to influence.

The best time to create an anchor is when the client is accessing the desired state, so, for instance, you might want to anchor "rapport" at the beginning of a meeting, having built it to a satisfactory level.

The outcomes

People buy from people they like. One of the keys to success is ensuring that your client has a positive experience when meeting you and, in future, that they associate you with that positive feeling. You may achieve this already with many of your clients, and anchoring will help you to be successful with others too.

⊚ exercise

The procedure

1　Take time at the beginning of a meeting to build rapport with your client.

2　Decide what resourceful state you would like to anchor in your client, such as a feeling of being in rapport, enthusiasm, curiosity, interest, decisiveness, or whatever.

3　Encourage your client to access the desired state, with the use of language, rapport skills, appealing to values, or else have the client tell you about something you know they are interested in or enthusiastic about.

4　Pay attention to the client's behavior, so that you notice when the state intensifies.

5　Anchor the desired state using a word, statement, smile, a gesture or, perhaps, a certain movement.

6　Break the state by changing the subject.

7 Repeat the same anchor, precisely, to test the response, then watch for the same external behaviors associated with the desired state.

8 Fire the anchor again to recreate the state when appropriate in that meeting and at future meetings.

How much more successful can you possibly be when you use this approach to create a positive response in your client right at the very start of your meeting?

Presentations

A range of anchors can be used to enhance the effectiveness and impact of your presentations. Create a resource anchor to access a positive state, such as confidence, calmness, alertness, enthusiasm, or all of these, before commencing your presentation. The procedure set out for the "Managing your resourcefulness" technique earlier in this chapter can be used to anchor a positive state for presenting.

Another effective use of anchors in presentations is to utilize spatial or stage anchors. It may be that you have a mixture of good and bad news to deliver or perhaps you are following a speaker you don't want to be associated with or else you may want to focus the audience's attention on future visions and ideas.

◉ exercise

Ideas for stage anchors

1 Decide the states you wish to anchor – interest, enthusiasm, alertness or motivation, for example.

2 Identify any states that you might want to change, such as disinterest, boredom or tiredness.

3 Select a space on the stage where you would not usually stand – for instance, over to the right-hand side – and reserve this for delivering any news that may be unpopular – never stand there to deliver your good news.

4 If you want to pace and lead your audience and generate enthusiasm for plans and ideas, consider using gestures that direct their attention up and to your left. For the majority of your audience, when their eyes look in this direction, they will see imagined or constructed pictures of the future you are presenting.

5   Similarly, consider marking out the past, present, and future on the stage, with the past being to your right and the future to your left. You can use these positions as anchors and communicate more effectively and clearly with your audience.

6   Use language to help your audience access resourceful states. Encourage them to imagine what it will be like or to remember a time when they have been successful.

Meetings and the workplace

It is useful to notice anchors that have already been created, or that you create without realizing, and check that the associated responses are helpful and desirable. For instance, do you hold regular meetings in the same place and at the same time? What feelings and states have been anchored to these places and times? How do people feel about always meeting on a Friday afternoon? Do people always sit in the same place? What feelings might be anchored to previous experiences or meetings? How resourceful would you expect a member of staff to be if the last time they met with you in this same office, with the same seating arrangement, they were receiving negative feedback?

How resourceful would you expect a member of staff to be if the last time they met with you in this same office, with the same seating arrangement, they were receiving negative feedback?

Use the following suggestions for any meeting, whether on a one-to-one basis or with a group or team and, more generally, for maintaining a positive state in the workplace.

The outcome

Increased awareness of negative anchors that might hinder performance will enable you to remove them. You can then replace them with positive anchors to get the best out of your meetings.

exercise

Suggestions

1   Vary the location, time, and arrangements for meetings that are proving unproductive.

2   Alter the seating arrangements, encourage attendees to access different states, and think differently.

3 Alternate the role of chairperson and minute taker.

4 Take time to build rapport and help others access positive states. Create positive anchors for future meetings.

5 Use words, statements, movements, and gestures to anchor resourceful states in others during the meeting.

6 Reserve certain areas or places for negativity that are away from the normal area of work.

7 Use specific words and positive language to anchor resourceful states and responses during telephone conversations.

Collapsing negative anchors

The process allows you to counterbalance a negative anchor with an even more powerful positive anchor and collapse the negative anchor, resulting in a neutral or even positive feeling being associated with the original experience.

There are various ways of achieving this. The example of the technique described below is one way that can easily be used for yourself or with someone else to help change a negative feeling attached to a previous experience. Note that this technique is unsuitable for major negative experiences and trauma. It is best used for minor events; for instance, you may have delivered a presentation or run a meeting that didn't go as well as you would have liked and, as a result, you feel disappointed about it.

The outcome

By collapsing the negative anchor, you will be able to replace an unresourceful state with something more positive.

⊚ exercise

The procedure

1 Think of a past event that, as you think about it now, creates a negative feeling. Choose something fairly small that you would like to change.

2 Also, think about a positive experience you have had that brings back enjoyable memories. Choose a situation where you were having a very enjoyable time.

3 Mark two locations on the floor at least four feet apart. On one location put a piece of paper with a minus sign written on it, on the other, one with a plus sign.

4 Stand on the minus sign and talk about your negative experience.

5 Break state by moving off the sign and thinking about something else.

6 Stand on the positive sign and talk about your positive experience.

7 Try to retell your negative experience while standing on the plus sign and notice how the old feelings that you had have now changed or disappeared.

This technique works only where the positive experience greatly outweighs the negative. As long as that condition is met, you have a simple technique you can use for any number of work-related situations that deplete your inner resources.

Summary

Pay attention to anchors that you create, notice those that already exist, and check that the associated response for you, and others, is useful. Become more aware of your own state and that of your colleagues and customers. Where appropriate, practice some of these techniques to create more resourceful states. When you experience a really positive state or feeling, "bottle it" by creating a resource anchor for yourself, in the moment, when the feeling is at its strongest.

As you become more aware of the anchors affecting you and continue practicing and using these techniques, you will create even more choices for your state and for how you feel. These, in turn, will have an enormous impact on your performance and results.

24

Reframing – forming new perspectives

Most people working in organizations want to succeed. At least that is their intention, but sometimes their thinking can get in the way and the resultant behavior fails to have the desired effect. Progress can be impeded because people are slaves to their thinking and the more they think about a situation in the same way, the more entrenched the problem becomes for them. Reframing is a way of releasing people from this mental slavery.

❖ example

A young manager, Jamul, was told that he needed to work more creatively with his team. His style was very prescriptive, leaving little scope for the team to contribute to how things were done. There was just one way – Jamul's way. I was assigned as his coach and discovered that he was driven by results and enjoyed getting things done. Creativity was pretty low on his value hierarchy – he didn't believe that he had a creative mind, nor that creativity would lead to better results. Even though his thinking was getting in the way of promotion, the more he thought about it, the stronger his beliefs became.

Everyone has creative ability, so I used a reframe to help Jamul find his. I suggested that the next meeting be held around the corner from his office, in the Sherlock Holmes museum. Jamul thought this a little odd, but I wanted to get him away from the business environment. As we walked around the museum, Jamul began to tell me how he had read Arthur Conan Doyle as a young boy, but that now he preferred modern films with special effects. He went on to tell me how he really enjoyed watching films such as *Star Wars*, recounting some of the key characters and storylines.

We were moving towards a more creative style of conversation as we left the museum and walked into St James' Park. We stopped for a coffee and I looked out at a futuristic-style table and chairs. I asked Jamul how the table and chairs could be used to describe one of his problems at work and he began to create a rich metaphoric link between the table and chairs and a technical problem he was currently dealing with. It was time to offer the reframe. I said, "That's very creative, to be able to make links like that – does your manager and team know you have this ability to think creatively?"

In order to process this reframe, Jamul had to accept the presupposition that he is creative, then realize that he hadn't shown this creative ability in the work context. The remainder of the coaching consisted of helping him to identify opportunities for using it with his team.

Reframes can be used in less time than the example above, where I wanted Jamul to experience his creativity and diminish his limiting belief. This type of reframe is called a *context reframe* and is appropriate where behavior in one context is useful in another. Another type of reframe is the *meaning reframe*, where an alternative meaning is offered for particular behavior.

> Reframing is a way of releasing people from mental slavery.

Think about the slavish thinking that goes on in your organization and the phrases used to communicate it. I'll use some that I have heard recently to demonstrate both types of reframe. In each of the responses, there is a pacing statement and a reframe to lead the thinking towards a more positive perspective.

"My people don't like change."

"I know people like that, and isn't it reassuring to know that you can rely on them being consistent when you want them to be?" (*Meaning reframe*)

"He makes me so angry."

"We all have the right to get angry when we choose. What causes you to choose anger in response to him?" (*Meaning reframe*)

"I keep an idiot list of the names of people I meet in the company who make life difficult for me."

"Lists are good when you want to remember things. Do you have a bad memory or is the list your best way of dealing with failed attempts to influence difficult people?" (*Meaning reframe*)

"It's stressing me out, having to make all these young people redundant."

"Giving bad news can be stressful, but have you thought how uplifting it might be if, instead, you were to give these youngsters a start on the next step of their careers?" (*Meaning reframe*)

"I get too involved with details."

"Details can be involving I know and you wouldn't have made it this far in the company had you not known when to get involved in the details." (*Context reframe*)

"I know the best way to do this job."

"There's always a best way for someone. I wonder how many other 'best ways' are being blocked by thinking in this way?" (*Meaning reframe*)

"My boss is so indecisive; I often have to wait weeks for a decision to be made."

"So your boss is indecisive. Isn't it reassuring to know you have a boss who takes his time with important decisions involving you?" (*Meaning reframe*)

"I don't feel confident joining in the discussion at Board level, so I just listen."

"Not joining in the discussion gives you a chance to practice your listening skills – wouldn't that be useful with your peer group sometimes?" (*Context reframe*)

"The parent company wants to know so many details before it will authorize expenditure. It's such a painstaking process."

"They want to know so many details before authorizing expenditure. Is it reassuring to know that they are careful with the company's money, especially when there is such a poor record of cost control?" (*Meaning reframe*)

"The team leaders are so busy with day-to-day operations that they're not interested in attending my project meeting."

"They're that busy? They must be very diligent and conscientious in their work." (*Meaning reframe*)

▩ The six-step reframe

This procedure is useful for dealing with indecisiveness, when someone is torn between taking two courses of action. It can also be used to resolve conflict in a person,[1] between two people or two groups of people. The objective is to separate the behavior from the intention and create some new options that result in a win–win for both sides. The following procedure is a modified six-step reframe for use with teams in conflict.

It is a good idea to bring the conflicting groups together initially using an *agreement frame*, which might go something like this. "If your company were to give you time to resolve this issue for good, would you be interested in finding a better way to work together?" Assuming you get a "yes" answer, ask, "Will you both agree to this and be fully committed to finding a solution?" You are looking for both teams to agree to work together towards a solution – that's often a big step forward for conflicting teams.

Separate the behavior from the intention and create some new options that result in a win–win for both sides.

An option, before beginning the procedure, is to pace and lead each team into a state of cooperation, which you can anchor to the physical space you will be using for the six-step reframe. You might ask them to think back to a time when they were enjoying a cooperative interaction with another team. Calibrate their states for cooperation to check for congruence at the end of the exercise.

Note that calibrating the states of individual team members requires highly developed sensory acuity, but it is a skill well worth developing.

Remember that pacing is important at every stage in the procedure. Respect each team's map of reality, no matter how childish or unrealistic it may seem.

◎ exercise

The procedure

1   Identify the conflicting behavior, as described by each group. For example, "When this happens, they do (X) and we respond by doing (Y)." It is very unlikely that descriptions of behavior will match, but that's OK, just pace each group and respect what they say. As a facilitator, it's important that you stay out of the content and work with the process of conflict resolution.

2   Ask each person to individually recall the last time conflict occurred and to rerun the events in their mind. Ask them to identify the exact moment when they realized "it's happening again" and to describe their feelings at that specific moment. Calibrate their states as you watch them doing this activity.

This calibration will be used to compare with the state you notice at the end of the exercise. You are looking for a contrast that tells you the teams have fully internalized the changes they have committed to on completion of the exercise.

3   Next, get each individual to ask, "What is the positive intention behind my behavior in response to this moment of conflict?" After this stage, you can bring people together in small groups to share their findings and compile a team list of positive

intentions. The next task is to determine, collectively, "What function is being accomplished here?"

Typical functions teams come up with are at a higher level than the behavior, such as efficiency, effectiveness, learning, cooperation, and so on. It is common for teams to describe the same or similar function. It is important to work with whatever they come up with.

4   Ask the teams if they are willing to explore alternative ways of achieving this function. The procedure now enters a creative stage and you can offer them any number of ways to do this, depending on the nature of the conflict, time, and creative ability of the teams. Try the Walt Disney strategy (described in Chapter 21) or simple brainstorming techniques. The objective is to generate a number of alternative ways of accomplishing the stated functions.

5   The next question for both teams is, "Will you accept responsibility for using one or more of the alternatives you have come up with to accomplish this function?" If there are conditions attached to a "yes" answer, the solution is unlikely to last very long. The closer you get to an unconditional agreement, the better. If conditions can be agreed on easily, it may be the best possible solution at this time. One alternative is to agree the process by which future problems will be resolved, thereby reducing the possibility of conflict arising again from an unmet condition of the solution.

6   Before implementing the new options, future-pace the teams through the solution. Have all your sensory receptors on alert here, looking for congruity. Have each team imagine a scenario where the initial problem recurs, then have them implement their chosen solution. Lead them through the reality, step by step, and ask them to be aware of any objections to the solution. If the team encounters objections, go back to the beginning of the exercise and start again from step two or four, depending on the strength of the objection.

The outcomes

The six-step reframe exercise is really useful for bringing dysfunctional teams together. Because of the nature of organizations, keeping them working in harmony requires much more than this. In my experience, the major causes of team dysfunction are not within the team, but with senior roles.

Many CEOs, presidents, vice-presidents, and divisional heads are unaware of how their behavior affects teams at the functional level. Teams take their cues from the senior role models around them, so damaging team behavior is often the result of political positioning among the top team.

When this happens, it is extremely difficult to get results by working with the team in isolation. Thus, the more factors in the systemic equation you can include, the more complete and robust the solution will be.

Note

1   For comprehensive coverage of the six-step reframing procedure for personal conflict, as well as other reframing techniques, see Richard Bandler and John Grinder (1982) *Reframing*, Real People Press.

Section 4

Modeling excellence:
how to be the best

Introduction

Do you know someone who can perform a particular skill exquisitely? Getting great results time after time? Have you ever wondered how they do this? Have you ever wished you were able to get the same results?

Well, in this section you will discover the makeup of any skill and learn how to model it and install it in yourself. This is where NLP began, after all, when Richard Bandler and John Grinder[1] modeled the success patterns of leading therapists Fritz Perls, Virginia Satir, and Milton Erickson[2] in the early 1970s. They proved that it is possible to learn just about anything you want – all you need is a suitable model and the techniques of modeling. They proved it by being able to get the same results as their model subjects, and it didn't take them long to realize the vast possibilities of this as they began to model top people from other professions.

> *It is possible to learn just about anything you want – all you need is a suitable model and the techniques of modeling.*

Much of what exists as NLP today is drawn from those early modeling experiences – taking the best from top salespeople, negotiators, public speakers, storytellers, Olympic sports men and women, great thinkers, business leaders, and models from many other disciplines. Today, there are few skills that have not been modeled and, while there are some generic models available, such as the creativity strategy of Walt Disney,[3] the skill of modeling gives you the ability to replicate any model of success you want that is within the physical limitations of your body. So, let's get down to some modeling.

Notes

1   Richard Bandler and John Grinder (1979) *Frogs into Princes*, Real People Press. Also Richard Bandler and John Grinder (1975) *The Structure of Magic*, vol. 1, Science and Behavior Books.

2   Richard Bandler and John Grinder (1975) *Patterns of the Hypnotic Techniques of Milton H. Erickson, M.D.*, vol. 1, Meta Publications, Inc.

3   Robert B. Dilts (1994) *Strategies of Genius*, Meta Publications, Inc.

25

Method and technique

You will recall from Chapter 5 how we respond to external events from the internal representations we make as a result of filtering sensory input. The filters we use act to generalize, delete, and distort sensory information, and this is how we each form our own unique model of the world. This is the process of modeling. When we want to find out how a person performs a particular skill, we need to discover how they are generalizing, deleting, and distorting to create their unique model of the world in the context of performing the skill.

> To find out how a person performs a particular skill, we need to discover how they are generalizing, deleting, and distorting to create their unique model of the world in the context of performing the skill.

Some years ago, I modeled the memory strategy of someone who had the most phenomenal memory you can imagine. I wanted to have his ability for recalling details and facts instantly. This particular project has a twist in the tail and emphasizes an important cautionary aspect of any modeling project – the possibility that a key part of your model's success strategy may be incompatible with your personal values. For this reason, it is an ideal example to demonstrate the technique of modeling, which has four distinct parts:

◆ *strategies* the sequence of internal processing;

◆ *values* the motivation to succeed;

◆ *physiology* physical components of the strategy;

◆ *language* how distinctions are coded.

Before we get into the details, let me tell you something about the incredible memory man, who I will refer to as William. He is a teacher and within a few days of taking a new influx of 30 or so students, he would have all their names committed to memory. Mention any past experience and, in just a short time, he will tell you the date, what he had for lunch, who he spoke with, and any other significant events occurring on that day. He frequently quotes the Classics, which he learned as a young student, and can remember names, dates and details that, to most people, are unimportant and insignificant. There seem to be few boundaries to William's ability to recall details. He is also able to quickly tell you that six weeks next Friday will be August 19, which is the day before so and so's birthday, three days after his first date with his wife, and a celebratory day in some obscure part of Belgium!

Strategies

You were introduced to strategies in Chapter 7, learning about communication channels and eye accessing cues. When you consider a skill, it is important to know where it begins – that is, what triggers the strategy or strategies. You will need access to your subject to ask a series of questions and observe both verbal and non-verbal components of their communication. It is widely known that successful people find it difficult to tell you how they achieve their success. They may have a feeling or a notion, but few people understand the strategies they use. So, skill in eliciting a strategy is key to modeling. With this topic, I wanted to know not just William's memory recall strategy, but how he memorized information as he experienced it.

> *When you consider a skill, it is important to know where it begins – that is, what triggers the strategy or strategies.*

Some useful questions to ask are:

◆ "How do you know when to (commit something to memory)?"

◆ "Think back to the most recent time when you (committed something to memory). What drew your attention to it?"

As you ask the question, you need to watch and listen for the strategy working as it is replayed. Notice eye movements, voice tones, the words used, value and belief statements, and physiology. Your subject will not give you what you want in the sequence you ask for it. Be prepared for anything – have your sensory acuity finely tuned and be in total uptime.

Here's a transcript of the initial session with William.

DM: "Think back to the most recent time when you committed something to memory. What drew your attention to it?"

William's eyes focused slightly left and ahead.

DM: "What are you looking at now?"
William: "I'm looking at my diary, which is on my desk in the study."
DM: "What is important about your diary?"
William: "It contains all the anniversaries, holidays, birthdays, and celebrations I need to remember."
DM: "Do you have a memorable event yet?"
William: "Yes, I was in France on February 18 with a bunch of kids from year ten."
DM: "Choose a particular memorable moment from that day and recall the events leading up to it."

At this point, William's physiology changed. He began to frown, his face got redder, and his breathing speeded up, so I got the next question in quickly.

DM: "What are you thinking right now?"
William: "I won't be seeing my wife for three days and I can't phone her."
DM: "What does this mean?"
William: "At the end of each day, I have to tell my wife everything that has happened in the day and I don't know if I'll be able to remember it all over three days."
DM: "Why is this so important?"
William: "It's uncontrollable – I can't do anything about the strong urge I have to tell my wife all the details."
DM: "What would life be like if you couldn't remember these things?"
William: "There would be no enjoyment."

At this point, William's eyes made a quick left pass and his physiology changed again. His breathing slowed, there were crow's feet around the eyes, he sat back, and his voice softened.

DM: "What memories were you recalling then?"
William: "My father always used to tell us stories after Sunday dinner. He would tell us about his past and things that happened to the family. We would all join in and tell stories about each other, the things we did, and the trouble we got into. Those were really happy times."
DM: "Recall the last time you went home and told your wife about the day."
William: "That was on Monday. I had the worst bunch of kids imaginable to try and teach ... ."

DM: "Recall actually telling your wife, in your home, after you returned from work."

William: "Jill was in the kitchen and I remembered that, as I left the house that morning, I saw my neighbor looking out of the window. He should have been at work at that time. I told her how he was probably bunking off work."

William continued to provide details about his day, in a very passionate style. What I considered to be tedious detail, William was totally passionate about.

DM: "Recall the moment you saw your neighbor through the window, and rerun that from just before leaving the house."

William: "I opened the door, walked out, saw him, and thought about how I would tell Jill when I returned home that evening."

William's eyes made a series of movements that told me he was constructing the dialog he would have with Jill when he returned home. A strategy was becoming clear, and it seemed to be taking up huge amounts of processing power. I now wanted to find out the end of the strategy.

DM: "How do you know when the memory is secure in your mind?"
William: "I don't know."
DM: "What tells you it is OK to think about something else? Go over that last example again and notice at what point your focus of attention moves to another subject."

At this point, William made a facial gesture resembling a smug grin, with some internal dialog, so, again, I was quick with the next question.

DM: "What did you just say to yourself?"
William: "Just as I thought – a lazy good-for-nothing."
DM: "What was the very next thought that came into your mind?"
William: "My lesson schedule."

I elicited a few additional examples and discovered the same end point to the strategy. He would punctuate the memory with a short piece of internal dialog. So, the strategy can be represented with the notation and TOTE, as in Figure 25.1.

I also wanted to know what happened when he was with his wife. In this situation, the urge would be to tell his close friends. In fact, after I had identified this, I noticed how many times he would punctuate his conversations with, "I must tell Jill (or whoever)." This strategy told me how William committed experiences to memory, so, next, I wanted to find out his retrieval strategy.

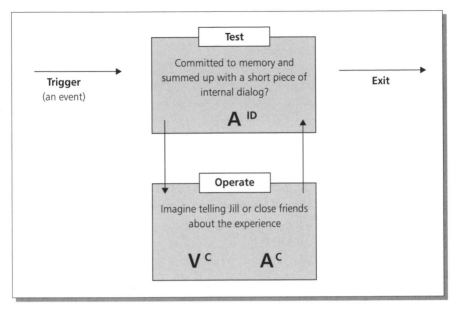

Fig 25.1 ◆ TOTE for William's memory strategy

This was very clear, and consistent. The important job of getting events into his memory had been done, and retrieval was simple. The strategy consisted of three stages:

◆ visual recall

◆ auditory recall

◆ kinaesthetic.

William's lead system was visual, and his preferred representation system kinaesthetic. In notation form, the retrieval strategy is written as:

He would use a visual to locate the date and time in his diary, then recall the words he used to punctuate the "commit to memory" strategy, then he would associate with the experience and relive it for his audience. During the process of eliciting this strategy, I also asked William to describe the qualities (submodalities) of the images, sounds, and feelings of his internal representations. I would need these to install the strategy and use it for myself.

The next thing I wanted to know was which experiences William chose to commit to memory using the strategy shown in Figure 25.1, and here we need to look at his value system.

Values

William is a very warm, extrovert, tactile, and humorous person – often the life and soul of the party. He has many friends and is well known in the community. His life is spent with other people, enjoying their company. His conversations are predominantly about other people – a clear metaprogram pattern is in operation here. Memories tend to revolve around people rather than activities, places, things or information. At the centre of each memory is a person or group of people.

A high-level means value of William's is "enjoying the company of others". When asked, "and what does this get for you?", he replied, "an opportunity to talk about life." Further questions revealed an end value of "telling others about me" that I am sure comes from his childhood evenings of storytelling with his father. Supporting the end value is the powerful belief that his urge to tell others about his day is uncontrollable. Also, in support of his memory retrieval strategy was a very powerful belief in his ability to remember just about anything.

Physiology

During the modeling interviews and general observations, I calibrated a number of distinct states. The first was at the beginning of the TOTE, which told me William had selected an experience to commit to memory. Interestingly, if he were to read a school document, he would quickly find someone to discuss it with. Following this, all other accounts would be about the discussion he had, rather than his first experience of reading it – for example, "I told Mike that I thought the document had missed the mark." William selected all experiences that involved an interaction with someone else. If he went for a bicycle ride, he would tell you about it only if it involved him interacting with someone on the journey – "I was riding my bike into town when I saw young Fred coming out of the Hare and Hounds; he looked completely drunk," for example. I have never heard William say, "I was sitting thinking about this."

The second state was the "uncontrollable urge" state, when he was constrained from telling others about his experiences. The third state was at the end of a TOTE when he summed up an event with internal dialog. These were the really distinct states that formed the "committing to memory" strategy. There were quite a few others related to the process of retrieving a memory and giving an account of it to other people. The state at which he was most animated was the moment he switched from auditory recall to kinaesthetic in the recall strategy. At this moment, his entire body would be upright, chest out, arms extended in gesture, breathing fast, and voice volume significantly higher than normal.

Language

Language gives so many cues to a person's strategy. While the tone of voice may indicate state changes, the actual words used contain lots of process information about values, beliefs, meanings, options, necessities, and unique distinctions being made in the particular subject context. In the case of William, the cues from language were rich and coming at me thick and fast. Did you notice the modal operators of necessity?

"… birthdays and celebrations *I need* to remember."

"*I have to* tell my wife everything."

As an extrovert, he loves nothing more than to talk about himself. In fact, at the very first interview, as I thanked him for his time and poured him a beer, he replied, "No problem, dear boy, I've been looking forward to this. I enjoy nothing more than talking about my memories." You see how values and predicates just jump out at you from everyday conversation?

Getting the most from modeling

The key to getting the information you want is the questions you ask. Notice what the eyes do and ask your subject to describe their process – for example, "What do you see now?" or "What can you hear as you think about that question?" If you interpret the eye cues accurately and the remainder of the physiology also, you are most likely to get what you want from your subject.

The key to getting the information you want is the questions you ask. Notice what the eyes do and ask your subject to describe their process.

You want them to replay their strategy for you, so you can record it, learn it, and install it for yourself. Review the information in Chapter 7 to help you with this process.

So, suppose you have accurately recorded a strategy from a worthy subject, what next? In the example given, where I successfully elicited William's memory strategy, I realized that I didn't want a brilliant memory that badly. His strategy did not support my own values as a coach and people developer. I had spent years learning how to subdue my personal agenda so I could listen to other people and understand their model of the world. So, clearly, a strategy centered on the extension of one's ego was diametrically opposed to some of my highest values and beliefs. I decided not to install it and, instead, look for an alternative way to improve my memory. But what if you do want to install a strategy, how is it done?

Strategy installation

I will use the memory example to demonstrate the process of strategy installation. This is what I would have done had I wanted to install it. You might like to try it for yourself.

◎ exercise

1 Create the internal experience of seeing the diary with dates and times. Replicate the exact same submodalities of the image – that is, in front, as a timeline running from left to centre, then the future going directly upward – a two-page, colorful diary out in front, marked clearly with date, day, and anniversary reminders.

2 Identify a number of future events to begin with, and select a person on whom to center the experience. If no person exists, select someone to tell about the experience soon afterwards. Picture that person with a visual name tag on their head (this is William's "pupil name remembering" strategy).

3 Decide whom you will be reliving your experiences with and use your internal dialog to remind yourself throughout the day, "I must tell so and so about this later."

4 Each experience you have during the day that you want to remember must be linked to a person. If you have a very different metaprogram, you can either change it using the technique in Chapter 17, or change this strategy so that experiences are linked with your primary area of focus (people, information, activity, places or things – see Chapter 9). This option may not work if the metaprogram is key to the strategy. You will only find out by installing and testing it.

5   As you take in an experience, create an internal image of it surrounding the link person, and imagine telling it to your chosen person (using a visual and auditory construct). Then come up with a few words of internal dialog to summarize it, and go on to the next experience.

6   Repeat the above procedure for all the experiences you want to remember, and relive each one with your chosen person (trust that they will tolerate your story-telling).

7   Test the effectiveness by asking someone to question you on past events. Notice any improvements you have made.

In addition to the procedure above, you need to make sure that your values, physiology, and language support the strategy. You may not want to adopt the values of your subject, but remember that the more you alter the strategy, the less it is likely to work for you.

Next steps

In the next chapter, there are two further modeling case studies to demonstrate the flexibility and range of the technique. If you are drawn to install the memory strategy covered in this chapter, I wish you every success. William is a superb model for effective memorizing and is well known for his unique ability. Bear this in mind when you select modeling subjects – you don't want someone who is just average at something – choose someone with a high degree of success and consistency in the skill you want to model, then be curious to learn what distinctions the person is making as they respond to external events.

When you select modeling subjects you don't want someone who is just average at something.

26

Modeling case study: customer service skills

In this chapter, you will learn how the method and technique of modeling has been applied to elicit excellence in customer service skills among a group of computer service analysts at Computacenter (UK) Limited.[1] This project was undertaken in 1996 and played a major part in realigning the business model to the marketplace.

The project came about as a result of being asked to design a training course to help computer service analysts deliver higher levels of customer delight. The request begged the question, "What do you mean by customer delight?" and so the project was set up to find the answer. In fact, there were two distinct projects – one involving customers and a second involving analysts.

The customer project

So, what is customer delight? To answer this question, I interviewed ten customers from different types of companies to find out first hand what aspects of service delivery delighted them the most. The answers I came back with were extremely varied and invaluable as input to the selection, management, and training of service analysts. Here are some of the customers' responses.

"I would be delighted if the analyst would spend some time showing me how to get the most from the computing equipment we have in the office. Can we share printers? How do we transfer files between computers?"

This customer wanted help to maximize productivity. He was asking to be educated, and it would take an analyst only a few minutes of extra time each visit to provide this additional service. It would cost the company very little in comparison to the value it would add to the service for this particular customer.

"I would be delighted if, when we have a major problem with one of the critical systems, we could be informed of progress every 15 minutes – even if there is no change. This would allow us to make decisions on resource sharing across the rest of the network in real time."

This customer wanted improved communication – very easy to do, at no cost at all.

"I would be delighted if your analysts would be more proactive in anticipating problems before they occur. A high number of incidents could have been avoided if they had been monitoring the usage on our network."

This service would also be easy to provide. There would, perhaps, be a little up-front cost involved, but the customer would probably be happy to pay something for it.

"I would be delighted if you could do some trend analysis and show us how to eliminate repeat problems. We seem to be experiencing a high number of similar problems and if you could help us to reduce that, we would be very delighted indeed."

Each customer I interviewed told me a completely different way in which they could be delighted, so how is it possible to train analysts in customer delight and cover all potential scenarios?

It seemed, from what customers said, that "delight" is about adding value.

I realized that the conventional idea of "delight" – that is, the "be pleasant, smile, and treat the customer as king" approach – was totally inadequate. The question this brought to my mind was, "How can analysts delight customers, in the way that they want to be delighted?" It seemed, from what customers said, that "delight" is about adding value, so the answer had to lie somewhere else – not in the standard training we had been doing over the years.

▪ The analyst project

Working through the service delivery managers, we enrolled 12 analysts on the project. Half of them were getting average or below-average scores on customer feedback forms, and the other half had been receiving high scores consistently over a year or more.

The two groups allowed comparisons to be made between the strategies of low- and high-scoring analysts in this area. The objective was to model the analysts' strategies that were responsible for delighting customers. The method used was to model each of the analysts for half a day and observe the responses of customers during interactions. Each modeling session finished with a half-hour interview to elicit values, beliefs, and metaprograms. The strategies were recorded as I followed each analyst, asking questions on the move.

There were some astounding differences between the two groups. The lower-scoring group used effective strategies in some situations, the higher-scoring group was effective in all situations. There was a clear difference here in the consistency of application.

One of the top scorers, Mike, had an intriguing strategy I named the "corridor" strategy. He worked in a large office block and was supporting thousands of computer users. Between calls, of which he took about 12 per day, he would take a detour via another floor and hurtle down the corridor to spend a couple of minutes with a user he had visited the previous day. His conversation would be tailored to the particular user, sometimes technical in content, sometimes focused on the user's business, but always with the aim of ensuring that the user was still happy (almost like reminding them how happy they were yesterday when he had visited them).

Another top-scoring analyst, James, combined excellent teamworking skills with an almost meditative style of problem solving. On being allocated a fault call he was not sure about, James would spend ten minutes asking experts for their opinions. Armed with this information from his team, he would take the minimum number of tools to the call. His first-time fix rate was among the highest in the company.

In contrast to this, the lower-scoring analysts tended to consider each of their calls as a personal challenge and rarely used the team for help until they got really stuck with a protracted problem. They also took an overcautious approach to problem solving, often taking numerous spare parts and tools to the call, most of which were unnecessary, putting extra burden on spare parts inventories.

James was always calm and in control. When he entered the user's office he would immediately relax into their environment as if he were a part of the user's team. When things didn't go well, he would become even more relaxed and focused on finding a solution. In similar situations, the lower scorers would become stressed and irrational in their problem-solving methods.

Some interesting visual strategies were used by both groups to help them imagine the environment before reacting to the call. One of the lower-scoring analysts, Dave, would visualize the user's environment and consider the best approach to take with the call. For example, on one occasion, he had been allocated a call relating to a keyboard being used by a secretary. As he started to visualize the secretary using the keyboard, he decided to take a new, replacement keyboard rather than attempt to fix the problem key. His rationale for doing this was that secretaries needed a 100 percent fully functioning keyboard, whereas less demanding users would put up with one or two dodgy keys. During the interview, Dave revealed that a secretary to a top manager had once castigated him in front of his colleagues and he has been nervous about secretaries ever since.

Nigel, one of the top performers, used a visual strategy to remember the location of all the key computer systems in the office block. As he went about his daily calls, he would look out for any changes to this visual image – any new, changed, moved or removed computer systems. He kept a mental map, whereas other analysts had to refer to documentation that was mostly out of date.

Another prominent difference between the two groups was the problem-solving method used, which seemed to be influenced by the options–procedures metaprogram. The more procedural the analyst, the more mistakes he would make due to the urgent necessity to fix things. On a number of occasions, I observed interventions that even I (a novice in this area) knew would worsen the situation. One time, I watched as a user's documents were deleted by mistake. Higher-scoring analysts were more options-oriented and it seemed as though the lack of necessity was more responsible for their success than the ability to consider options. This group made hardly any silly mistakes and were much more thorough in their diagnosis of the problem.

> *It became clear that certain combinations of strategies, values, language, and physiology were responsible for delighting customers, and that the analysts with a particular combination did it naturally, for all their customers.*

It became clear that certain combinations of strategies, values, language, and physiology were responsible for delighting customers, and that the analysts with a particular combination did it naturally, for all their customers, regardless of status, role, technology or problem situation.

The interviews

The interviews were used to elicit values and test some of the strategies I had observed. There were a number of differences between the two groups, the main one being the metaprogram primary interest. I repeatedly asked the question, "What do you enjoy most about your job and why?" The low-scoring group were consistent in giving "technology" as the answer to this, with "because there are always new products and features to learn about." All the top scorers gave "people" as their answer, because "there are so many different people to relate to every day." Also, outside work, the top scorers' hobbies and interests involved people and activities unconnected with computers, such as hang-gliding, music, and team sports. The opposite was true for most of the lower-scoring analysts, who all spent a good deal of time on their home computers, improving their performance by continually upgrading.

During the observation stage, I noticed a difference in the way calls were being handled throughout the day. The lower-scoring group would often have unfinished calls at the end of the day; the more dedicated and conscientious would work late to complete as many of their own calls as possible before going home. This was caused by their single-minded approach to call allocation. They considered the calls their personal challenge and would hang on to them even when things went drastically wrong. To be beaten by a call was considered a failure.

The higher-scoring group, on the other hand, would reallocate and swap calls as they went through the day, passing tough ones to specialists in the respective product or technology. They would rarely have to carry unfinished calls over to the next day, except in situations outside their control, such as the user being unavailable or parts being in short supply.

During the interviews, I was able to establish a timeline variation accounting for the difference in call management between the two groups. The more team-oriented, flexible approach of continual reallocation was possible because the top scorers were predominantly "through time" (see Chapter 11). The lower scorers tended to be "in time", causing them to stick with problems for extended periods of time, eventually running out of time mid afternoon and becoming increasingly stressed and tired as the day progressed.

The results of this modeling project were described within eight categories and summarized as follows.

Physiological characteristics

◆ *High-scoring analysts*

Relaxed; taking some time to think before reacting to a call. Remaining relaxed and calm even when working against the clock and when pressurized by the customer. Can work fast and remain in a relaxed state throughout the day.

◆ *Low-scoring analysts*

Get easily stressed when things go wrong. Often impatient to get to the call and fix the computer, performing problem analysis on the way. Jobs are often rushed, with negative consequences. Stress levels rise as the day progresses.

Time orientation

◆ *High-scoring analysts*

Through time. Good planning at the start of the day. Reallocation of calls among the team according to skill match and personal workload. Most calls resolved by the end of the working day.

◆ *Low-scoring analysts*

In time. Less time spent planning. Strong need to own calls, rarely reallocating among team members. Regularly delayed at calls, building up through the day. Calls are often left unfinished at the end of the day. Lose track of time easily.

Teamworking

◆ *High-scoring analysts*

Gather knowledge and experience from others before leaving to attend a fault call. Not concerned at showing a lack of knowledge or skill. Very curious to understand more about a problem before attending the call.

◆ *Low-scoring analysts*

Calls are personal challenges. Do not draw on the combined strengths of the team. Like to be seen to be coping well without help from others. Progress throughout the day is kept a secret from the rest of the team, except for the most urgent priority calls.

Work values

◆ *High-scoring analysts*

Enjoy being part of a team and interacting with customers. Get a buzz from the process of helping people. The metaprogram of attention direction is strong on the side of others (refer to Chapter 9). Hobbies are varied and tend to exclude computing, although computers are considered very interesting and working with them is a challenge.

◆ *Low-scoring analysts*

Enjoy technology above interaction with people. Computing tends to take up much of their life, both at work and home. Techno-chat is frequent with like-minded colleagues and people are a less important focus. The metaprogram of attention direction is strong on the side of self.

Confidence
◆ *High-scoring analysts*
Happy to ask others for help and knowledge before attending a call. Act as though there are no limits to their capability, frequently involving other members of the team in their calls. Use the least possible physical resources and the most intellectual resources to solve problems.

◆ *Low-scoring analysts*
Secretive about own progress. Work considered a personal challenge. Use the most physical resources and the least intellectual resources. Act as though there are no limits to their capability, but often end up in trouble.

Response when things go wrong
◆ *High-scoring analysts*
Deeper relaxation and more focused thinking. Ask more questions and involve the customer and the team. Ongoing problems are not considered personal failures. Able to remain emotionally dissociated from situations where the customer is emotionally charged.

◆ *Low-scoring analysts*
Stress increases as the day progresses and this is amplified when things go wrong. Emotionally associated, causing thinking to become muddled. Keep the customer and the team at arm's length as ongoing problems are considered a personal failure.

Thinking strategy
◆ *High-scoring analysts*
High use of the visual channel to pre-empt problem scenarios. Use of the auditory channel to ask questions and open up the problem space before searching for a solution. Dialog indicates an options orientation.

◆ *Low-scoring analysts*
No common elements noticeable, but dialog tends to be more about "necessity" than "options", causing them to act before adequately thinking the problem through. Whatever channel was being used to consider the problem, diagnostic time was minimal.

Relationships with customers

◆ *High-scoring analysts*

Friendly, informal, and also very professional in approach. Will spend time talking with a customer before trying to fix the computer. Blends into the user environment and develops rapport quickly. Will take detours when going between calls to check on the more problematical calls from the previous days or weeks.

◆ *Low-scoring analysts*

Very formal. Minimal dialog with the user, preferring to get quickly involved with fixing the computer. Stands out in the user environment, awkward at times. Often fails to create any rapport with the user.

The results

At the end of the project, it was very clear how the high-scoring analysts achieved their results. Less clear was the training required to help others match their performance. It was obvious that conventional methods would be inadequate, as the changes required were at higher logical levels than behavior. Any analyst wanting to improve their customer satisfaction scores would have to be prepared to modify their values, strategies, and metaprograms. The approach taken was twofold. First, we designed new, high-impact training based on teamworking and strategies and, second, we worked through the management team using their coaching skills to create the necessary value and metaprogram shifts.

Any analyst wanting to improve their customer satisfaction scores would have to be prepared to modify their values, strategies, and metaprograms.

Managers with more highly developed coaching skills got the best results. In some areas, where managers had either not been trained in coaching skills or were not applying their training, very little change occurred in the customer delight measurements. We realized that achieving the desired change would require the ongoing effort of managers working with the analysts on the job. The focus turned on to that particular area and the project evolved into a manager development initiative. It also provided some new dimensions to the recruitment process, ensuring that future recruits fitted the ideal profile more closely.

Also, as a result of this project, and of other research being done in the customer environment, the company changed its high-level business model. Much more effort and focus was put into motivating and rewarding analysts who today still benefit from one of the most comprehensive employee-focused management systems in the industry.

Note

1   David Molden (1999) "What NLP did for Computacenter", *IT Training Magazine*, November.

27

Modeling case study: generative excellence modeling in a top tax consultancy firm

Brad Waldron

Generative excellence can be described as performance with built-in learning processes. Some people perform well, but are static and don't progress, while others instinctively seem to know how to continuously improve. It is this built-in learning that makes the project I shall describe in this chapter so interesting.

The project occurred in early 1994 and I shall refer to the consulting firm as Tax Inc. as many of the people involved have moved on due to a merger and permissions to publish names have proved difficult to obtain for that reason. The objectives of the project were to discover how certain star performers achieve their results and how they generate new learning, document the findings, create a template for training, and develop standard training courses for the consultancy firm. The overall aim of the project was to grow the capability for generating new business for the firm.

> Generative excellence can be described as performance with built-in learning processes.

The project began with modeling consultants from London and two other regional offices. A small number of star performers were enrolled, along with a similar number of average performers. Performance was measured on the amount of new business generated per consultant over a given period. In this case, the average performers were relative newcomers to the business and less mature than the star performers in relation to their industry experience. The approach taken was to accompany each modeling subject on sales visits and record their strategies, values, beliefs, language, metaprograms, and physiology.

■ General observations

The project revealed some common areas between star performers and highlighted one person in particular. Melvin had some extremely effective patterns, putting him way above all the other consultants in terms of consistent performance. Melvin's strategies are invaluable to anyone involved in consultancy, and you may find it interesting to compare the similarities and differences between Melvin's approach and the common approach of the other star performers. The general and collective observations of the star performers were described using a collection of ten statements, as follows.

◆ **It's more than just selling *per se***
Selling is a secondary issue supporting their identity as a consultant.

◆ **Constant drive to be market leader**
They perceive their role as far bigger than as a sales generator, with compelling desires to serve Tax Inc., their teams, clients, industry, and themselves. There is an almost obsessive drive for professional delivery and advice.

◆ **Selling is a byproduct of passion**
This is not to decry selling – it is a component of personal performance described in terms of quality, management, and leadership. Selling is described as the ability to complete a service and maintain further services provided as an extension to the overall relationship.

◆ **Tax Inc. sells by example**
The partners communicate that Tax Inc. has a better ability than other firms to think about and solve financial problems. The backing for this statement comes from national and international resources. They do not sell tax accountancy; they sell profits and their ability to solve the client's problems. Having established credibility, it is only a matter of time before a need manifests.

◆ **A strong utilization of resources**
The star performers see themselves as resources and coaches to other Tax Inc. teams.

◆ **Develop a "hero" culture**
They consider the client's lead person a hero, making him or her less of a buyer and more a colleague. They also ensure that heroes are recognized

in Tax Inc., increasing their commitment to pull out the stops to earn and keep the hero accolade.

◆ **Tax Inc. makes you more profitable**
Their job is to make the customer more money than Tax Inc.'s fee. Until the client can see that Tax Inc. will profit them, you are just an additional financial burden on top of their tax burden.

◆ **Get clients curious to know what you can do for them**
Use the unexpected to get and maintain interest. If you first get under the client's skin, you can then give them the benefits of your advice. Be flexible to do whatever is necessary to get the client interested, using unexpected twists and perspectives.

◆ **Maintain your presence in the marketplace**
Show the client that you know more about their market dynamics than they do, and use your knowledge to interpret the client's own figures in the context of the wider picture.

◆ **Empower others by personal leadership**
Learning how to process information and respond according to the situation. Paying attention to the needs of others and bringing your resources to bear on developing the capability of the client, and your team. This is the core of generative excellence – that is, excellence with the ability to generate ever-increasing levels of excellence.

In addition to these common attributes of the star performers, some effective patterns were found among individuals and across different regions. For example, outside London, marketing was mainly centered on a variety of networking initiatives, including belonging to a club, lunching with clients, doing small personal tax jobs for free, and playing host to the region's top businesses. The overall marketing strategy in the regions outside London concentrated on gradual building of relationships with clients and in the business community. In London, marketing was more evenly spread across a larger variety of activities, such as:

> *The core of generative excellence is excellence with the ability to generate ever-increasing levels of excellence.*

◆ networking
◆ conferences
◆ workshops and seminars
◆ mailshots

- internal publicity
- press releases
- TV and radio appearances
- creating and publicizing databases
- representations to government
- brainstorming
- recommendations to industry bodies
- referrals
- telesales
- invites to lunch and other social events
- corporate events.

The star players maintained successful marketing activities by focusing on four areas:

- doing what you can do while maintaining balance with other roles, not stretching yourself across too many activities;
- delegating activities among the team;
- monitoring the effectiveness of marketing activity and following up initiatives;
- keeping up appearances.

Values and beliefs

A sale is defined as the activity that takes place once an introduction has occurred, so there is some overlap between selling and marketing. Selling efforts can pass with very little impact if the partner has inappropriate values and beliefs, generally about their own capability, but also about clients' needs and expectations. A sale can be sabotaged by the underlying fear of the partner trying to achieve the sale. This fear, in some cases, seems to be the fear of rejection and hearing the word "no". The star performers rarely face a rejection such as this, but, on the rare occasions when they did, several responses were noted:

- "How can I improve what I did in this case?"
- "No means no for now, but not for ever."
- "Next prospect please!"

There were also several presupposed conditions supporting the star performers' sales results that came out of interviews to elicit values and beliefs. These were the following.

◆ Identify the key decision makers in the client organization. We learned that an aspiring partner was conducting all his communications through an "influencer" and, when it came to securing the business, he was unable to get the decision maker to ascertain the influencer's buying concerns.

◆ Maintain personal contact. Every star performer, without exception, stated that "we are, first, a people business and, second, an advice business". Comments were made about aspiring partners "staying in their boxes" and not getting close enough to the client.

◆ An ability to analyze the challenges facing a client's business and understand clients' needs from a commercial perspective.

◆ The ability to communicate tax as a profit-generation activity and/or cost-cutting activity. Companies do not want to hear about tax analysis, they want to hear about bottom line, so it is imperative that the partner can talk in bottom-line language.

◆ Sell the success of your clients, not the success of Tax Inc. When selling to a new, prospective client, they will require proof of what you have achieved in the past with similar clients. They want to hear how you can help them in the same way you have helped previous clients. This is what they are buying. Your capabilities are already presupposed by your previous successes.

Melvin's approach

Melvin embodied most of the common attributes of the star performer group and enhanced them with some elegant aspects unique to him. We recorded the main stages of his approach to obtaining new business from target clients.

The goal

To obtain chargeable work from the client.

Objectives

1 To identify an appropriate contact within the organization. The quality of the contact is vital to ensuring an appropriate level of authority for commissioning work.

2   Set up a meeting with the client (possibly lunch).

3   Prepare for the meeting.

4   At the meeting.

◆ Develop rapport with the target client and understand the company's problems from a commercial perspective.

◆ Make the target client impressed with Tax Inc. and establish credibility.

◆ Anticipate and overcome objections to moving forward with Tax Inc.

◆ Secure agreement to a brainstorming day on international tax-planning ideas on a non-fee-paying basis. Invest in developing the relationship by giving a favor.

◆ At the end of the meeting, leave the target client with a calling card that looks impressive, restates the points made at the meeting, and shows how the client will get good value for money and excellent service by using Tax Inc. The calling card is actually a complete A4 booklet, bound and printed on glossy paper. The quality of the booklet, like the no-fee brainstorm, indicates to the target client that Tax Inc. is investing in the relationship.

5   Prepare for the brainstorming day.

◆ Obtain agreement from the client to provide information useful to the brainstorming day in advance.

◆ Use material provided by the client.

◆ Use whatever Tax Inc. resources are appropriate, including specialists and people from the international network.

6   At the brainstorming day.

◆ Come up with some different and interesting ideas.

◆ Grade the ideas according to a cost–benefit analysis.

◆ Obtain agreement from the client to perform further work on the best ideas on a fee-paying basis.

◆ Leave the target with the impression that further ideas would be forthcoming from a continuing relationship with Tax Inc.

◆ Carry out the work, meeting the key objectives of a high-quality product produced on time and to budget.

In addition to this quite structured approach, Melvin used a number of very effective techniques to convince the target client to buy. Three very distinct techniques are described below.

Contrasts

One of the ways in which Melvin would deal with a cost-related objection was with a contrasting example that would go something like this:

> "If we wanted to increase profits by X percent, how could we do that?"
>
> We could increase sales by 80 percent.
>
> We could reduce overheads by 30 percent.
>
> More creatively, we can reduce your tax burden by 1 percent, saving you $Xm."

Example

> "One client had a potential tax bill of $80,000,000.
>
> Tax Inc. reduced it to $80,000.
>
> The fee charged was $1,000,000.
>
> Saving the client $78,920,000.
>
> This type of contrast demonstrates that Tax Inc.'s fee is negligible in the face of a pending tax bill. Until clients can see that, there is a danger that Tax Inc. considered an additional burden on top of the tax threat."

"Money as energy" metaphor

Using metaphors helps people to understand large amounts of information. In this case, Melvin described money as energy, helping him to simplify the financial profile of the client company. Using the metaphor, he would regard money coming into the company as an energy flow and consider debt as lost energy. He would include the amount of tax shelter as stored energy, where running low would indicate potential disaster.

Using metaphors helps people to understand large amounts of information.

In this way, Melvin was able to take a complicated cash flow situation and represent it straightforwardly using the energy metaphor. This allowed him to keep a clear image in his mind of the big picture while discussing the details. Where most other partners saw tax, Melvin saw energy.

Throne concept

Melvin had a particular strategy that made him the focus of attention at meetings with clients. The other partners would position themselves behind the weight of Tax Inc., and make their presentations as if on behalf of Tax Inc., using the generalization "we" when discussing Tax Inc.'s capability. In contrast to this, Melvin would make his presentations personal, using the word "I". Melvin would become Tax Inc. He would embody the company identity, values, and capabilities, and these would be expressed in his words and physiology. He would talk as if from a throne of credibility and confidence, bringing in Tax Inc.'s resources and successes, but always suggesting what he could get out of his organization.

Conclusions

Although the star performers had been trained in selling skills, it was clear that sales techniques played only a small part in their success. The key dynamics seemed to come from their presence and how they integrated Tax Inc., displaying confidence and compliance as "leaders of the finest tax advisory practice anywhere". This statement is confirmed by powerful values and beliefs driving a capability to communicate and understand their clients' needs from a commercial perspective.

They communicate that they are champions on behalf of their clients, being an ally of their clients' goals and mission. They approach problems with excitement, treating them as opportunities for personal growth. Their ability to harness vision is allied with attention to detail. They are fastidious in meeting deadlines and are able to identify significant personal needs in their clients. In essence, if we were to put the star performing partners in a melting pot, we would be graced with the presence of a fine individual with the following characteristics:

◆ a primary focus on people, with a passionate desire to serve;

◆ strong loyalty towards themselves, their team, the client, and Tax Inc.;

◆ trustworthy;

◆ fosters empowering beliefs about Tax Inc.'s capabilities and is modest about their personal capabilities;

◆ thrives on interpersonal relationships, fun, intellectual stimulation, and challenges;

- conversant with how to exercise influence in a way that is non-manipulative and totally congruent with themselves;

- proactively takes responsibility for generating new business and will employ a multitude of proven marketing activities to increase their client base;

- never settles for less than what they want to attain – being second best, for some, is a fear driving them towards perfection;

- demonstrates most of the classical selling skills naturally, showing a good integration of learned skills.

- a strong desire to demonstrate brilliance by working in unison with the client and continually exploring ways to exceed everybody's expectations;

- carries financial concepts with a simplicity that gives the freedom to engage in solving complicated problems.

These qualities were to form the template for the training program, consisting of two components:

- internal selling – working with personal values, beliefs, language, and metaphors;

- external selling – addressing the relationship aspects of working with the client.

This was a particularly insightful project and anyone looking for a suitable model for business growth in a consultancy firm stands to reap many benefits from the findings in this chapter. If this is you, then let me know what you achieve.

28

Kill the habit – for ever!

Some habits are useful, others damaging. Think about the habits you experience every day in the workplace, such as the way you respond to certain people or the way you feel when confronted with a difficult situation.

> *"The chains of habit are too weak to be felt until they are too strong to be broken."*
>
> *Dr Samuel Johnson*

In this chapter, you are going to learn how to break any habit – no matter how strong a hold it has on you – and you will break it for ever. To explain the technique, I have chosen an example where I have broken the habit of a lifetime – smoking.

Seven years ago, I smoked between 20 and 30 strong cigarettes each day. I loved the burning sensation in my throat, the relaxing feeling of inhaling, and the social aspect of group smoking. I was a true smoker through and through, addicted to the buzz of nicotine, from early morning to the last thing at night. If I could have smoked in my sleep, I would have done so.

I have chosen an example where I have broken the habit of a lifetime – smoking.

I started smoking at the age of 14, but by 25 I was trying anything to stop the habit, even though I enjoyed it. I knew that the longer I smoked, the harder it would be to stop. I tried cutting down gradually, I tried downgrading to lower and lower tar levels, I tried patches, hypnotherapy, and willpower, but the best I ever achieved was six months of non-smoking and that was six months of agonizing deprivation.

In 1993, I became a non-smoker. I have never once been tempted to have a cigarette since and I can be among smokers without feeling the urge to smoke myself. I am cured.

I did it in five minutes while on a flight over Europe and all I used was NLP. I have since revealed this "wonder strategy" to a number of people, all of whom have achieved similar results. I would have written a book about it had I not been too busy doing other things. So, I now make it available to others by including it as a practical example of NLP's modeling process in this book.

I will explain the process I used to design the strategy and outline the procedure so that you can use it to break other habits, such as nail biting, overeating or excessive TV watching. This chapter will give you a procedure for designing your own wonder strategy to break just about any habit, regardless of the hold it has over you.

The design process

I wanted to discover my strategy for smoking. This would allow me to redesign the strategy to get a different result – that is, not to smoke. I knew that my values (why I smoked) and beliefs (supporting my values) were important, as was the language I was using to talk about smoking and not smoking, and my physiology. I also realized that a strong motivation to stop would require both "moving away from" and "moving towards" values. I had been strengthening my values for health and fitness for some time and so these were beginning to take a higher-level priority than my values for smoking.

Values – towards and away

My "towards" motivation was health, longevity, and the realization that to develop and grow a consultancy business would require lots of energy and stamina. Also, how could I be sincere with my clients, helping them to achieve more for themselves and their business, if I couldn't use my NLP skills to stop smoking?

So, as I thought through all these aspects of smoking, my hierarchy of values was changing. It ended up looking something like this:

◆ **ends value**
be around to support my family (towards);

◆ **means values:**
long-term success (towards);
health and longevity (towards);
bad influence on my children (away from);
sincerity and congruence (towards);
smoke-stained hands (away from);
smoke-infested clothes (away from);
dirty, over-filled ashtrays (away from).

Beliefs

My belief structure was being reshaped also. Over a period of months leading up to the point at which I stopped, I developed some powerful beliefs to support the change I was ready to make. I believed that:

◆ I would succeed;

◆ my family's future depended so much on my stopping smoking;

◆ my children would be more likely to take up smoking if I continued to smoke;

◆ the more times I failed, the more difficult stopping would become;

◆ I am living in a time when smoking exists, but, in 100 years, no one will smoke, so, just because it exists now, doesn't mean I have to do it and, although others can choose to smoke, I can help to create the non-smoking future 100 years from now.

Strategy

This was the most significant part of the entire process for me, and was responsible for my breaking the habit. The work I did with my values and beliefs had set the foundation for a strategy to work and would sustain a change of habit into the future. So, first of all, let me tell you how I elicited my smoking strategy and then I'll explain the changes I made to it.

I began by realizing that when I said, "I am a smoker", I was generalizing something I did intermittently. I didn't always smoke. There were times when I was smoking a cigarette and times when I wasn't. This caused me to ask the question, "How do I know when to smoke?" I had previously determined that the main reason for my smoking was to enjoy the taste of the smoke as it traveled through my throat. I would even smile as I described the sensation this brought me. Next, I wanted to discover the trigger that started the smoking strategy.

I knew that to smoke a cigarette, I would have to first take one out of the packet, but how did I know when to do this? I became more aware of this each time I felt like a smoke. Eventually, I realized that the throat sensation kicked the whole thing off. Then I noticed that, between this sensation and reaching for the packet, I would visualize bringing a cigarette to my mouth, with my right hand. As the cigarette got closer to my mouth, so the sensation grew stronger and that was the specific moment I decided to have my next cigarette. Eureka! I had it.

In NLP notation, this strategy is described as:

$$K \longrightarrow V(c) \longrightarrow K \longrightarrow A(i)$$

Key:

K =   throat sensation

V(c) =   construct an image of my right hand bringing a cigarette up to my mouth

K =   stronger throat sensation

A(i) =   tell myself it's time for the next cigarette.

Redesigning the strategy

The next step was to change the strategy so that the end result would be different, preferably one that didn't include smoking another cigarette.

It all started with the throat sensation, made stronger by the image of the cigarette. I wondered what would happen if the cigarette were to taste differently. What if the cigarette diminished the throat sensation, rather than strengthened it? What could I use for this? I began to think of the worst-tasting food I had ever swallowed and I recalled my kindergarten days, probably at the age of four or five.

> *What if the cigarette diminished the throat sensation, rather than strengthened it? I began to think of the worst-tasting food I had ever swallowed.*

I recalled being served lunch by a very large dinnerlady who would stand over me and make sure I ate all the food on my plate. I am sure she was well intentioned, but a monster nonetheless. Most days this was OK, but on some days I would be served with mince, followed by tapioca pudding – my worst nightmare! What could I do? There was no escaping the white-coated monster towering over me, so I would cram the meat into my mouth, wait for the tapioca, and shovel that in with the meat. Then, when we were allowed outside, I would run into the playground and empty my mouth into the nearest bin, hiding the evidence under some waste paper. I would get very hungry on those days, but hunger was a small price to pay for avoiding having to swallow the worst food on earth. So, now I had the worst taste ever for my strategy.

I ran the smoking strategy again and turned up the submodalities of the visuals so that I could see the tip of the cigarette more clearly. Then I changed the image by replacing the filter tip with a potent mix of mince and tapioca pudding.

I ran the strategy again and, *voilà*! As the cigarette came closer to my mouth, I saw the disgusting mixture inside it, imagined what it would taste like, and threw the cigarette away. At the same time, the throat sensation changed from a pleasurable nicotine taste to the awful meat and tapioca concoction.

I had done it! I ran the new strategy a good dozen times to make sure it was stronger than the old one and it worked a treat. Since that moment, I have never yearned for nicotine, not even once.

◼ What about other habits?

The process I have described can be used to change any bad habit. I hear many stories about people who want to lose weight, get fit, respond more sympathetically to their children's needs, or break a lifetime habit, yet fail very early on. Managers tell me how they want to be better listeners, coaches, facilitators, and leaders, but their habitual responses to pressure hold them back. Even with the best strategy or support system, if the value and belief systems are not aligned with the desired "new you", failure is very likely. The following procedure can be used to break any habit, whatever the context.

> *Even with the best strategy or support system, if the value and belief systems are not aligned with the desired "new you", failure is very likely.*

At this point, you might find it useful to refer back to the various chapters in the book for help with the process, which consists of the following stages.

1 Listen to the language you use to talk about the habit. Use the metaprogram model on your language, looking in particular for:

   ◆ generalizations
   ◆ nominalizations
   ◆ complex equivalences

- ◆ cause effects
- ◆ universal quantifiers
- ◆ modal operators
- ◆ comparisons.

This will give you insights into your strategy, values and beliefs.

2 Create a value hierarchy to support the desired change. Make sure it contains both "towards" and "away from" values. The "end value" and higher "means values" should be "towards".

3 Create as many beliefs as you can to support your new value hierarchy. Think laterally about beliefs you may not have considered before. Do what you want to do, not what you think will fit in with other people – they have their own lives to live, so concentrate on taking charge of your own.

4 Ask yourself two key questions to discover the trigger to your habit strategy:

- ◆ "Why do I ...?"
- ◆ "How do I know when to ...?"

Try these questions also:

- ◆ "How do I know when to stop doing ...?"
- ◆ "What does ... get for me?"

5 Determine the strategy from beginning to end and think how you can change it so that it results in you not doing the habit. The earlier in the strategy you can make the change the better – either step one or two.

6 Design the new strategy and run it a good ten times to burn it in.

Does it work? If it does, well done. If not, have you been thorough enough? Have you defined the strategy correctly? Do your values and beliefs support the change you want? Can you get any more information from your language or physiology?

This is a very powerful technique and the contexts in which it can be used are unlimited. I would be very interested to hear from anyone using this strategy to stop smoking or to break any other kind of habit. You can send me your feedback about your results to the Quadrant 1 e-mail address at the back of the book.

29

A model team

David Robinson

My first exposure to NLP was unintentional. I was a junior manager and, as part of my personal development plan, I attended several courses that used NLP techniques, presented under the heading "management training". I found the courses extremely practical and the techniques eye-opening. This was to become the start of a journey of discovery, although I didn't know it at the time.

NLP changed my whole way of thinking and gave me real tools that worked in everyday situations with my team and with my own abilities. It was reassuring to discover that NLP was a way of modeling excellence, not a hard-to-explain indoctrination based on some obscure Eastern teaching.

I recall making significant progress in my ability as a manager. I developed the ability to help others achieve their goals – a very powerful management tool. I stopped making excuses when things went wrong, which had a big impact on my energy levels. As I improved my sensory acuity, I knew, more often, when I was getting the responses I wanted from people. NLP gave me a window into other people's thinking. This was a powerful tool in business, and it gave me a real edge in a very competitive industry.

> *NLP changed my whole way of thinking and gave me real tools that worked in everyday situations.*

Since this experience, I have been managing teams for five years, using NLP to help achieve team goals. During this time, the business environment has been hectic, with high sales growth and intense bursts of activity. Despite this, we have been able to deliver high levels of service to clients, even with their increasing demands for extended service provision.

As I look back on the experience, I recall a thoroughly enjoyable time, having succeeded in achieving business goals and working with a team with whom I have shared the highs, lows, and the many celebrations of achievement. There have been good times, and the key ingredient underpinning our success has been the very positive attitude of my team.

I know that I can only be successful with the team. If the team fails, then so do I. This is why I have dedicated at least 75 percent of my time to meeting my team's needs and I make this a priority. I have involved my team leaders and managers in workshops that have been designed to achieve a particular goal, such as planning a large office move involving over 2,000 people, personal effectiveness training, and teamworking skills. These workshops have been designed and delivered using NLP principles and techniques.

For the planning workshop, we had three goals:

◆ plan the office move;

◆ equip my team to be able to do it;

◆ get individual buy-in to the whole process to the point that everyone took responsibility for their particular part of the move.

We used timeline techniques during the workshop and the whole team came away with a complete mental picture of the processes needed to complete the task successfully. The team also used a timeline after each stage of the move to adjust the model we were working to, ensuring that we met all our deadlines, which we did.

I remember organizing a coaching workshop that included Latin American dancing as the coaching metaphor. The course was a great success. The team learned how to coach, some of them learned to dance the Salsa, and we all thoroughly enjoyed the experience. They also bonded as a management team and were keen to use the newly acquired skills within their own teams.

I firmly believe that skills are like muscles – if you don't use them, they waste away. I had empowered my team and developed their capability with the NLP-based workshops, and now I had to support them. We all came away from these courses with one clear lesson learned: "Have the destination in mind before you start out and make sure you enjoy the journey." If you can embed this principle in your team, you are well on the way to success.

Skills for inspiring team success

NLP offers the manager all the ingredients needed to help a team succeed. In my experience, when I have come across teams performing badly, it is nearly always caused by an incompetent or uncaring manager. NLP can help the manager to develop a high-performance team by the approach taken in a number of key areas as follows.

Setting goals and outcomes

Use the acronym PRIEST (see Chapter 17) with the team to agree well-formed outcomes linked to business goals. Encourage team members to continually define the outcomes they want before engaging in new tasks and projects. Become outcome-focused, not just results-oriented. Outcomes cover wider consequences of the team's efforts, such as learning from the experience, increased confidence and ability, creating new options, and improving how things are done in the future. Outcomes include the personal elements of achieving business objectives and it is this that boosts motivation. With outcomes, you include the "What's in it for me?" aspect of work, which is so crucial to getting full commitment from the team.

Creative problem solving

Encourage the team to come up with innovative ideas using the Walt Disney strategy (see Chapter 21) and help all to become familiar with the process.

> With outcomes, you include the "What's in it for me?" aspect of work, which is so crucial to getting full commitment from the team.

The best-performing teams are those that make communication and problem solving a team activity rather than an individual process. This is a superb way of helping the team to understand more about how each individual thinks and to develop their creative thinking ability. You can also build creativity in the team during everyday contact by using simple techniques such as asking "what if ... ?" questions and taking time to consider possibilities and alternative options before taking what might seem like the only course of action. Observe more opportunities to open minds and widen the horizons of thinking ability.

Facilitating meetings

Don't chair meetings with your team, facilitate them instead using information frames (see Chapter 20). The more you can ensure that your team gets value from the time spent in meetings, the happier everyone will be about attending future meetings with you. Elicit their outcomes and agendas, not just the ones you think they have or, even worse, just your own. Encourage team members to help with the facilitation and to adopt a more open style in their own meetings. Think of yourself as a team facilitator rather than a team manager and provide them with support and direction instead of management and bureaucracy.

If you think your job is to manage the team, that's what you will end up doing, and you will limit their potential. Reframe your role and become a person whose job is to feed and nurture the team, giving it a direction in which to grow, noticing when it requires attention. As you make the journey to work each day, ask yourself this question: "What does the team need from me today?" You might call this leadership.

Planning

There are lots of techniques to help you and your team plan success. Timeline and outcomes techniques (see Chapter 17) are excellent for this purpose. Identify the more visual members of the team and engage them in visual-type activities. Auditory types may prefer to discuss their ideas, while kinaesthetic types are usually very happy to record ideas on flipcharts. Avoid forcing people to engage in ways they do not find easy, unless they express a desire to do so of course.

A timeline exercise can deliver excellent results, identifying many people-related issues and communication problems often overlooked when using a computer planning system alone. Use your imagination to provide planning meetings that utilize the unique strengths of each individual and their preferred communication styles.

Coaching

There is no more satisfying reward for a manager than to see the members of their team develop and achieve more for themselves and the company.

Outcomes are important for motivation, and language patterns will help you to phrase some effective coaching questions (see Chapter 8). Coaching, however, is significantly more than this. It requires all the knowledge and skills NLP has to offer. By understanding your people better and pacing their models of the world, you can lead them in ways that will make them more capable, both as individuals and as a team.

Coaching need not be restricted to something the manager does with the team; it can also be used by team members, coaching each other in difficult or new tasks. This is a superb way of encouraging a supportive climate of continual learning and improvement. Indeed, people often ask me, "What happens when two people, who are both trained in NLP, come together in a work situation?" The answer to this is simple. The business gets double the benefit as they are able to coach each other. If this sounds peculiar, check out your beliefs about learning.

Giving and receiving feedback

Feedback is a vital component of performance improvement and learning. Everyone should get some direct feedback every day. The person who thinks they can get by without it should play no part in organizational life.

> Everyone should get some direct feedback every day. The person who thinks they can get by without it should play no part in organizational life.

Companies are systems and so are people. All systems require feedback about their behavior if they are to survive and grow. Everyone should be trained in giving and receiving feedback because, in my experience, it is not a natural human trait. It is more natural to criticize, but this needn't be the case. Learn to use the feedback sandwich and be sincere in your intentions to coach and develop your team.

> You did a good job at (X), **and** ...
> I think you could improve (X) by doing (Y), **and** ...
> Your (Z) was excellent – well done!

In this example, the request for improvement is sandwiched between two slices of positive feedback. This makes the improvement much easier to digest. The key word is (can you guess?) "and". You will more often hear people say something like, "You did a good job, but ... ." The "but" negates the statement preceding it, so it is wasted. Use the sandwich and get better results with your feedback.

Improved communication among the team

People need to talk. If people don't talk they bottle up their feelings and become insulated from events going on around them.

At work, there are many ways in which team members can become insulated from external events. Too many individual tasks, time pressure, e-mail, working from home, traveling, feelings of insecurity or inadequacy, the belief that no one cares, the perception that no one is listening – I'll stop there, but you get the picture.

Someone has to be the champion of communication, inspiring action by means of the interactions of the team. You cannot leave it to chance because it will, most often, choose to reduce in quantity and quality. This is an area requiring proactive initiatives to bring people together and create ways of facilitating meaningful communication. Involve the team. Find out what they need and want to know and encourage sharing of both experience and technical expertise.

Performing as a team

If the team members merely discharge their individual responsibilities and meet personal goals, they are not embracing the concept of the team.

Teams can achieve extraordinary performance when they really come together and approach future success from a collective perspective. To achieve this, a team needs to attend to four areas of being a team,[1] namely:

◆ **team orientation**
  the importance, or value, of belonging to a team and what this means to each team member;

◆ **team communication**
  the style, content, and frequency of communication among the team;

◆ **team support**
  a genuine and sincere desire to help each other succeed;

◆ **team process**
  how the team makes decisions and solves problems.

As a leader, you will be working with the team to create an environment that will facilitate these four aspects of being a team. This is the process of teamworking, not the content of how the team goes about achieving its goals.

Be a role model of excellence

Whatever your style of communicating, be positive and upbeat. Teams often adopt the style of the leader, so be aware of the influence you have, even when you are doing nothing. If you show a pessimistic view of the future, don't be surprised when your team delivers to your expectations. Be the person you want your team members to be.

> *"You must be the change you want to see in the world."*
>
> *Mahatma Gandhi*

So, be creative, communicate, connect, listen, facilitate, coach, try new ideas and techniques, learn, be approachable, and provide direction. Whatever else you do, be human and enjoy life.

Note

1   You can download a team performance questionnaire from www.quadrant1.co.uk

Glossary

Accessing cues

Subtle behaviors that indicate which representational system a person is using. Typical accessing cues include eye movements, voice tone and tempo, body posture, gestures, and breathing patterns.

Align

Arrange so that all the elements being aligned are parallel and, therefore, moving in the same direction.

Ambiguity

The use of language that is vague or abstract.

Analog

Having shades of meaning, as in an analog watch (a watch with minute and hour hands), as opposed to a digital one that has a discrete (on/off) meaning, like a light switch.

Analog marking

Using your voice tone, body language, gestures, and so on to mark out key words in a sentence or a special piece of your presentation.

Anchor

Any stimulus that is associated with a specific response. Anchors happen naturally and they can also be set up intentionally – for example, ringing a bell to get attention or, subtler than this, standing in a particular place every time you introduce humor into a presentation, thus setting up the expectation that humor is coming whenever you stand on the humor spot.

Anchoring

The process of associating an internal response with some external trigger (similar to classical conditioning) so that the response may be quickly, sometimes covertly, reaccessed. Anchoring can be visual (as with specific hand gestures), auditory (by using specific words and voice tone), and kinaesthetic (as when touching an arm or laying a hand on someone's shoulder). Criteria for anchoring are:

◆ intensity or purity of experience;

◆ timing at peak of experience;

◆ accuracy of replication of anchor.

As if frame

Pretending that some event has happened. Thinking as if it had occurred, encourages creative problem solving by mentally going beyond apparent obstacles to desired solutions. Ask, "What would it be like if I could … ?"

Association

As in a memory, looking through your own eyes, hearing what you heard and feeling the feelings as if you were actually there. This is called the associated state.

Attitude

A collection of values and beliefs around a certain subject. Our attitudes are choices we have made.

Auditory

Relating to hearing or the sense of hearing.

Backtrack

To review or summarize using another's key words and tonalities or, in presentations, a very precise summary using the same key words in the same voice tones as were originally used.

Behavior

The specific physical actions and reactions by means of which we interact with people and the environment around us.

Behavioral flexibility

The ability to vary one's behavior in order to elicit, or secure, a response from another person. Behavioral flexibility can refer to the development of an entire range of responses to any given stimulus as opposed to having habitual, therefore limiting, responses, which would inhibit performance potential.

Beliefs

Closely held generalizations about:

◆ cause

◆ meaning

◆ boundaries in:
- the world around us
- our behavior
- our capabilities
- our identity.

Beliefs function at a different level than concrete reality and serve to guide and interpret our perceptions of reality, often by connecting them to our criteria or value systems. Beliefs are notoriously difficult to change through typical rules of logic or rational thinking.

Calibration

The process of learning to read another person's unconscious, non-verbal responses in an ongoing interaction by pairing observable behavioral cues with a specific internal response.

Chunking

Organizing or breaking down some experience into bigger or smaller pieces. Chunking up involves moving to a larger, more abstract level of information. Chunking down involves moving to a more specific and concrete level of information. Chunking laterally involves finding other examples at the same level of information.

Congruence

When all of a person's internal beliefs, strategies, and behaviors are fully in agreement and oriented towards securing a desired outcome. Words, voice and body language give the same message.

Context

The framework surrounding a particular event. This framework will often determine how a particular experience or event is interpreted.

Criteria

The values or standards a person uses to make decisions and judgments about the world. A single criterion is composed of many elements, conscious and subconscious. The question to ask is, "What's important about … ?"

Deep structure

The sensory maps – both conscious and unconscious – that people use to organize and guide their behavior.

Deletion

One of the three universals of human modeling, this is the process by which selected portions of the world are excluded from the representation created by the person modeling. Within language systems, deletion is a transformational process in which portions of the deep structure are removed and, therefore, do not appear in the surface structure representation.

Digital

Having a discrete (on/off) meaning, as opposed to **analog**, which has shades of meaning.

Dissociation

As in a memory – for example, looking at your body in the picture from the outside, so that you do not have the feelings you would have if you were actually there.

Distortion

One of the three universals of human modeling, this is the process by which the relationships that hold among the parts of the model are represented differently from the relationships they are supposed to represent.

Down-time

Having all sensory input channels turned inward.

Ecology

The study of the effects of individual actions on the larger system.

Elicitation

The act of discovery and detection of certain internal processes.

Environment

The external context in which our behavior takes place. Our environment is that which we perceive as being "outside" of us. It is not part of our behavior, but, rather, is something we must react to.

Eye accessing cues

Movements of the eyes in certain directions indicating visual, auditory or kinaesthetic thinking.

Frame

To set a context or way of perceiving something, as in outcome frame, backtrack frame, and so on.

Future pacing

The process of mentally rehearsing oneself through some future situation in order to help ensure that the desired behavior will occur naturally and automatically.

Generalization

One of the three universals of human modeling, this is the process by which a specific experience comes to represent the entire category of which it is a member.

Gustatory

Relating to taste or the sense of taste.

Hierarchy

An organization of things or ideas where they are given a ranking based on their importance.

Identity

Our sense of who we are. Our sense of identity organizes our beliefs, capabilities, and behaviors into a single system.

Incongruence

State of having reservations, not totally committed to an outcome. The internal conflict will be expressed in the person's behavior.

Intention

The purpose or desired outcome of any behavior.

Internal representation

Patterns of information we create and store in our minds in combinations of images, sounds, feelings, smells, and tastes. The way we store and encode our memories.

In time

Being associated with memories and time. Being more conscious of the content of an activity than of the duration.

Kinaesthetic

Relating to body sensations. In NLP, the term kinaesthetic is used to encompass all kinds of feelings, including tactile, visceral, and emotional.

Leading

Changing your own behavior with enough rapport for the other person to follow.

Lead system

The preferred representational system (visual, auditory, kinaesthetic) that finds information to input into consciousness.

Logical levels

An internal hierarchy in which each level is progressively more psychologically encompassing and has greater impact. In order of importance (from high to low), these levels include:

- spirituality or purpose
- identity
- beliefs and values
- capabilities
- behavior
- environment.

Map of reality

Model of the world. Each person's unique representation of the world built from their individual perceptions and experiences.

Matching

Adopting parts of another person's behavior for the purpose of enhancing rapport.

Meta

Derived from Greek, meaning over or beyond.

Metamodel

A model developed by John Grinder and Richard Bandler that identifies categories of language patterns that can be problematical or ambiguous. The metamodel is based on transformational grammar and identifies common distortions, deletions, and generalizations that obscure the deep structure/original meaning. The model has clarifying questions that will restore the original meaning of the message. The metamodel reconnects language with experiences and can be used for gathering information, clarifying meanings, identifying limitations, and opening up choices.

Metaphor

The process of thinking about one situation or phenomenon as something else – stories, parables, and analogies.

Metaprogram

A level of mental programing that determines how we sort, orient to, and chunk our experiences. Our metaprograms are more abstract than our specific strategies for thinking and define our general approach to a particular issue rather than the details of our thinking process.

Milton model

The inverse of the metamodel. Using artfully vague language patterns to pace another person's experience and access unconscious resources. Based on the language used by Milton H. Erickson, MD.

Mirroring

Matching portions of another person's behavior, especially their body language.

Mismatching

Adopting different patterns of behavior from another person, breaking rapport for the purpose of redirecting, interrupting or terminating a meeting or conversation.

Model of the world

A person's internal representation of the condition of the world.

Modeling

The process of observing and mapping the successful behavior of other people. This involves profiling behavior/physiology, beliefs and values, internal states, and strategies.

Non-verbal

Without words. Usually referring to the analog portion of our behavior, such as the tone of the voice and other external behavior.

Olfactory

Relating to smell or the sense of smell.

Outcomes

Goals or desired states that a person or organization aspires to achieve.

Pacing

A method used by communicators to quickly establish rapport by matching certain aspects of their behavior to those of the person with whom they are communicating – a matching or mirroring of behavior.

Parts

A metaphorical way of talking about independent programs and strategies or behavior. Programs or "parts" will often develop a persona that becomes one of their identifying features.

Perceptual filters

The unique ideas, experiences, beliefs, and language that shape our model of the world.

Perceptual position

A particular perspective or point of view. In NLP, there are three basic positions one can take in perceiving a particular experience. The first position involves experiencing something through our own eyes associated in a first person point of view. The second position involves experiencing something as if we were in another person's shoes. The third position involves standing back and perceiving the relationship between ourselves and others from a dissociated perspective.

Physiology
To do with the physical part of a person.

Predicates
Sensory-based words that indicate the use of one representational system.

Preferred system
The representational system that a person typically uses most to think consciously and organize their experience.

Presupposition
A basic underlying assumption necessary for a representation to make sense. Within language systems, a sentence that must be true for some other sentence to make sense.

Problem space
This is defined by both physical and non-physical elements, which create or contribute to a problem. Solutions arise out of a "solution space" of resources and alternatives. A solution space needs to be broader than the problem space to produce an adequate solution.

Process and content
Content is what is done, whereas process is about how it is done. What you say is content and how you say it is process.

Rapport
The establishment of trust, harmony, and cooperation in a relationship.

Reference structure
The sum total of experiences in a person's life story. Also, the fullest representation from which other representations within some system are derived, so, for example, the deep structure serves as the reference structure for the surface structure.

Reframing

Changing the frame of reference around a statement to give it another meaning.

Relevancy challenge

Asking how a specific statement or behavior is helping to achieve an agreed outcome.

Representational systems

The five senses: seeing, hearing, touching (feeling), smelling, and tasting.

Resourceful state

The total neurological and physiological experience when a person feels resourceful.

Resources

Any means that can be brought to bear to achieve an outcome: physiology, states, thought, strategies, experiences, people, events, possessions.

Second position

Seeing the world from another person's point of view and so understanding their reality.

Sensory acuity

The process of learning to make finer and more useful distinctions about the sense information we get from the world.

Sensory-based description

Information that is directly observable and verifiable by the senses. It is the difference between, "The lips are pulled taut, some parts of her teeth are showing and the top edges of her mouth are higher than the main line of her mouth" and, "She's happy", which is an interpretation.

Sort

A computer term meaning to reorganize and/or to filter information in the process of the reorganization.

State

The total ongoing mental and physical conditions from which a person is acting. The state we are in affects our capabilities and interpretation of experience.

Stimulus response

An association between an experience and a subsequent so-called reaction; the natural learning process Ivan P. Pavlov demonstrated when he correlated the ringing of a bell to the secretion of saliva in dogs.

Strategy

A set of explicit mental and behavioral steps used to achieve a specific outcome.

Submodalities

The special sensory qualities perceived by each of the senses. For example, visual submodalities include color, shape, movement, brightness, depth; auditory submodalities include volume, pitch, tempo; and kinaesthetic submodalities include pressure, temperature, texture, location.

Surface structure

The words or language used to describe or stand for the actual primary sensory representations stored in the brain.

Swish pattern

A generative NLP submodality process that programs your brain to go in a new direction. Very effective in changing habits or unwanted behaviors into new constructive ways of doing things.

Systemic

To do with systems, looking at relationships and consequences over time and space rather than linear cause and effect.

Third position

When you observe yourself and others.

Through time

Being dissociated from memories and time, which is perceived as a linear sequence of events. Conscious attention is paid to the duration of an activity.

Timeline

The way we store pictures, sounds, and feelings of our past, present, and future.

Tonal marking

Using your voice to mark out certain words as being significant.

TOTE

Developed by G. Miller, E. Galanter, and K. Pribram, this acronym stands for the sequence test–operate–test–exit, which describes the basic feedback loop used to guide all behavior.

Trance

An altered state with an inward focus of attention on a few stimuli.

Uptime

A state where the attention and senses are committed outwards.

Values

The things that are important to us and so drive our actions.

Visual

Relating to sight or the sense of sight.

Visualization

The process of seeing images in your mind.

Voice quality

The second most important channel of communication and influence. Research suggests it is 38 percent of the total impact of the communication.

Well-formedness conditions

The set of conditions something must satisfy in order to produce an effective and ecological outcome.

Contributors to Sections 3 and 4

Alan Black

Senior Engineering Manager, Brown & Root Limited, Hill Park Court,
Springfield Drive, Leatherhead, Surrey, UK, KT22 7NL
Tel: +44 1372 862707 *Fax:* +44 1372 866559
e-mail: Alan.Black@Halliburton.com

Brad Waldron

Oxygen Learning Limited, 28 Bradmore Park Road, London UK W6 0DT
Tel: 0208 7414477 *e-mail:* brad@learningfun.co.uk
Website: Oxygenlearning.com

David Robinson

188 London Road, Wickford, Essex, UK, SS12 OET
Tel: 07968 870109.

Denise Parker

Quadrant 1 Limited, 75 Rose Hill, Oxford, UK, OX4 4JR
Tel: +44 (0) 1865 715895 *Fax:* +44 (0) 1865 717315 *e-mail:*
denise@quadrant1.co.uk *Website:* www.quadrant1.co.uk

Denise is a director with Quadrant 1 Limited and a certified trainer of
NLP. She has a background in financial services and is currently
working with a number of blue-chip companies as a coach and trainer.

Graham Yemm

Solutions International (Training & Development) Limited, Ashley
House, Bracknell Lane, Hartley Wintney, Hampshire, UK, RG27 8QQ
Tel: +44 1252 845944 *e-mail:* gy@solutions4training.com
Website: www.solutions4training.com

Jane Revell

KITE Courses/Saffire Press, 34 Park Hall Road, East Finchley, London, UK, N2 9PU

Tel: +44 (0)20 8444 0510 *Fax:* +44 (0)20 8444 4693

KITE Courses offers diploma and practitioner courses in NLP. Saffire Press publishes books about teaching and learning, specializing in the use of NLP in education.

Jon Symes

CPS International Limited, PO Box 2009, Chester, UK, CH4 7ZJ

Tel: +44 (0) 1244 629195 *Fax:* +44 (0) 1244 680733

e-mail: jsymes@cpsinter.com *Website:* www.cpsinter.com

CPS International works with organizations to develop people and teams in innovative and effective ways. Founder Director Jon Symes is a speaker, author, and co-author of *Realigning for Change* (FT Prentice Hall, 1999) with David Molden.

Marcus Muir

Change and Development Consultant and Coach,

Eagle-Oak Partnerships, 22 Firwood Avenue, St Albans, Hertfordshire, UK, AL4 0TF

Tel: +44 (0)1727 851575 *Mobile:* +44 (0)7971 810101 *Fax:* +44 (0)7970 213 695 *e-mail:* marcus.muir@talk21.com

Mark Underwood

Business Matters, 66 Belgrade Road, Stoke Newington, London, UK, N16 8DJ

Tel: +44 7074-BOWTIE (269843) *Fax:* 0207 249 7472

e-mail: businessmatters@geo2.poptel.org.uk

Quadrant 1

If you would like to energize people in your organization with courses and workshops designed to get the best out of everybody, then talk to us at Quadrant 1 Limited.

Our customers choose us for our unique ability to design customized solutions that deliver measurable benefits to their business. Join them and find out how we can do this for you via our:

◆ **NLP Business Masterclass Course**
equip yourself for success in business and your personal life by attending the ultimate NLP event – no prior training required (see Quadrant 1 website for details and dates);

◆ **Personal Performance Coaching**
to help you realize your full potential;

◆ **Customized Training Courses**
that motivate, develop skills, and build commitment to change;

◆ **Net-Coach**
personal performance coaching via the Internet to help you succeed, no matter what the challenge.

Widen your horizons with Quadrant 1 at

Websites:
www.quadrant1.co.uk
www.net-coach.net

e-mail:
energise@quadrant1.co.uk

Index

the bestselling guide to getting things done

SIMPLY BRILLIANT

The competitive advantage of
common sense
Fergus O'Connell

ISBN 0 273 65418 7

Simply
Brilliant

"Simply Brilliant is brilliantly simple – so much so that I might start coming to work to get things done." *Financial Times*

"Tears down management as a complex science, reducing it to life saving basics. This book does a good job – it may just help to simplify your working life" *Evening Standard*

"O'Connell's ideas for creating a better working environment are as simple as he claims and will provide welcome relief for anyone who is struggling to come to terms with the latest fad from the Harvard Business School…" *The Sunday Times*

Life is complicated enough. Yet many people go out of their way to create hoops to jump through, wrestling with tough problems and calling on the latest management fad to find that elusive solution to a problem. But it doesn't have to be that way. The best ideas aren't always complicated. The world is full of smart, experienced, skilled, brilliant people. However, many people – even smart ones – are lacking a set of essential skills that when pulled together can be termed 'common sense'. Shortlisted for the WHS Business Book of the Year 2002 and a runaway international bestseller, *Simply Brilliant* features a set of seven principles to make the bright better. Principles of common sense that can be adapted for attacking many of the problems that you encounter every day, be it in work or outside.

Simply Brilliant – you'll be amazed at the difference it can make.

Visit our website at
www.business-minds.com